IMAGES
of America

JAY

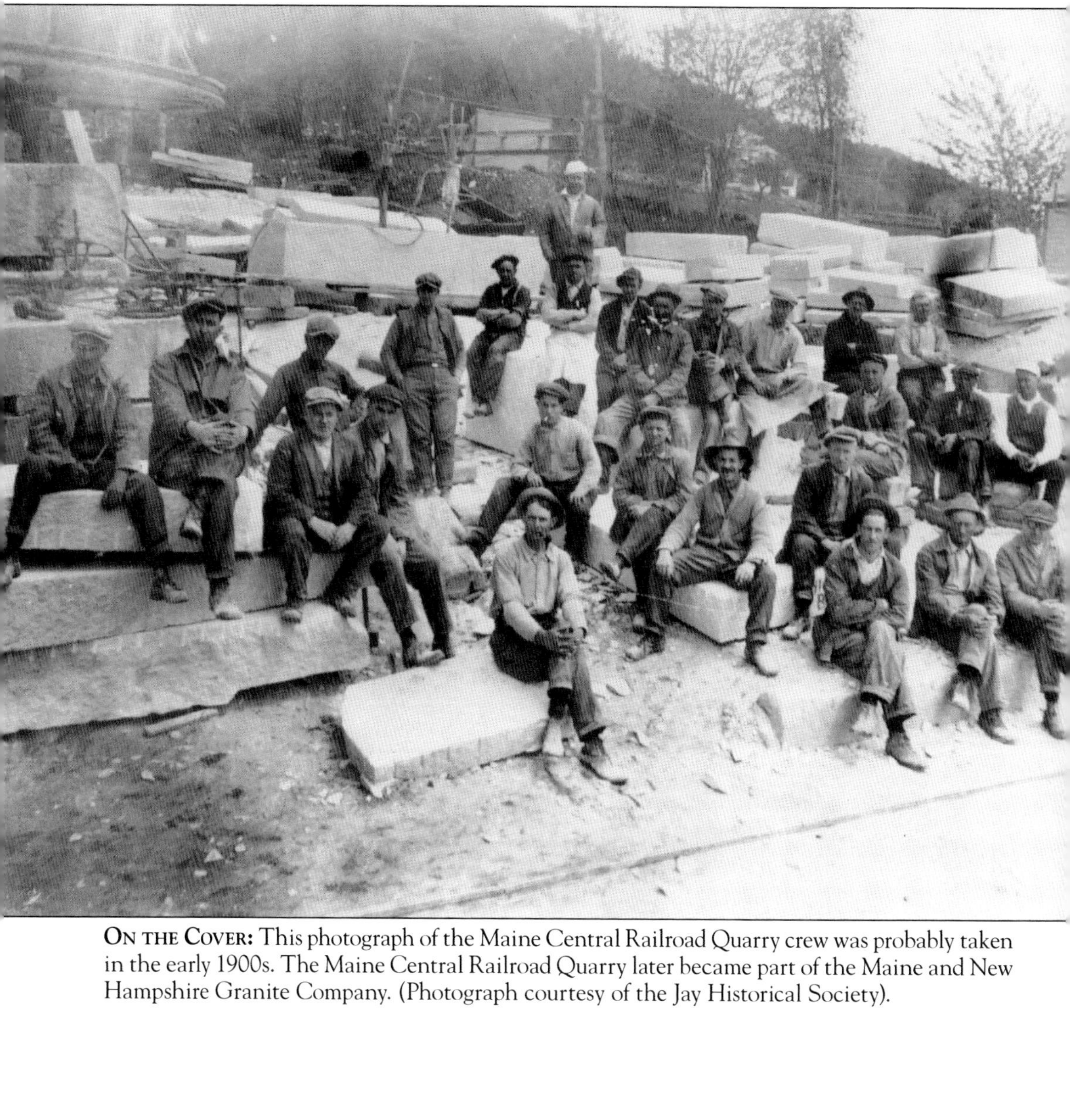

On the Cover: This photograph of the Maine Central Railroad Quarry crew was probably taken in the early 1900s. The Maine Central Railroad Quarry later became part of the Maine and New Hampshire Granite Company. (Photograph courtesy of the Jay Historical Society).

IMAGES
of America

JAY

Tamara N. Hoke

ARCADIA
PUBLISHING

ISBN 978-0-7385-7487-5

Published by Arcadia Publishing
Charleston, South Carolina

Printed in the United States of America

Library of Congress Control Number: 2010939072

For all general information, please contact Arcadia Publishing:
Telephone 843-853-2070
Fax 843-853-0044
E-mail sales@arcadiapublishing.com
For customer service and orders:
Toll-Free 1-888-313-2665

Visit us on the Internet at www.arcadiapublishing.com

To Sue McConnell, in whose memory I dedicate this book.

Contents

ACKNOWLEDGMENTS

Except where otherwise noted, all images in this book are used courtesy of the Jay Historical Society. The Jay Historical Society is a volunteer organization that exists because of individual donations and financial contributions from the town of Jay. The programs they have exist because dedicated volunteers believe in perpetuating the history of the town of Jay.

I am particularly grateful for the town histories others have written. Without their contributions, this book would not have been possible. The first comprehensive history was written by Rev. Benjamin F. Lawrence in 1912. The book was entitled *History of Jay: Franklin County, Maine.* The second book written on Jay's history, while smaller in scope, provided helpful town history details. This book, written in 1967 by Helen Cushman, was called *Horizons Unlimited: A History of Jay.* I am also exceedingly grateful to the comprehensive historical and genealogical work of Virginia Plaisted Moulton, *A History of Jay, Maine: from its settlement as Phips Canada*, which was published in 1995. I am also indebted to the local histories written by Brad Crafts as well as photographs from his collection, now in the possession of the Jay Historical Society. Lastly, I am indebted to the local history articles and town reports collected by my predecessors at the Jay-Niles Memorial Library. I found this information invaluable.

INTRODUCTION

This book, being a photographic history, does not go in depth where the early history of the town is concerned. However, I will endeavor to at least give a brief overview of some important events and people in the town prior to the advent of photography. The town's earliest inhabitants were Abenaki Indians, and they were settled at what was formerly Canton Point (then called Rockomeko). They are referred to by most, however, as the Rockomeka Indians. It is believed that most of the Rockomeka Indians were either decimated by disease before the town was settled or removed themselves to Canada where the population held less animosity towards them. The early written history is not kind to the native population and refers to them with terms such as "wily" or "cunning" savages. It is believed that the settlers first established themselves on the hills in Jay, especially the Jay Hill, where they felt more protected from the native population at Rockomeko. As history is often subjective, it is hard to know the real story of Jay's earliest inhabitants.

The area now known as Jay was granted to Capt. Joseph Phips and 63 others for services in the French and Indian Wars of 1755. It was for some time known as Phips' Canada. Jay was not formally settled until after the Revolutionary War. On March 15, 1770, David Phipps Esq., along with 71 veterans of the French and Indian Wars, petitioned the province of Massachusetts Bay for township status. It was granted in 1771. This area was 6.75 miles square, or approximately 30,000 acres. The stipulations for township included a plan of township to be returned to the court within 12 months. This required that 80 families be settled in the township, a "house for public worship of God" be built, and a "learned Protestant minister" be settled there per these stipulations. Divisions of lots soon took place. On April 12, 1774, the proprietors voted to give four pounds to each of the first 10 settlers who cleared 10 acres, seeded it with grass or grain, built a 16-square-foot house, and settled within one year and a half. This was to be accomplished within seven years. Due to the advent of the Revolutionary War, the proprietors had to petition for another seven years to complete the settlement.

Jay was finally incorporated on February 26, 1795, and named for the Honorable John Jay. There is no known connection between John Jay, the first chief justice of the US Supreme Court, and this town.

James Starr II once owned the Jay Tavern. He held office in the large front room. He issued the warrant for the first town meeting, which was held on the first Monday of April 1795 in the Baptist meetinghouse on Jay Hill. In 1830, Starr became the first postmaster in Jay. He was also a local judge, lawyer, banker, surveyor, and representative to the court of Massachusetts. He would travel on horseback to Portland and then get a ship or stage to Boston. He served as town clerk for seven years.

Moses Crafts was moderator at the first town meeting. He served as a town selectman for several years. He also served as town clerk in 1804.

Col. Daniel Merritt lived in a large house on the top of Jay Hill. He was head of the town militia for many years. The powder and lead balls used for ammunition were stored in a small stone building on Powder House Hill. Merritt was a leader in the community. He conducted cattle, sheep, and pig drives to the stockyards of Brighton, Massachusetts, walking this nearly 200-mile trip. Merritt held a number of town offices, but he also represented Franklin County in the state senate in 1842 and was high sheriff in the county from 1846 to 1850.

Maj. Stillman Noyes was part of the second generation of the Noyes family in Jay. He was a farmer and a lumber and cattle dealer. He built and operated the sawmill and gristmill at Jay Bridge alongside Francis Lawrence. From 1850 to 1851, Noyes represented the town of Jay in the Maine Legislature. He was a dedicated Baptist and provided for the parsonage on Jay Hill. Many of Stillman Noyes descendants were also involved in town affairs.

In 1839, Thomas Winslow and Francis Lawrence built the first mill at Jay Bridge just below its north end. This was taken out by a flood but rebuilt with a gristmill added by Noyes and Lawrence, which ran for a number of years. They owned the water rights to the area at Otis Falls for many years. These mills later burned, and the water rights were purchased by Alvin Record.

Prior to 1850, Aruna Holmes ran a large cabinet and furniture manufactory in a sizeable two-story building between his house and store on Jay Hill. He made Windsor chairs. His home was built around 1820. This homestead is now the location for the Jay Historical Society and is known as the Holmes-Crafts Homestead.

Hutchinson and Lane constructed a lumber steam mill between 1872 and 1873. Around 1880, this mill was purchased by R.H. Thompson, who operated it for four years. It was located just above Jay Village and had a novelty mill that employed many from the surrounding village. It burned and closed in 1884.

A carriage factory operated for many years in the Bean's Corner area of Jay. The carriages were constructed by I.B. Bean in the late 1800s and early 1900s.

The Impact of Industry on Jay

Jay has always been comprised of small villages, many with their own main street. These villages were North Jay (Bartlett's Corner), Bean's Corner, East Jay, Canada's Corner, Stone's Corner, Jay Village, Jay Bridge, Riley, Stubb's Mills, Jay Intervale, Canton, and Chisholm. Many residents still refer to themselves as being from certain areas of town, such as East Jay, Bean's Corner, or North Jay. The village of Riley has vanished. When the mill in Riley was running, there was a bustling population. International Paper closed the mill and built the Androscoggin Mill in the 1960s, buying much of the land and many of the houses so that they could destroy them and build the sprawling new mill complex.

Industry has been the backbone of this town. It has brought many settlers to the area. The population in 1870 was 1,490. In 1880, it was 1,291. By 1890, the population grew to 1,591. By 1900, it had grown to 2,758. Many immigrants came to Jay for work and decided to make the town their home. The immigrants who helped comprise the numbers in this growing town were of many nationalities, including French-Canadian, Italian, Lithuanian, Finnish, Czechoslovakian, and Polish. They came to work in the North Jay quarries and at the Otis and Riley Mills.

One

Agriculture

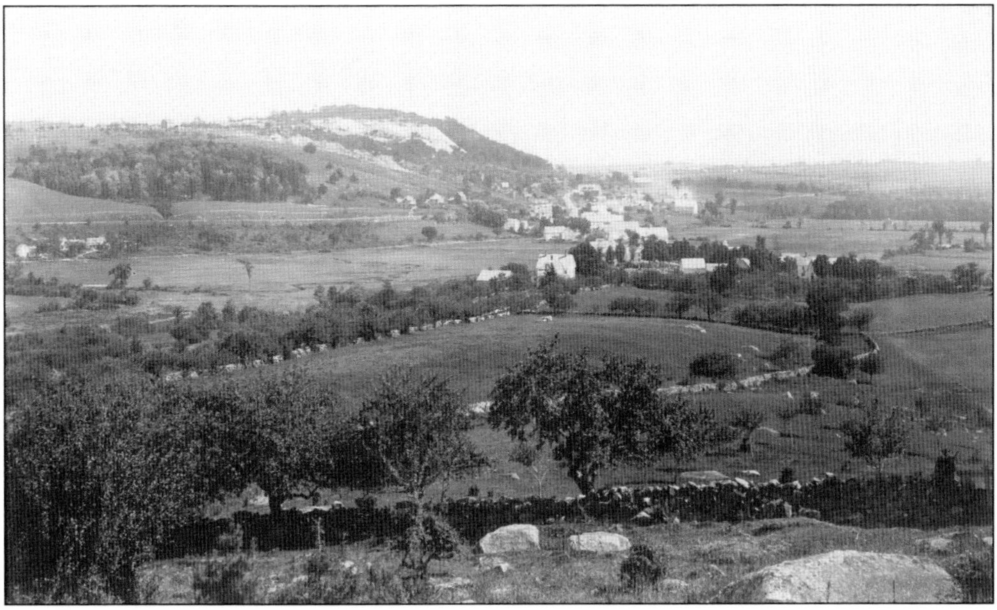

Farmland. This is a view of North Jay Village in 1904, taken from the Old Jay Road by S. Towle of Old Orchard, Maine. Stone walls had a number of agricultural purposes, including animal pounds, boundary and property lines, and animal fencing. Many of these stones were very likely granite, due to the proximity of the granite quarries. Granite is extremely hard and an optimum choice for building stone walls.

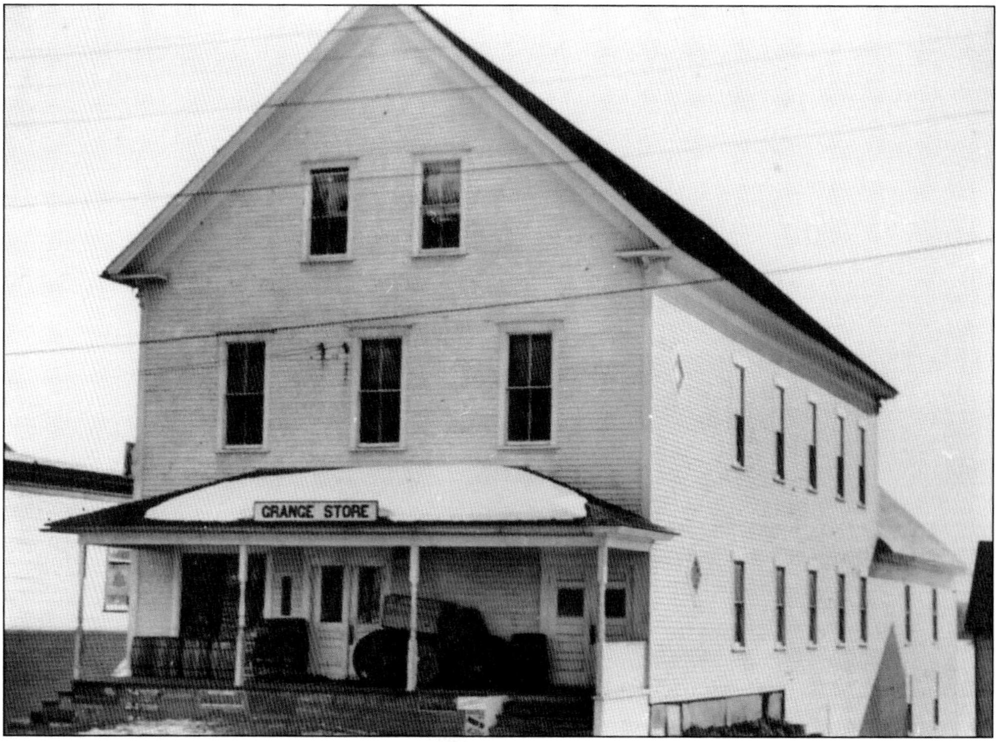

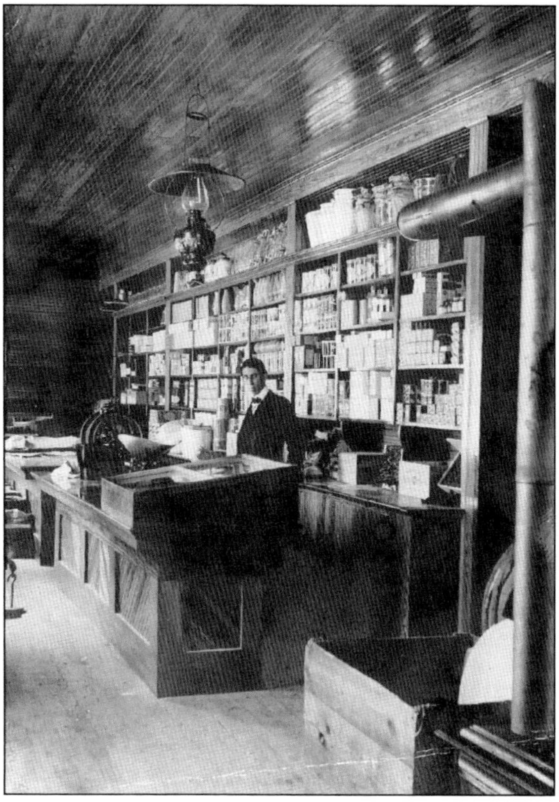

North Jay Grange Hall and Store, c. 1910–1915. The doors on the right led to the hall on the second floor, where Grange meetings were held on Saturday nights. The double-entry doors led to the store on the left, and the dining hall was on the right. Later, the dining area moved to the third floor and the store expanded.

North Jay Grange Store. Ernest Parsons (pictured) was an agent of the store starting in 1917. Parsons held his position for 29 years. The Grange Store had a general line of merchandise, including soda crackers, sugar, molasses, pickles, rounds of cheese, medicine, sticks of licorice, cloth, hardware, lollipops, ice cream, Johnson's wool pants, Fedco-Green Company aluminum siding, galvanized cans, BlueSeal feeds, horsehide gloves, Curity diapers, and flower seeds.

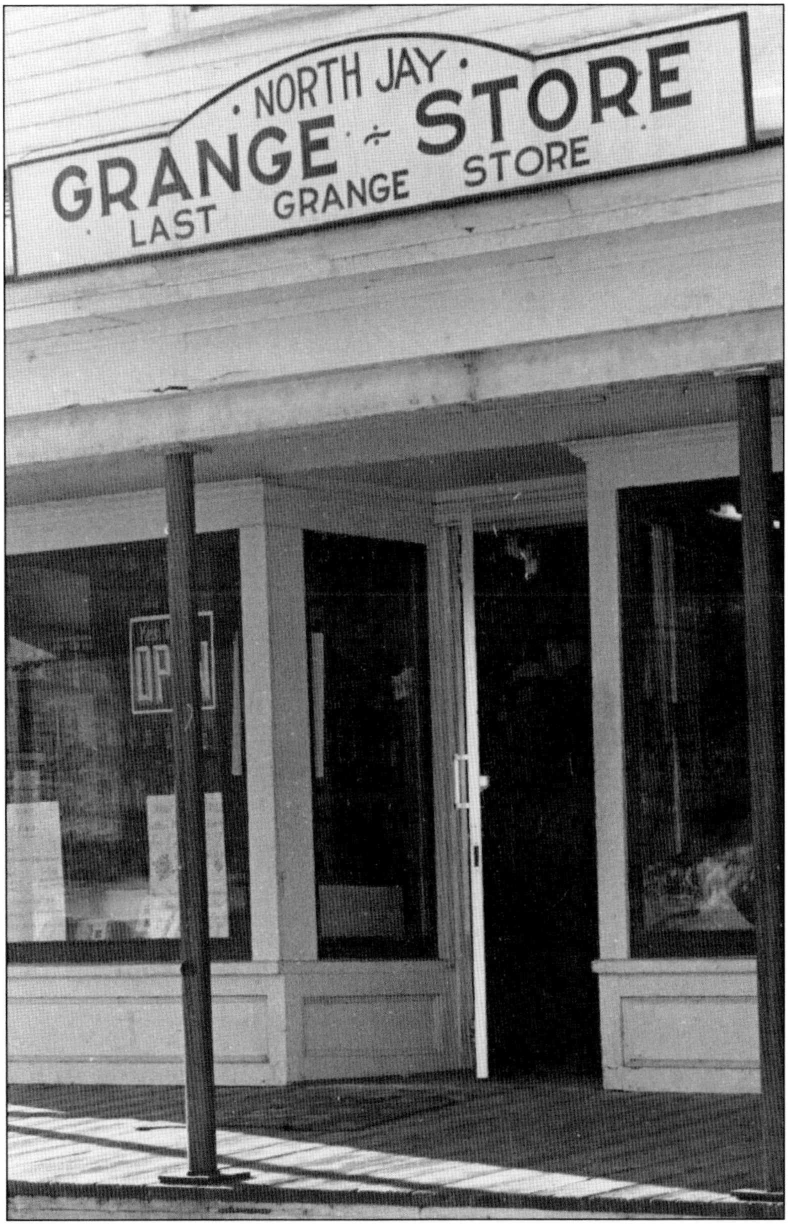

Last Grange Store. The North Jay Grange Store closed its doors in 1976. It is known as the last Grange store in the United States. According to a store trustee in 1976, dwindling local trade was the main reason for the closure. The Grange store had very modest beginnings. J.O. Kyes was the first master. The first store was run out of the Grange agent's shed. He was hired in 1874 and was paid $3.26 for an entire year's work. In 1875, a carload of corn and seven pairs of boots were ordered. Grange members were interested in goods that could be purchased by the group at prices that would benefit all. At this time, nearly everyone in the community farmed. The Grange store was established during a time when the nation was recovering from the Civil War. In 1889, a stock company was formed and a Grange hall was erected at the cost of $2,600. This hall was destroyed by fire in February 1895. The following summer, the members erected a new Grange hall at the cost of $3,000. It was dedicated on July 1895.

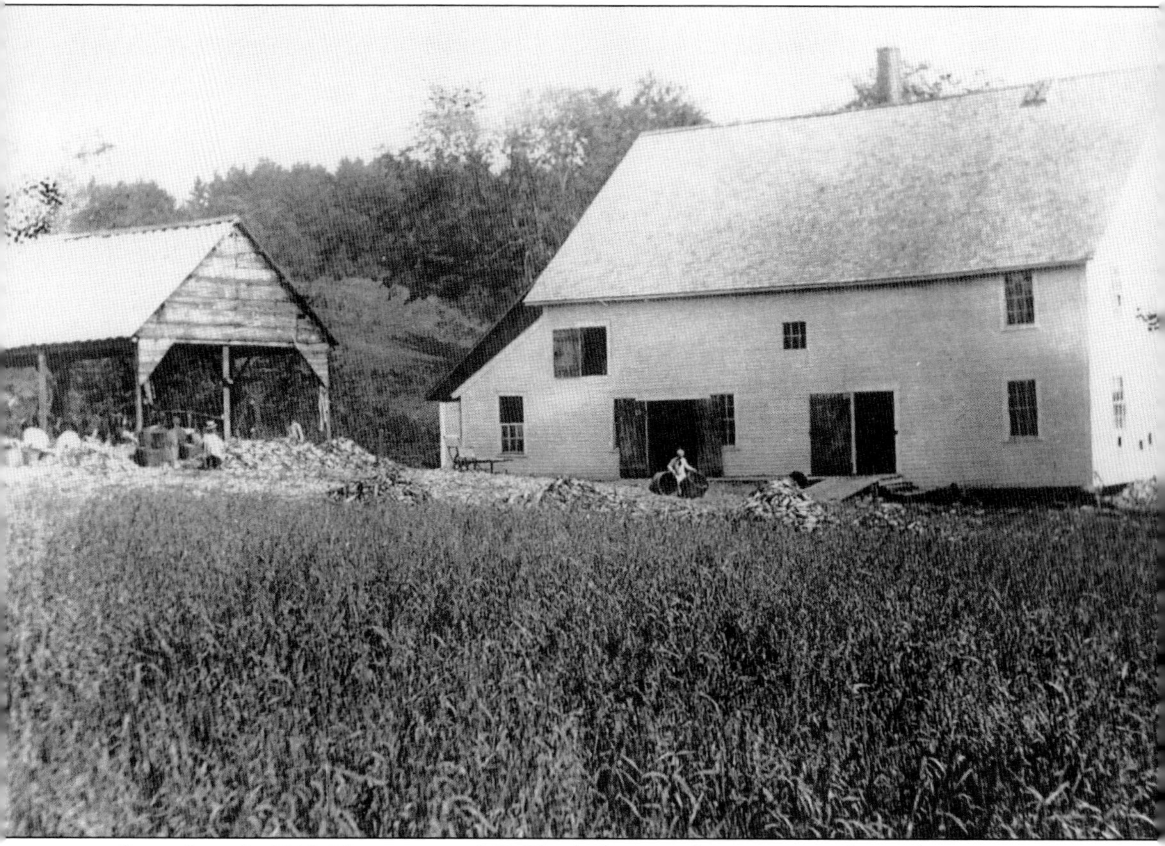

Corn Shop. In 1900, Thompson and Hall built the corn shop on Intervale Road in Jay. Tomlinson of Portland operated the canning factory for many years, with S.B. Farnum as superintendent. They canned corn, apples, and squash, mostly grown by local farmers. Many people were employed there during the canning season. This photograph was taken in 1908 and is part of the Brad Crafts Collection.

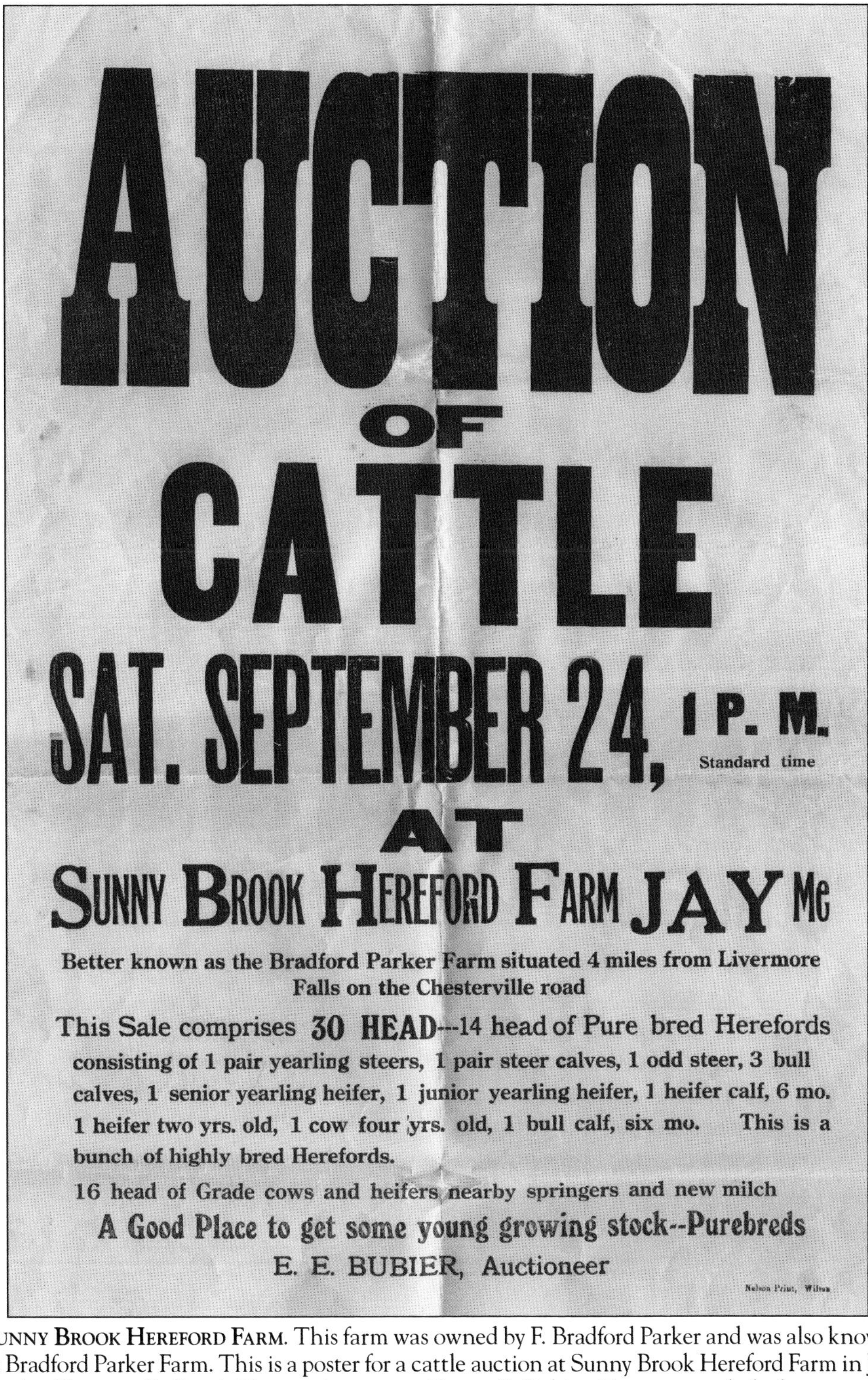

SUNNY BROOK HEREFORD FARM. This farm was owned by F. Bradford Parker and was also known as Bradford Parker Farm. This is a poster for a cattle auction at Sunny Brook Hereford Farm in Jay on the Chesterville Road. The auctioneer was Ernest E. Bubier. He was a stock dealer, an apple dealer, a granite-paving cutter, and deputy sheriff. This poster is likely from the 1920s.

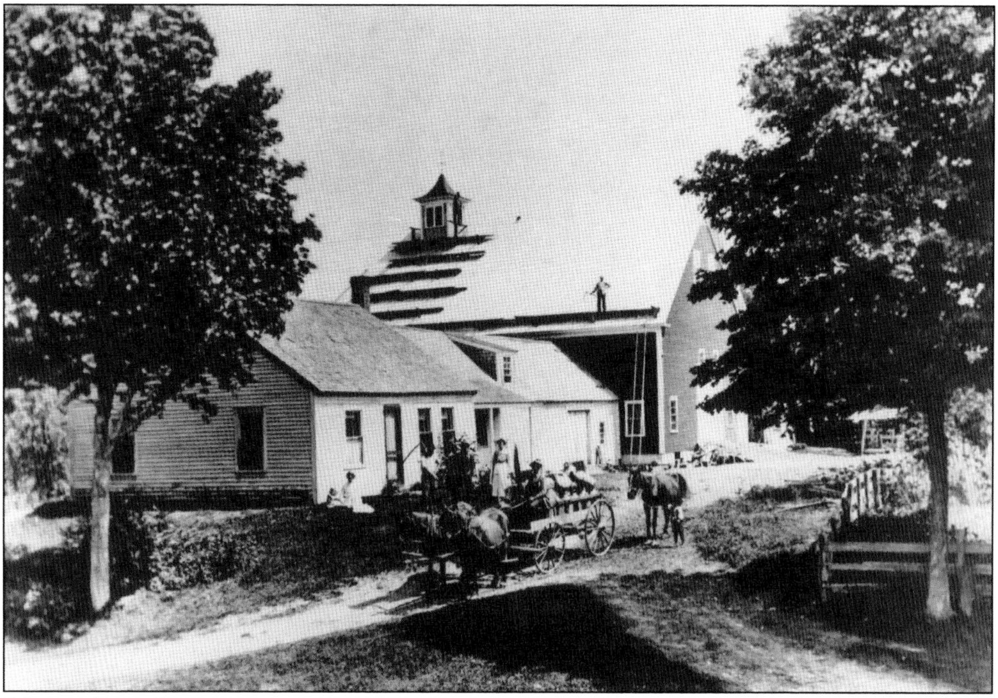

WALTER BEAN FAMILY AND FARM LIFE AROUND 1903. Walter Bean's home at Bean's Corner was built by his father, Isaac Bean. Isaac Bean was a farmer and carpenter, making carriages at his house, which held his shop.

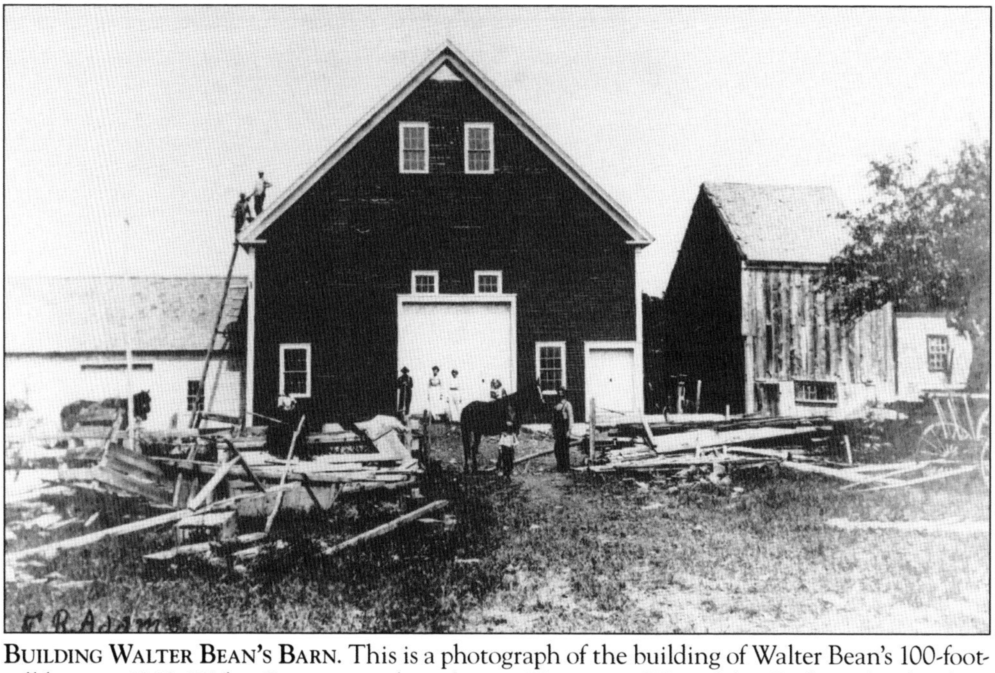

BUILDING WALTER BEAN'S BARN. This is a photograph of the building of Walter Bean's 100-foot-tall barn in 1903. Walter Bean was a dairy farmer. He married Dora May Goding, the daughter of Jonas Goding and Lucretia Bradford Smith Pike. They settled in Bean's Corner and had three children, Harold Gorham (whose twin did not survive) and Bertha Lucretia.

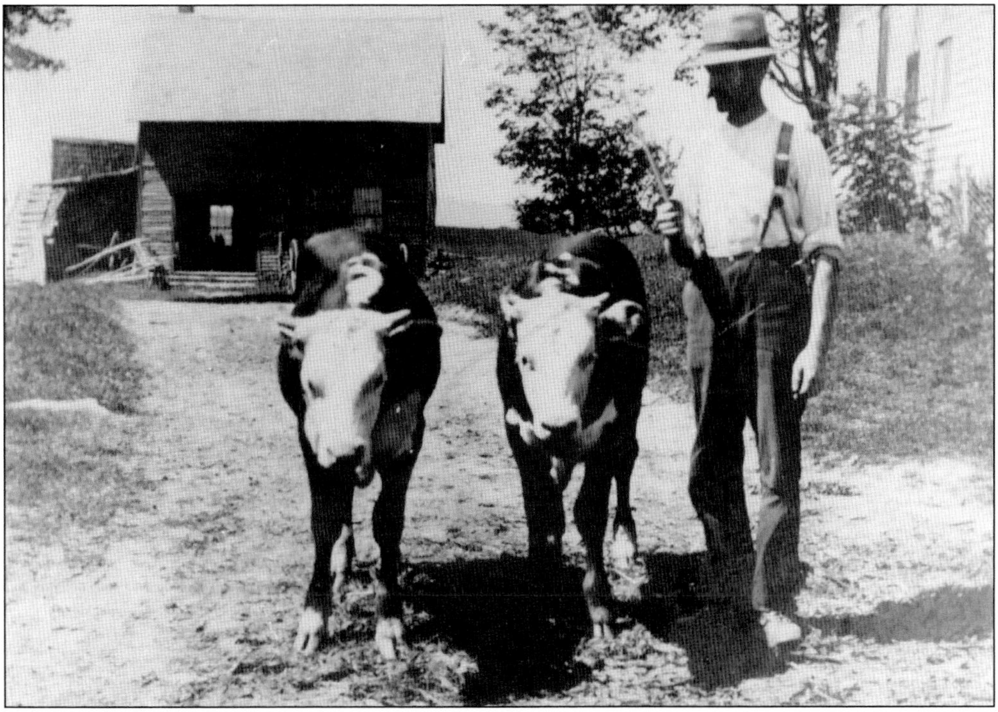

Walter Bean and His Steers. For many years, farming was the primary industry in Jay. This changed when other industries came to town. Here, Walter Bean can be seen working on the farm.

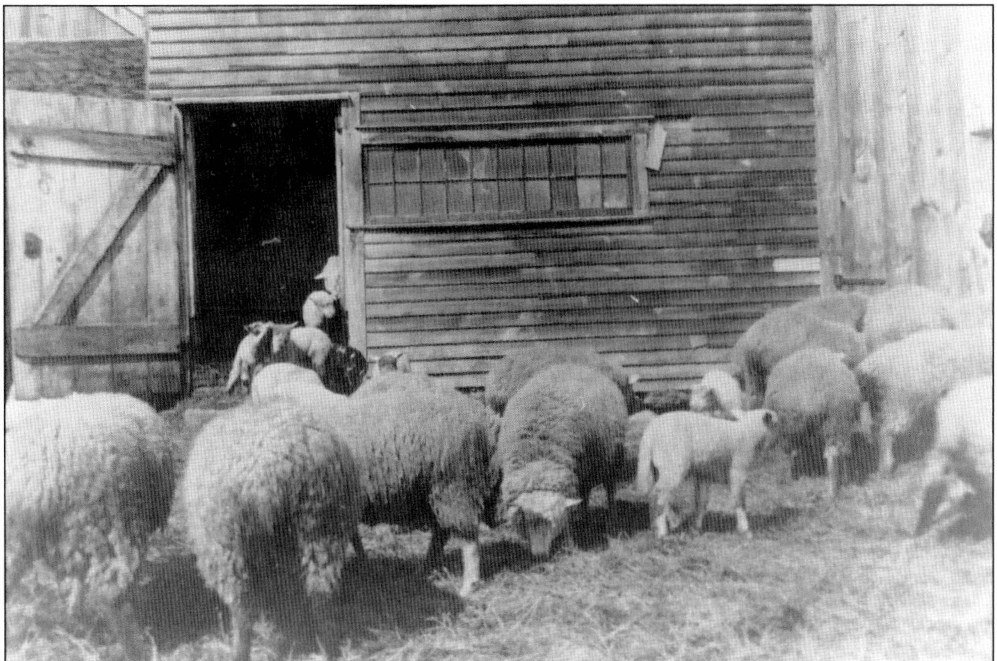

Sheep at Barn on Jay Hill. These sheep were likely raised to be shorn for their wool and eaten. The wool was spun into many clothing items, which would have been appreciated during the long and extremely cold winters in the area.

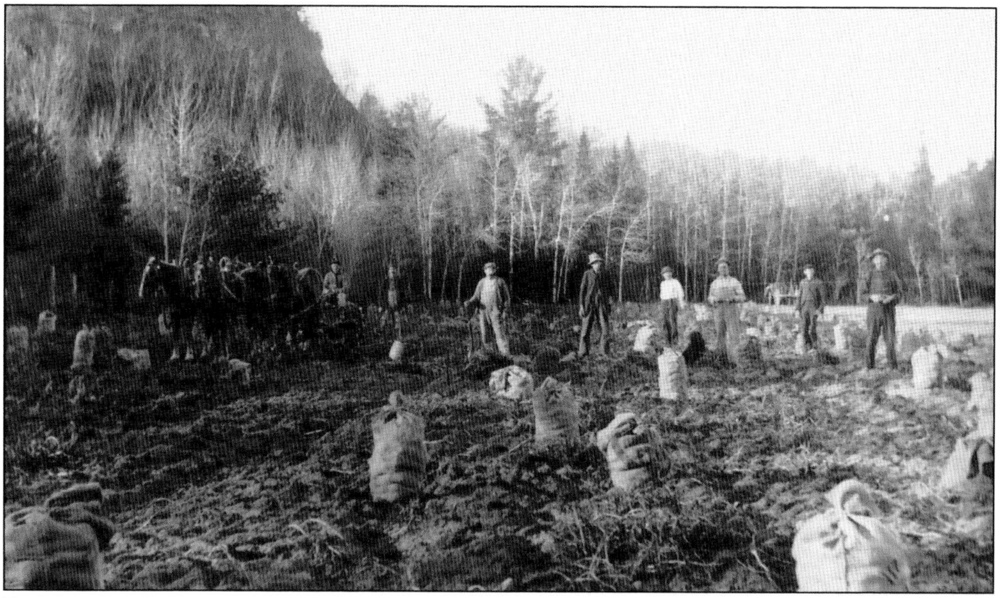

Potato Field at the Bluff on Jay Intervale. As autumn was harvest time, it was a very busy season for local farmers. There was the reaping and threshing of grain and the cutting and husking of corn to be done. Potatoes had to be dug and placed in what was called a potato hole near the homestead, for few homes in the early days had cellars. In later years, apple orchards were planted, so that fruit needed picking. Cider was made in the fall. Often, the apples were used to make applesauce and butter to be put away for the harsh winters.

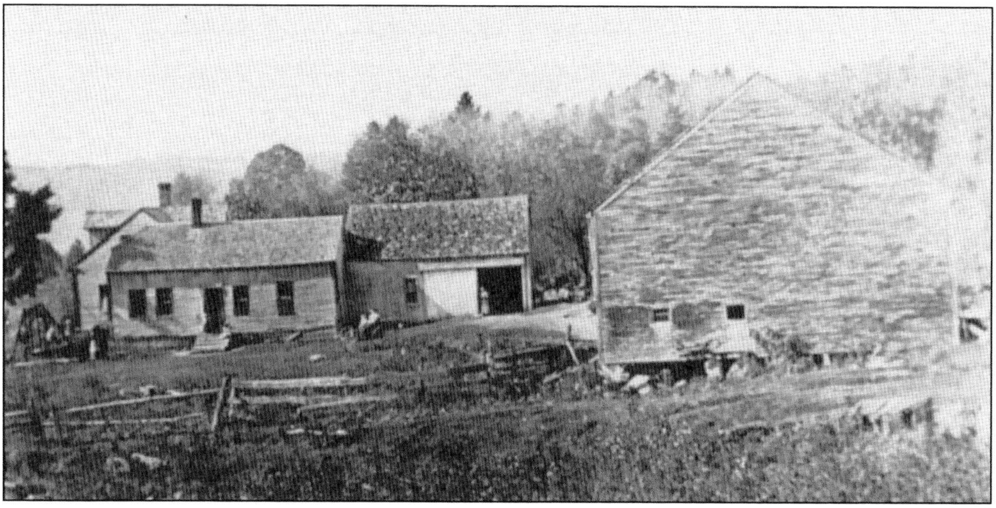

Frank and Daisy Latham's Farm and Home on Jay Intervale, c. 1911. Frank Latham was a laborer and farmer. He married Daisy Elva Moody, and they lived on the Canton Road. They had eight children—Maurice, Leona, George, Bernice, Mildred, Glennis, Ralph, and Martha. The land was ripe for farming throughout Jay, and the Intervale was no exception; it was found to be loamy and rich. The main crops that were found in abundance were hay, corn, wheat, squash, pumpkins, potatoes, oats, and apples. In the early years, Jay was a rural farming community. Food was grown and livestock raised, not only to eat but also for making clothing and other household items. Cows provided leather, sheep provided wool, beef tallow was used to make candles, and flax was used to make linen.

Two

INDUSTRY

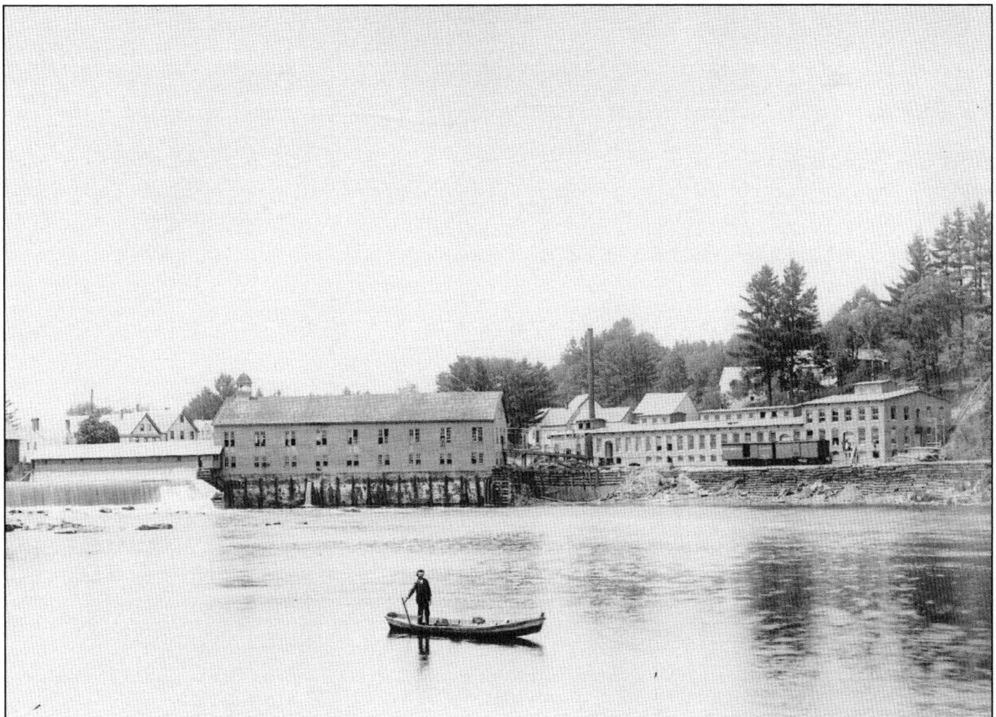

FALMOUTH PULP AND PAPER MILLS, C. 1894. The pulp mill was built by Alvin Record sometime between 1883 and 1885. Pulp manufacturing started in 1888, and in 1890 paper manufacturing commenced. In 1891, the Jay Paper Company was organized. A paper mill was added, the dam was built, and two paper machines were installed. These properties soon became known as the Falmouth Paper Company of Jay.

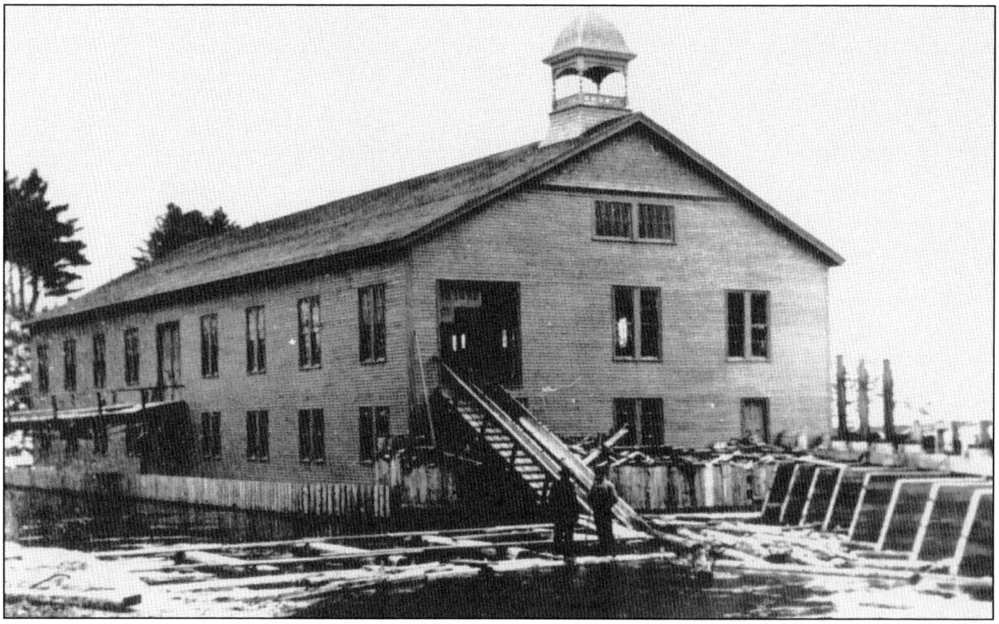

Jay Sawmill, c. 1891. Jay Sawmill became part of the Jay Paper Company and later the Falmouth Mill. This photograph was taken by Reginald Sturtevant and is now in the possession of the Jay Historical Society. This sawmill was at Jay Bridge. It was built by Francis Thompson, who operated it for four years. The large mill was above the village, and it had a novelty mill connected with it that employed many local people. It burned in 1884.

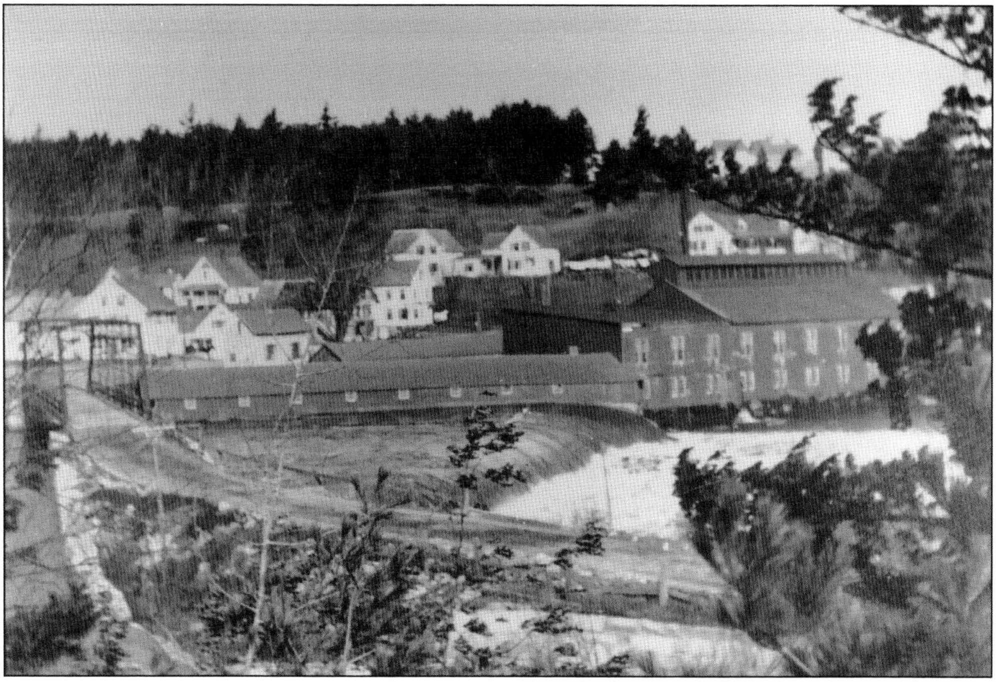

View of Jay Village and the Falmouth Mill. This photograph from around 1900 was taken looking east to the Jay Village settlement, which is visible in the background. It shows the Falmouth Mill and the metal bridge that replaced the covered wooden bridge.

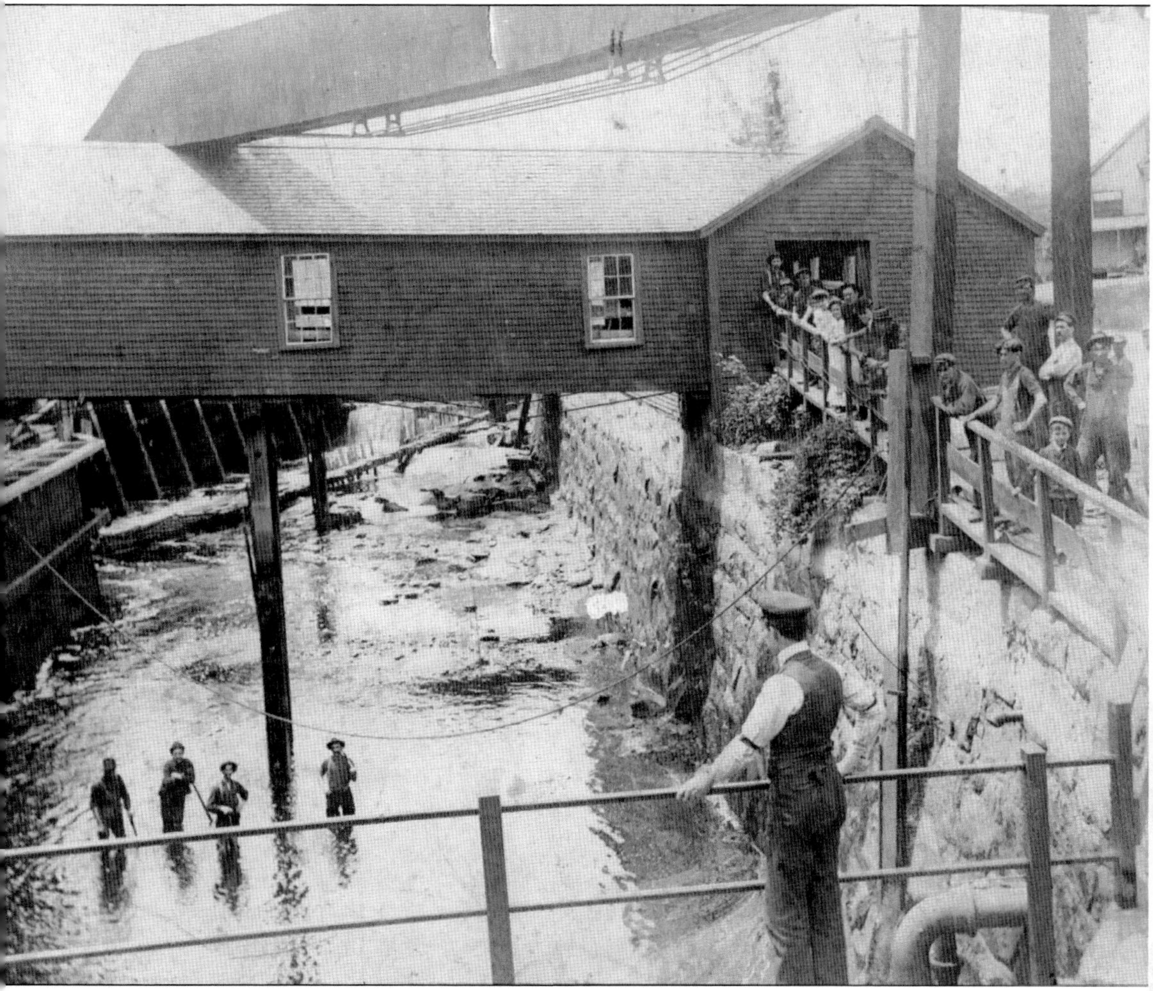

FALMOUTH MILL. This is another view of the Falmouth Mill with Jay Village in the background. The men in the water have shovels, but it is uncertain what exactly they are doing. They might be working on a cofferdam. This photograph was likely taken in the early 1900s.

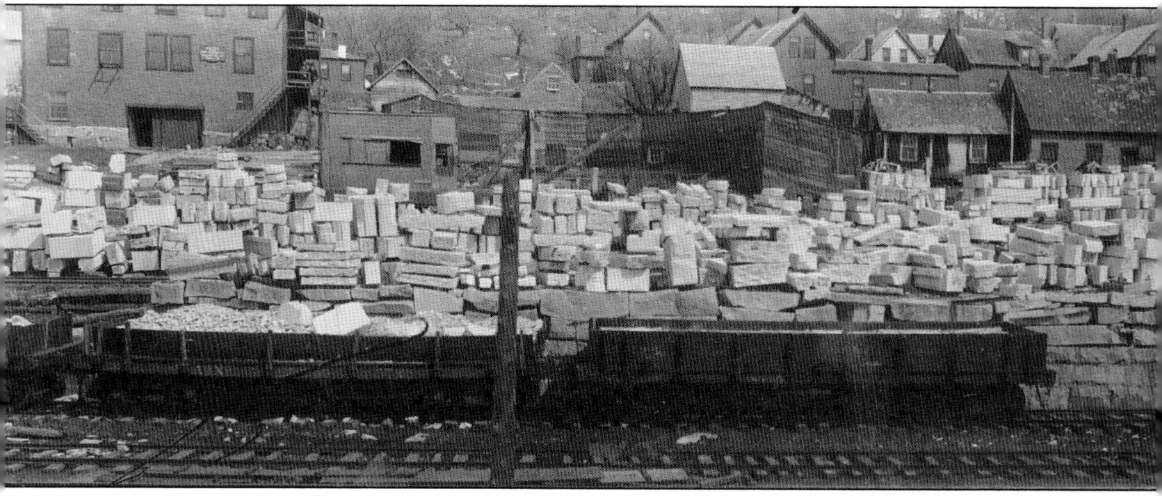

MAINE AND NEW HAMPSHIRE GRANITE CORPORATION, NORTH JAY. In this photograph are the main office and cutting sheds of the North Jay Granite Company. It was organized in 1884 by James H. Emery of Poland, Maine, and George W. Wagg of Auburn, Maine. This quarry supplied curbing and paving stones to several cities, as well as stone for monuments. In 1887, the company was reorganized and expanded and named the Maine and New Hampshire Granite Corporation.

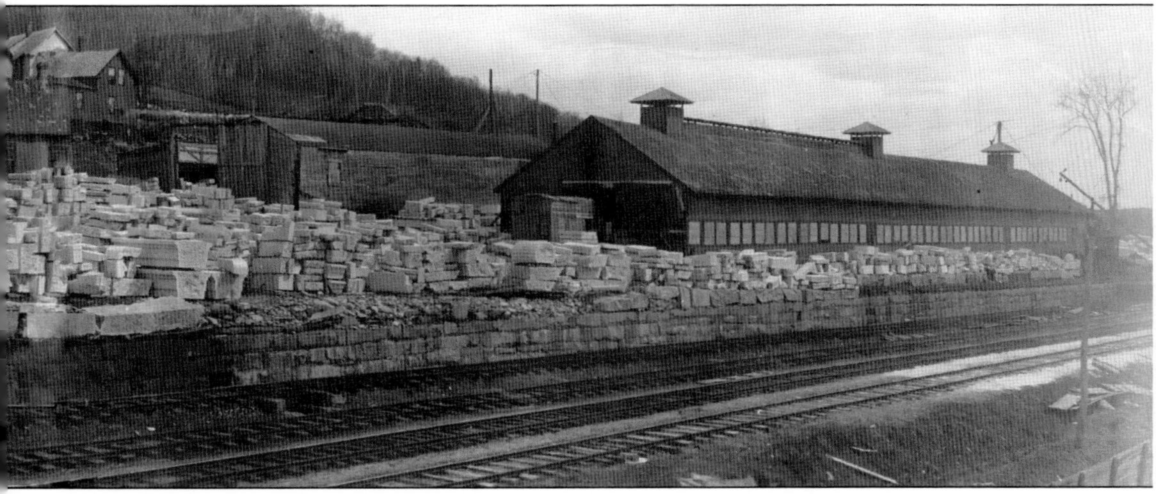

New cutting sheds were built and quarry operations enlarged. Payson Tucker, general manager for the Maine Central Railroad and Ara Cushman, a shoe manufacturer from Auburn, joined Emery and Wagg to form the Maine and New Hampshire Granite Corporation. J.P Murphy of Lewiston was hired as the general superintendent. He secured some very desirable contracts, including the R.H. Dunn Building in New York City and the Memorial Fairmount Park in Philadelphia.

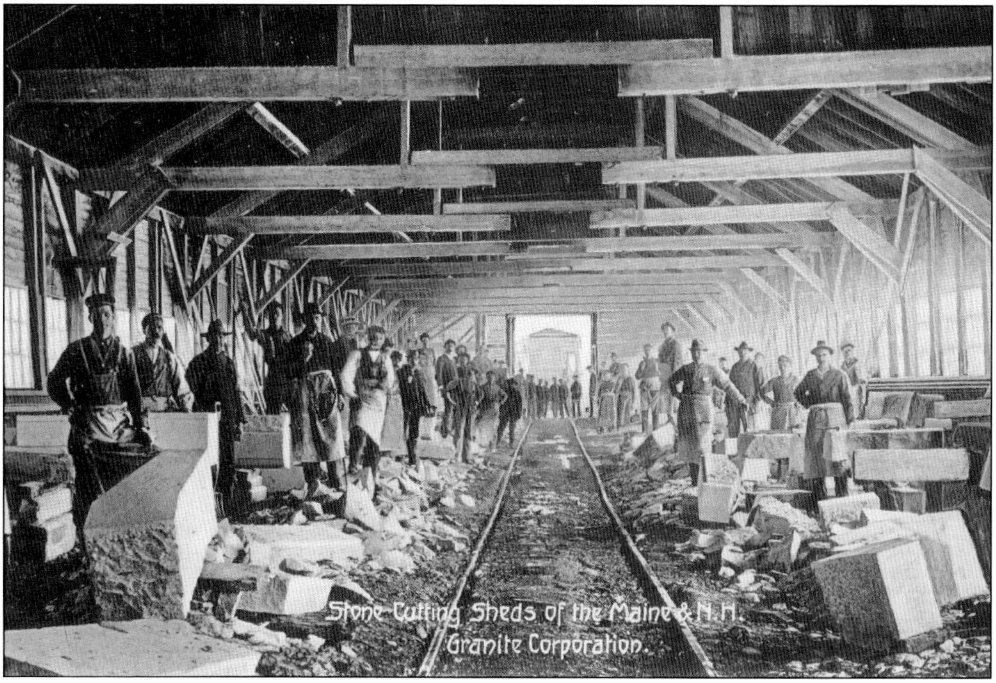

ONE OF THE MAINE AND NEW HAMPSHIRE GRANITE CORPORATION CUTTING SHEDS, C. 1930S. There are close to 50 men in this photograph. A railroad line was built to carry the cars up and down the hillside to and from the cutting sheds. This was accomplished by loading a car with granite blocks. Gravity would then move these blocks down the hill. The force of the filled car coming down the hill caused an empty car to return to the top to be filled again. Blocks in the quarry were moved to the line by pairs of oxen and horses.

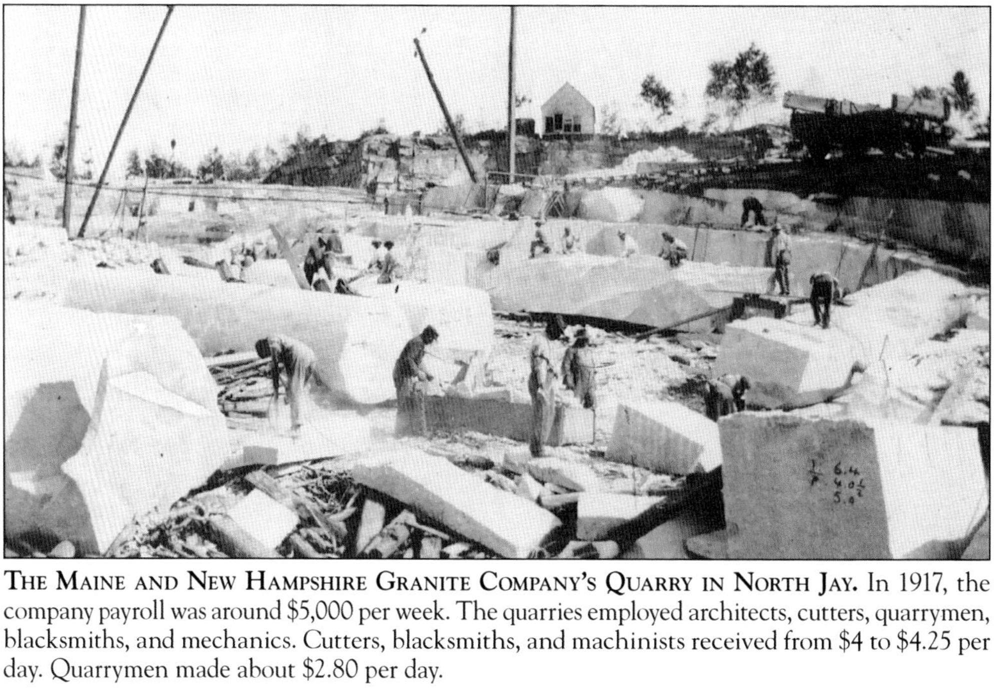

THE MAINE AND NEW HAMPSHIRE GRANITE COMPANY'S QUARRY IN NORTH JAY. In 1917, the company payroll was around $5,000 per week. The quarries employed architects, cutters, quarrymen, blacksmiths, and mechanics. Cutters, blacksmiths, and machinists received from $4 to $4.25 per day. Quarrymen made about $2.80 per day.

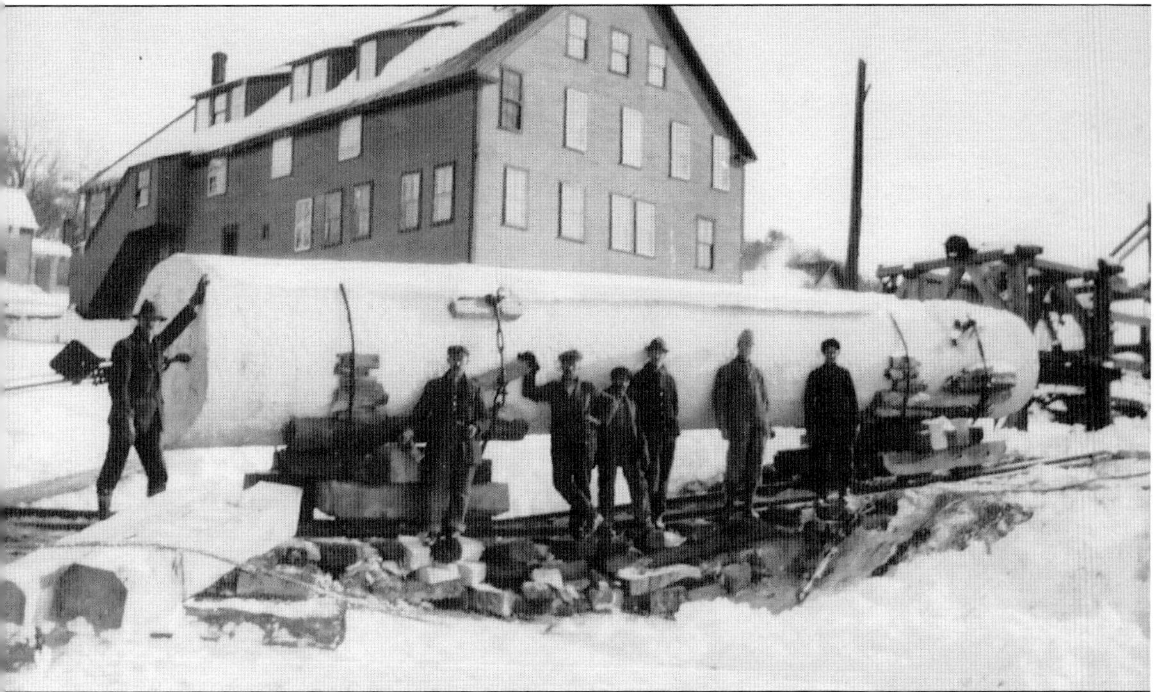

The Quarries and the Railroad. North Jay was in the path of the Maine Central Railroad, and the quarries were able to take advantage of this. One gets a sense of the size of this granite column by looking at the man standing beside it and the men in front of it. This photograph was likely taken in the early 1900s.

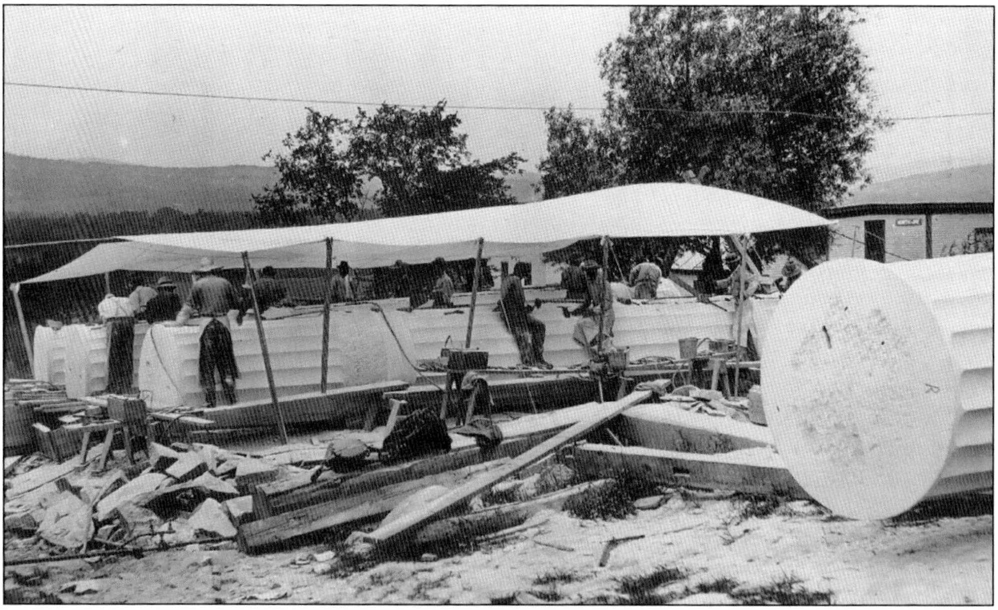

Columns of Granite Being Fluted. The photograph above shows a column of granite being fluted by hand before major machinery was invented to aid the process. This was a true art at the time. The photograph below shows a column of granite being fluted with the help of machinery.

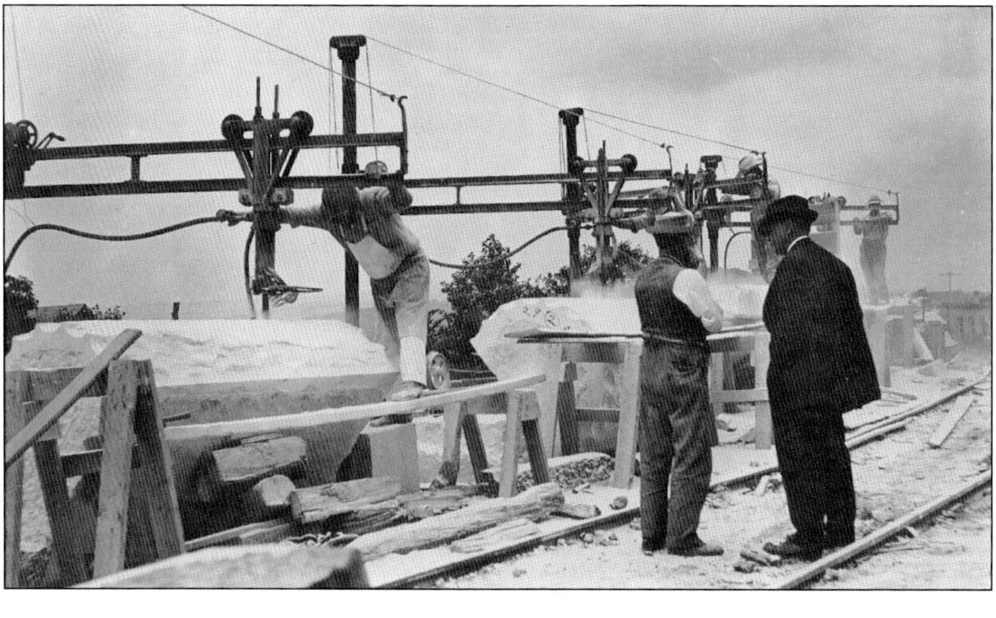

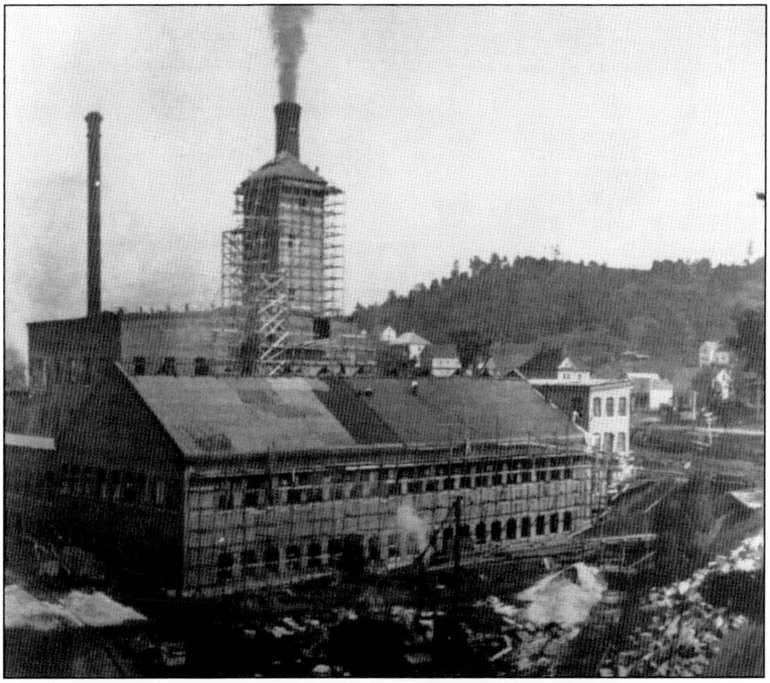

OTIS MILL UNDER CONSTRUCTION. Construction of the mill was started in 1892. The builder was John A. Greenleaf of Auburn. He had a history of building mills in Maine and beyond, and by this time, he had been constructing mills for 32 years. By 1898, eight paper machines were installed. The Otis Mill was soon considered the largest newspaper stock mill in the world.

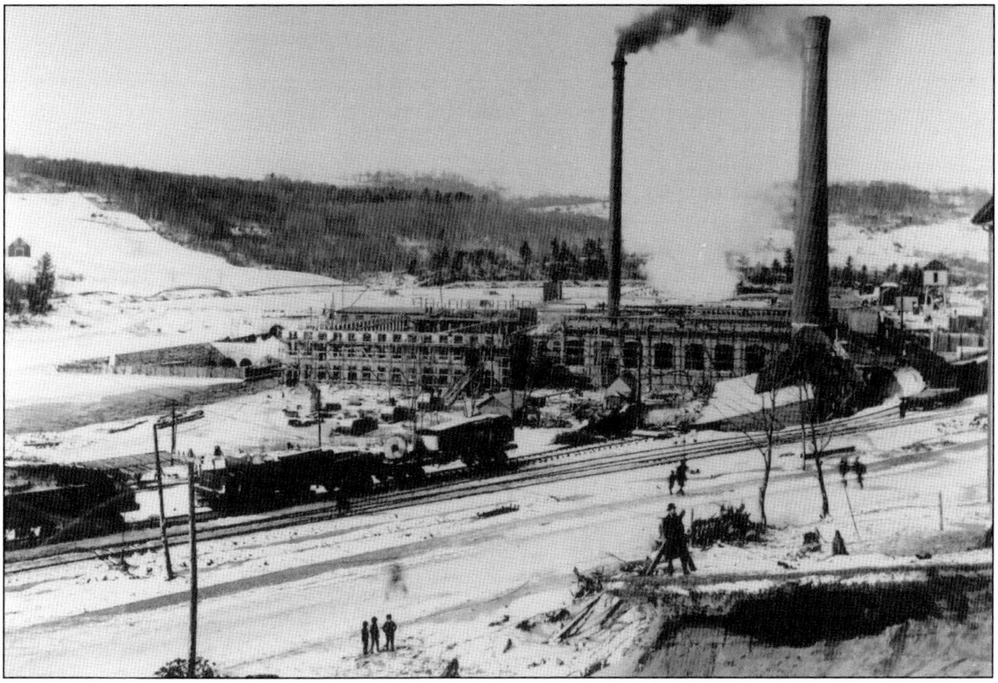

OTIS MILL BEFORE 1906. This photograph was taken of the mill at the time when the No. 9 and No. 10 paper machines were added to the complex. Otis Mill saw rapid construction. It had 10 paper machines, nine for newsprint and one for wrapping paper. Daily, 17 tons of wrapping paper were made from the waste. The pulp mill ground 60 cords of wood and the sulphite mill converted 100 cords of wood into paper each day. At this time, the capacity of the mill was 240 tons a day. It employed 550 men and generated 7,500 horsepower from the water.

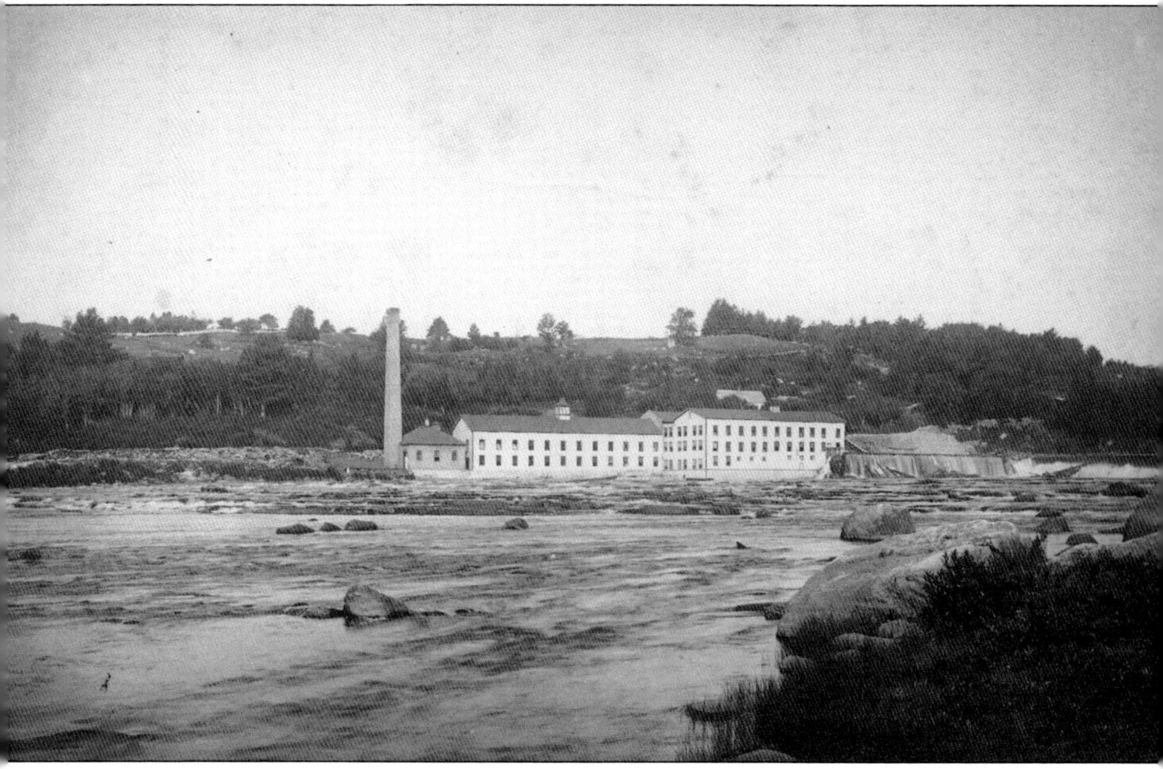

OTIS MILL, LATE 1800S. The village of Chisholm was named after the industrialist Hugh Chisholm. After he came to town, workers came to work in the mill, many from Quebec. The population of this area boomed, and it became the population center of the town of Jay. Eventually, this hillside was crowded with the homes of mill workers.

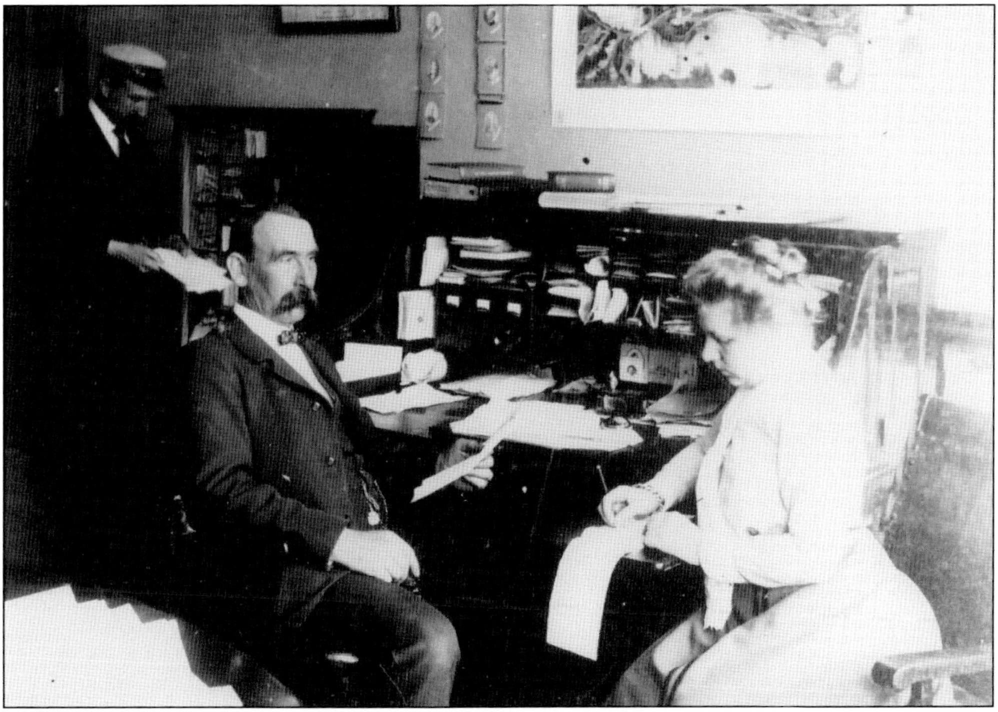

Otis Mill, 1892. In 1892, there were two Fourdrinier machines in use. Chisholm brought Edwin Riley (pictured) from Fort Edward, New York, to be the first manager in the mill office. Another pulp mill was built up the river, and the settlement there was named in Riley's honor.

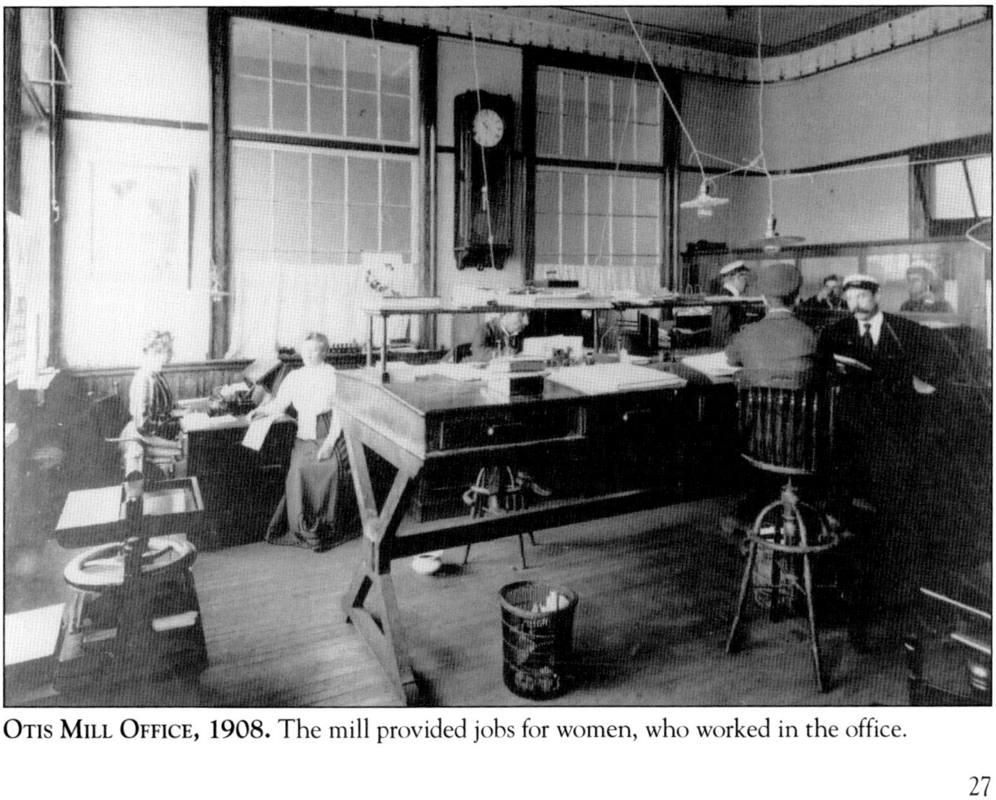

Otis Mill Office, 1908. The mill provided jobs for women, who worked in the office.

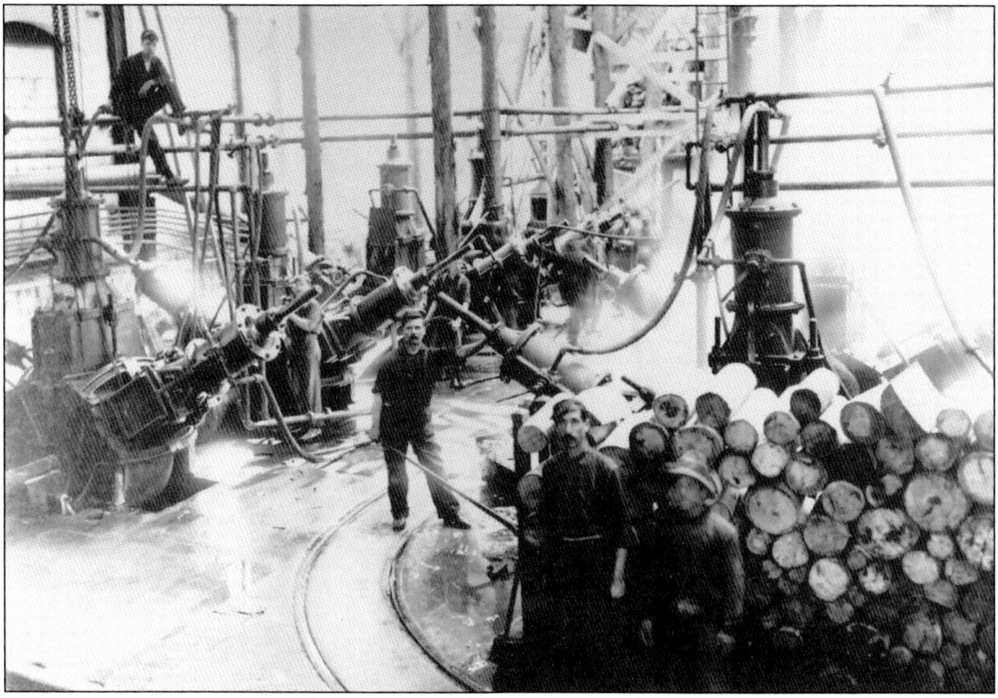

OTIS MILL CORLISS STEAM ENGINE, 1908. A Corliss steam engine is fitted with rotary valves and with variable valve timing patented in 1849. It was invented by and named after the American engineer George Henry Corliss. His engines were typically used as stationary engines to provide mechanical power to line shafting in factories and mills and to drive dynamos to generate electricity.

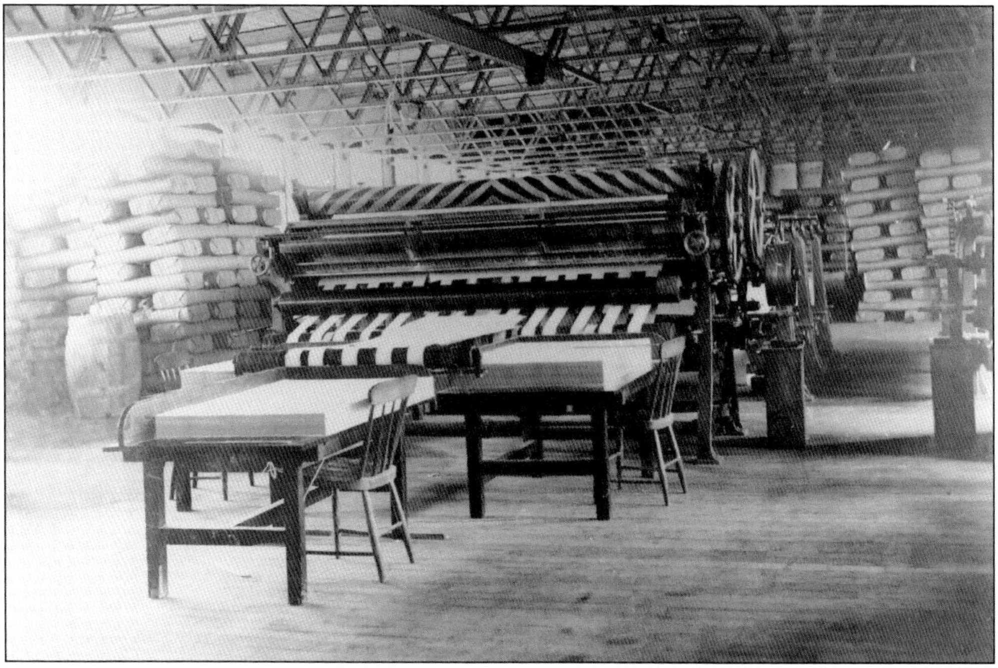

OTIS MILL FINISHING ROOM, 1906. This room was where the final touches were put on the paper, and it became a finished project.

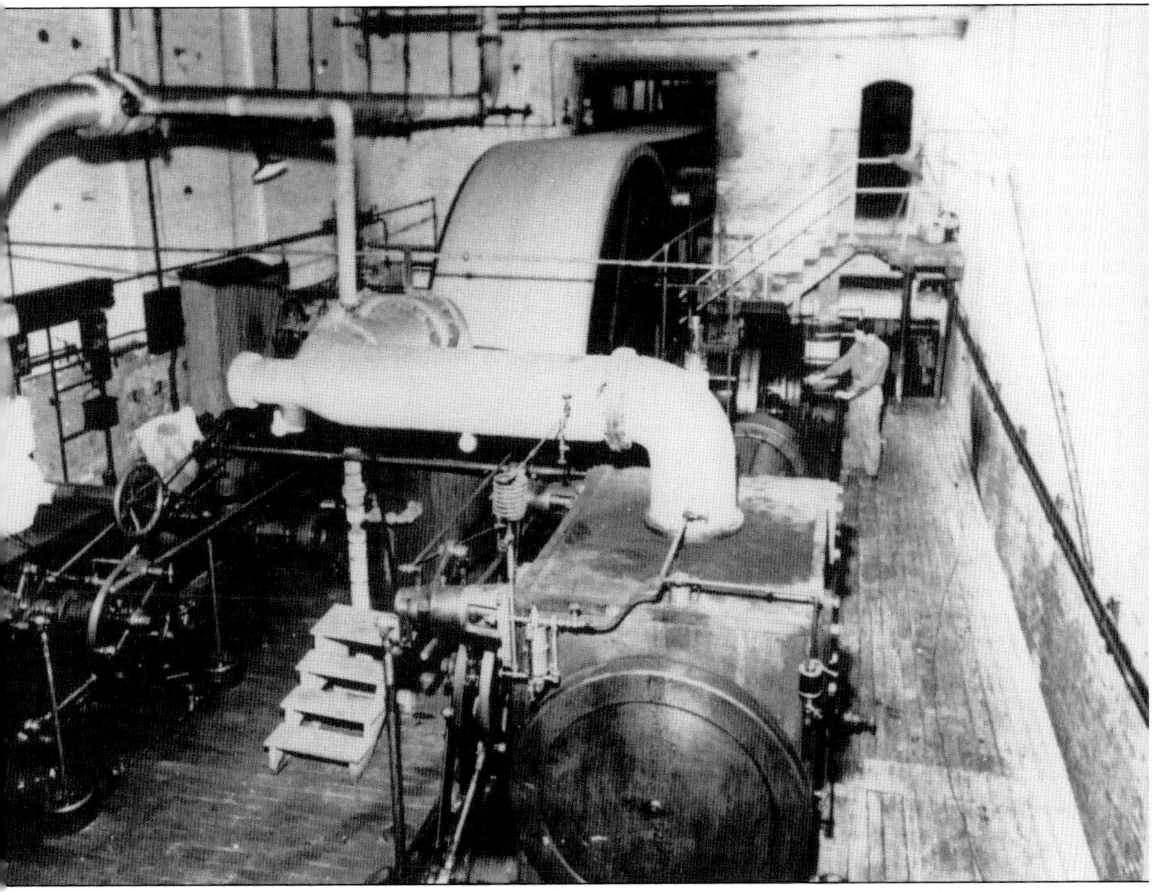

Otis Mill. The grinder room is shown at Otis Mill in 1908, when Edwin Riley was there. This is the room where the paper was ground into pulp, later to be made into paper.

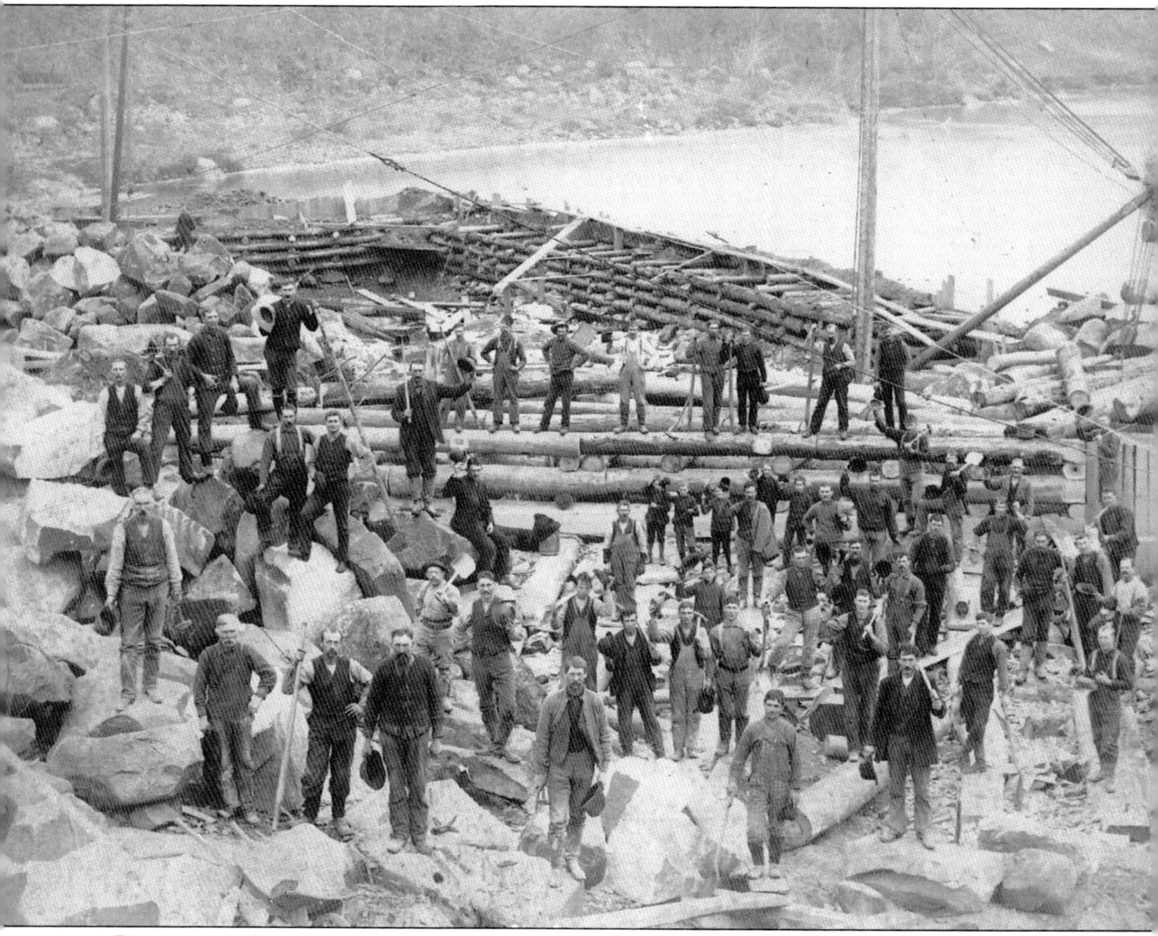

Building a Cofferdam at Otis Mill in the 1890s. This was the earliest dam built in this location. More effective dams were later built.

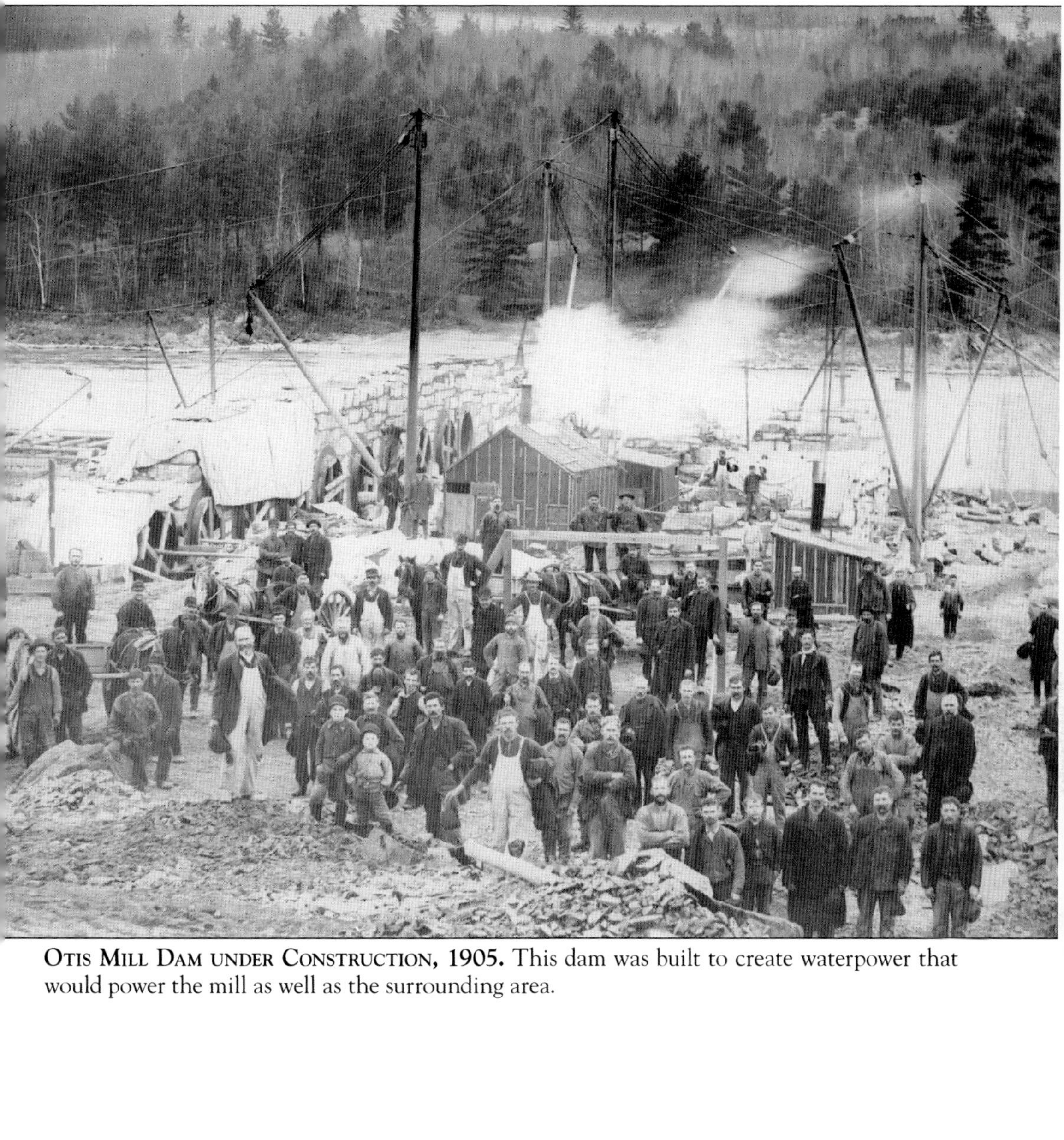

Otis Mill Dam under Construction, 1905. This dam was built to create waterpower that would power the mill as well as the surrounding area.

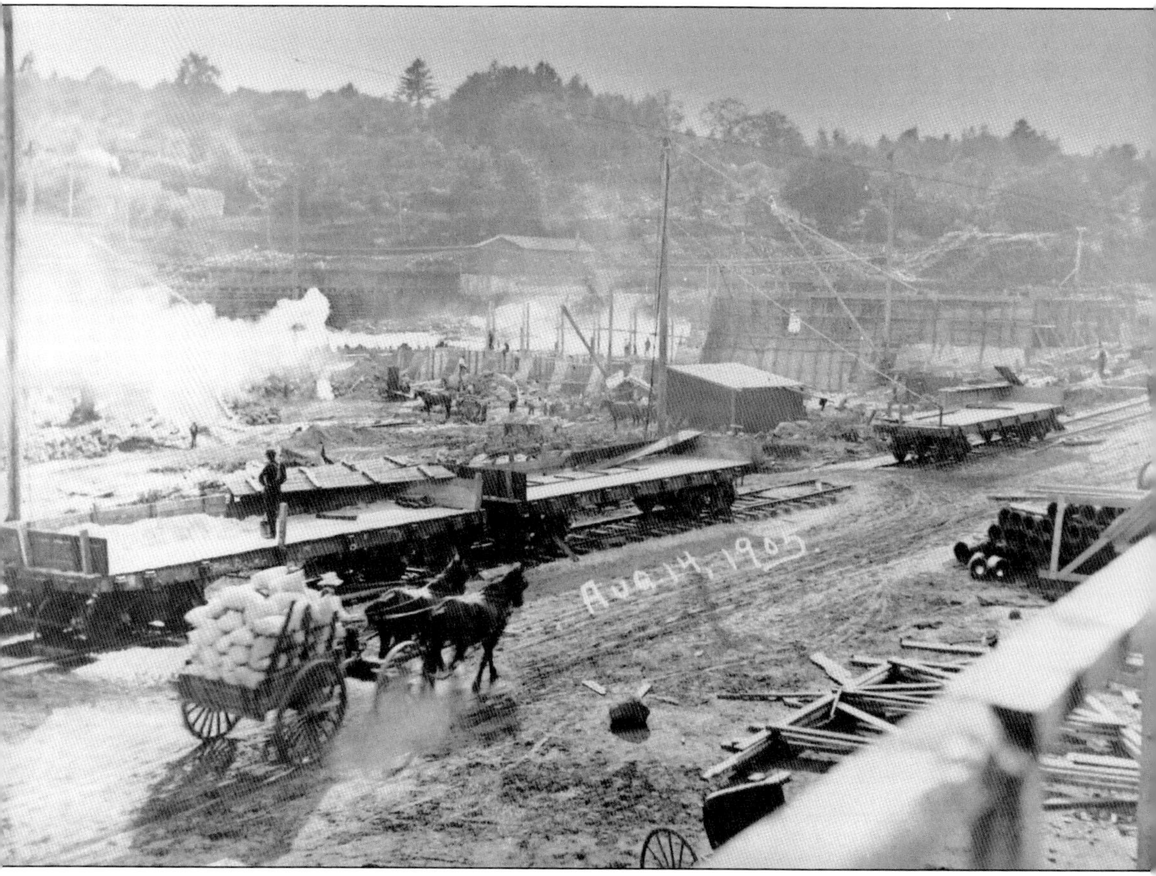

BUILDING OTIS MILL DAM, 1905. It was hoped the dams would help to alleviate flooding in addition to providing power. They helped with lesser freshets but were heavily damaged in the great flood of 1936.

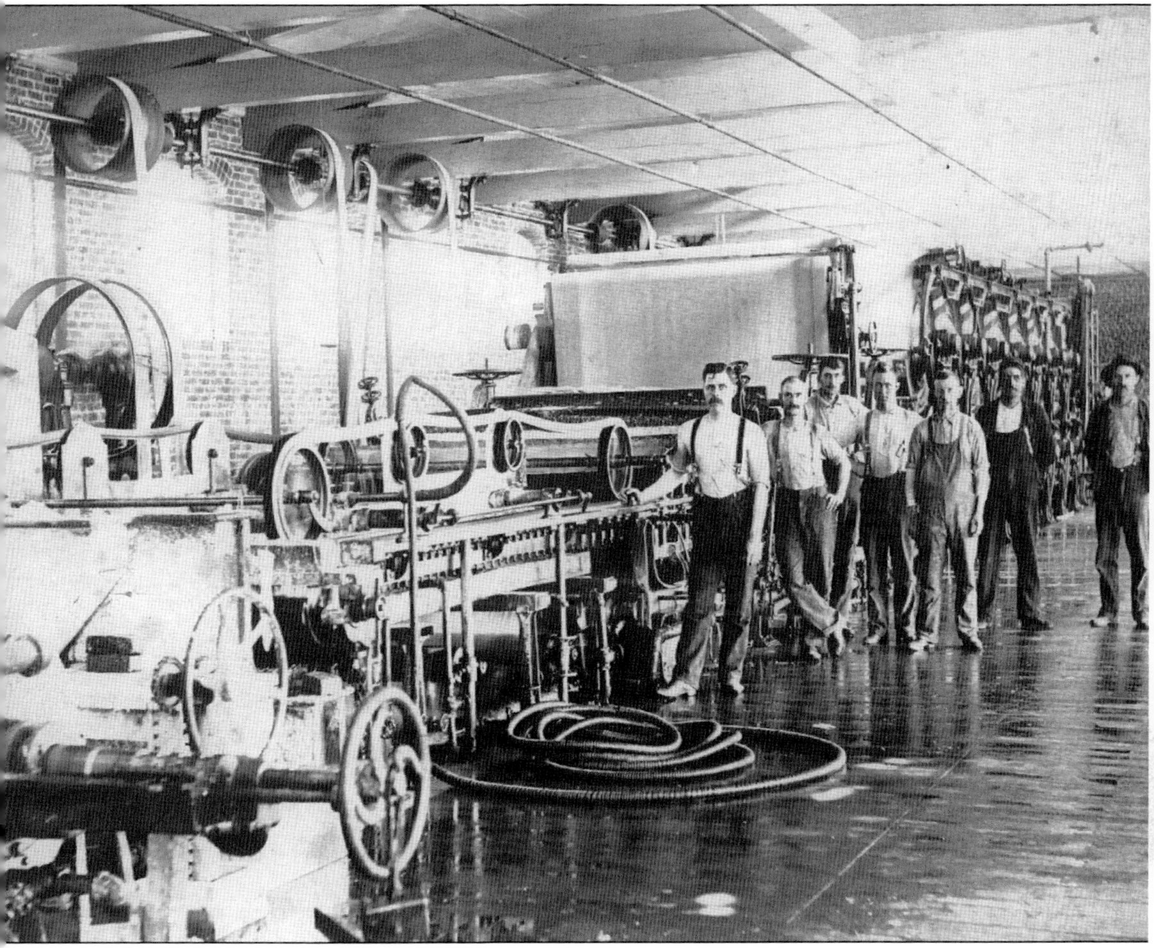

INSIDE OTIS MILL. For its time, Otis Mill had state-of-the-art equipment, which can be seen in this photograph from the early 1900s.

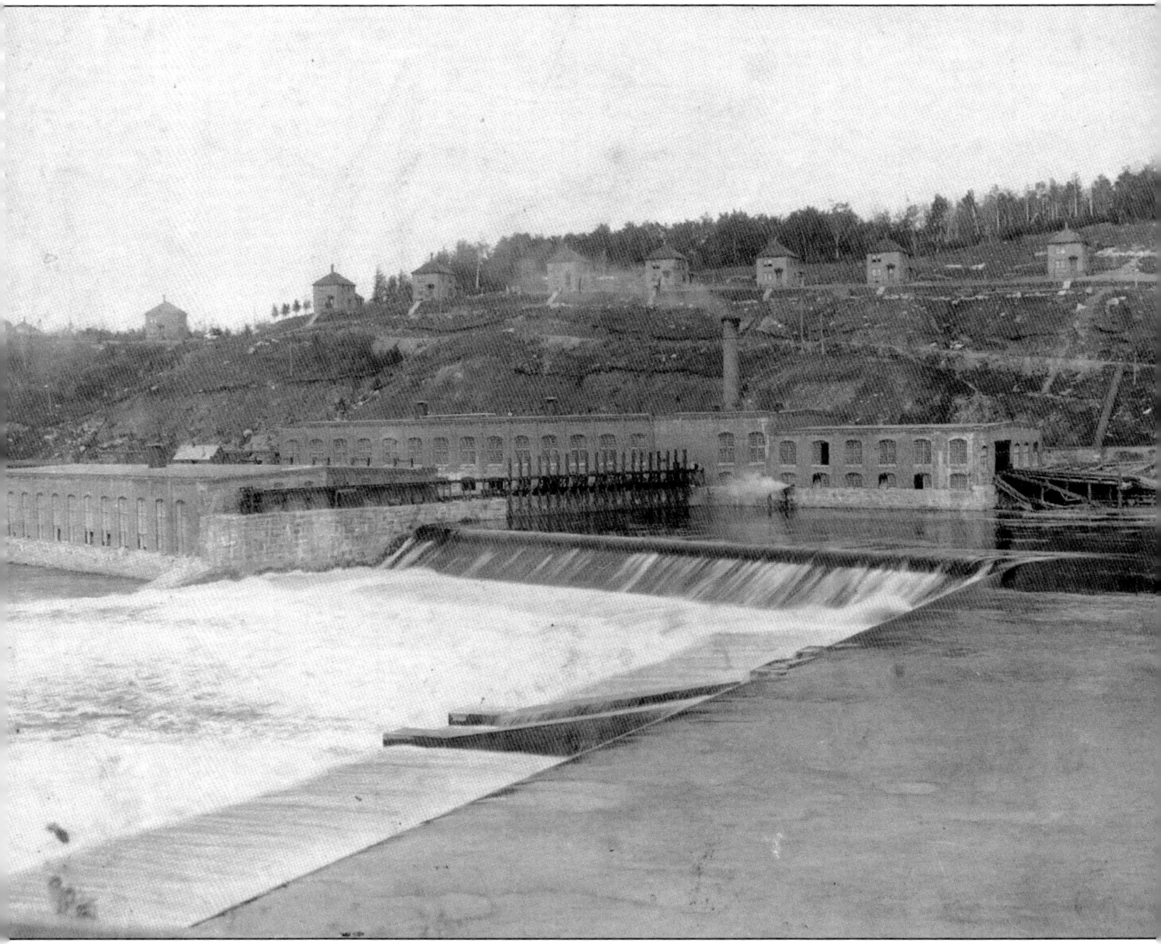

Riley Mill, c. 1900. The company houses in the background accommodated mill workers. At one point, there was as many as 20 company houses, and a school was constructed for the benefit of mill employees' children. A Catholic church, St. Mary's of the Assumption, was also erected for mill workers.

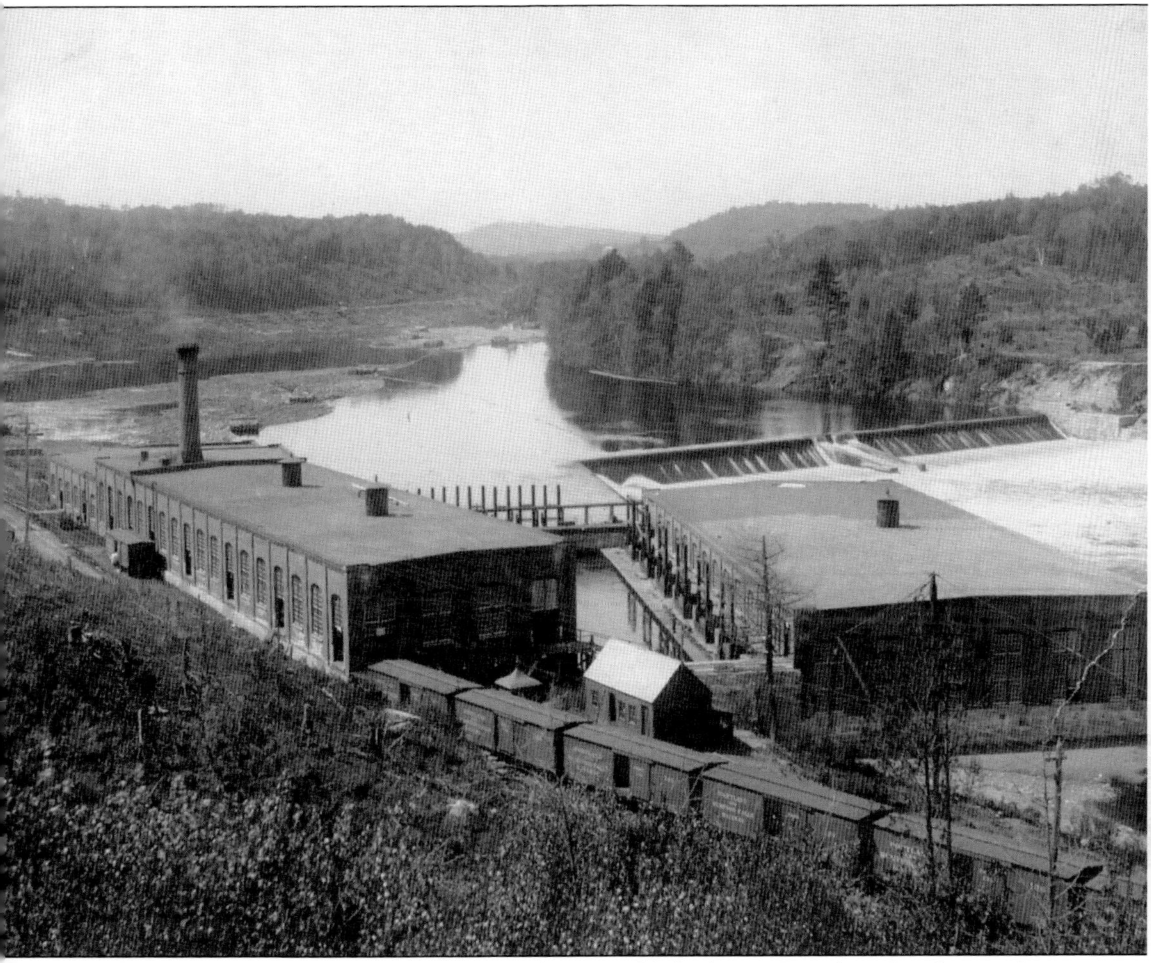

Riley Mill with Railroad Tracks. Riley Mill was established in 1897 and produced raw pulp for the Otis Mill. In 1898, the mill started up with 12 grinders and 17 wet machines. The pulp was dried on the wet machines and folded into bundles or "laps." The laps were loaded on railcars and shipped to the Otis Mill or the Chisholm mills in Rumford. Later, the pulp was transported by a pipeline that connected the two mills. It employed around 100 men. Eventually, this mill became part of the International Paper Company conglomerate.

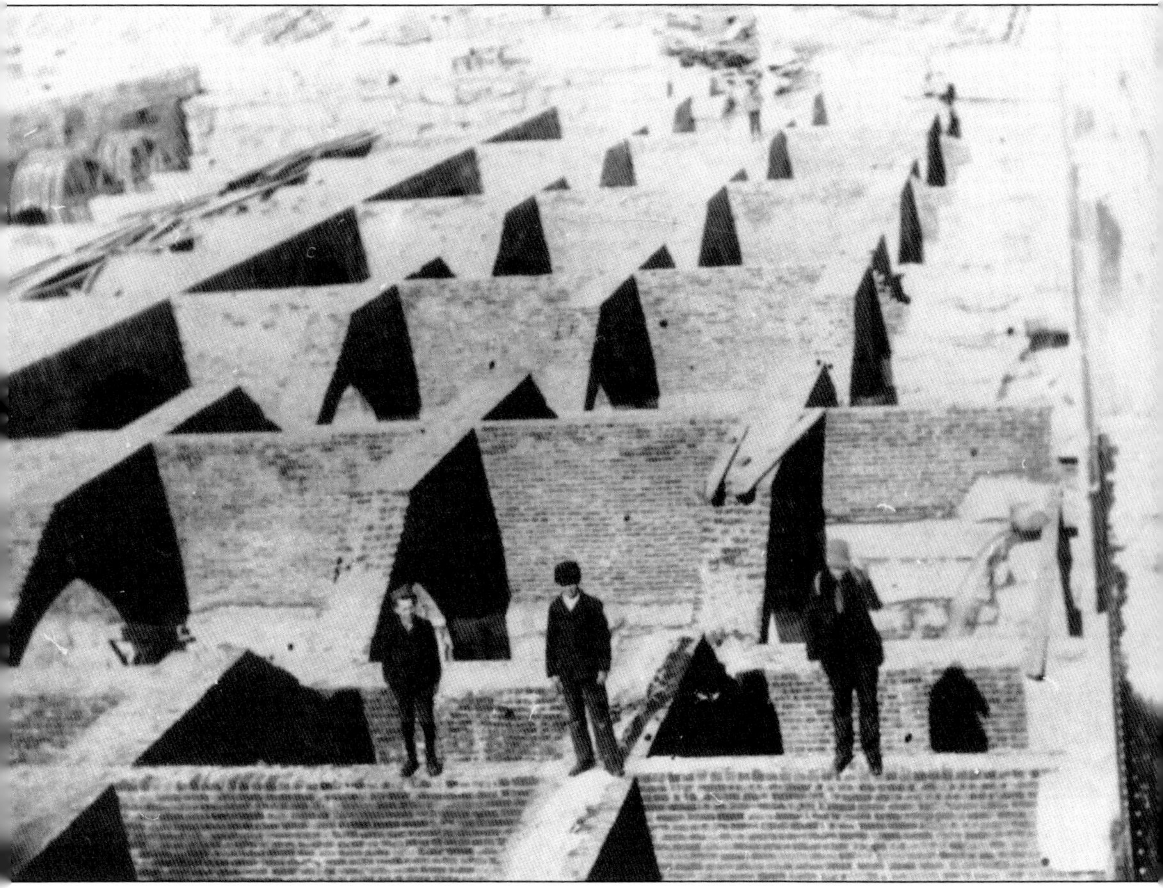

Riley Mill Foundation Construction, 1896. The new pulp mill at Riley was erected on what was previously known as the Peterson's Rips. In 1897, the Riley Mill had 22 grinders and a capacity of 100 tons per day.

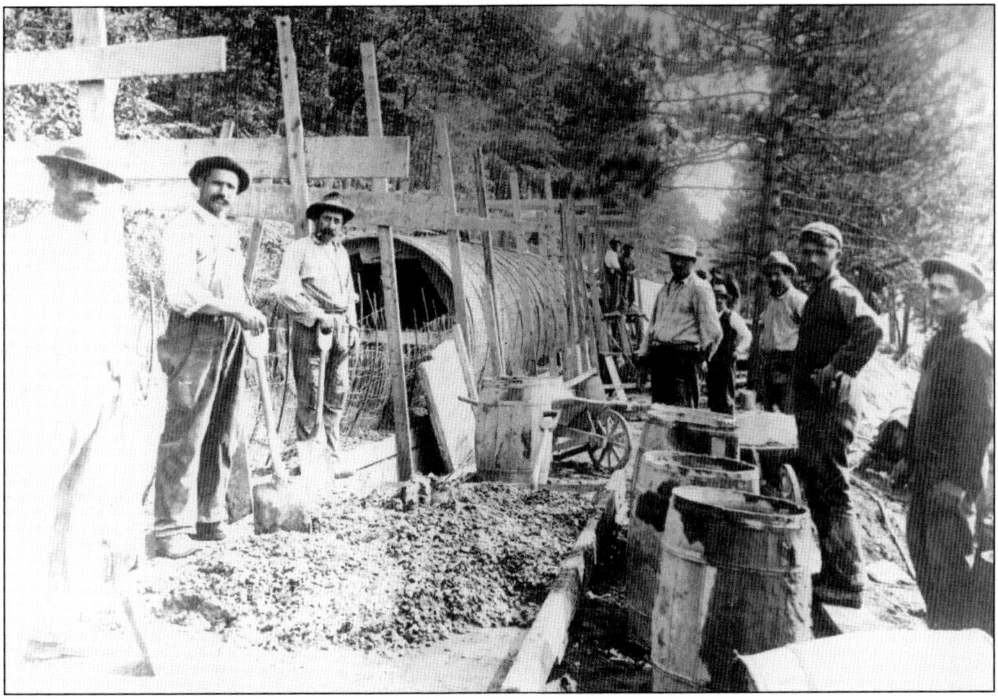

Building the Stock Line at the Riley Mill, 1897. The stock line was made of wood. It carried ground wood from the Riley Mill to the Otis Mill. The distance between the two mills was about two miles.

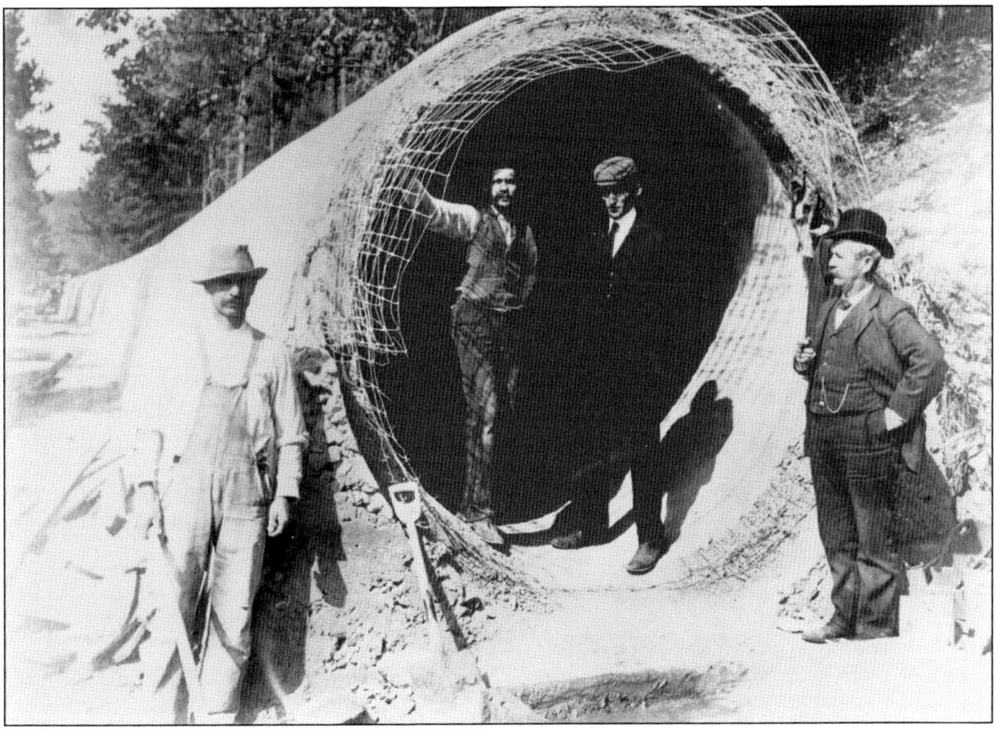

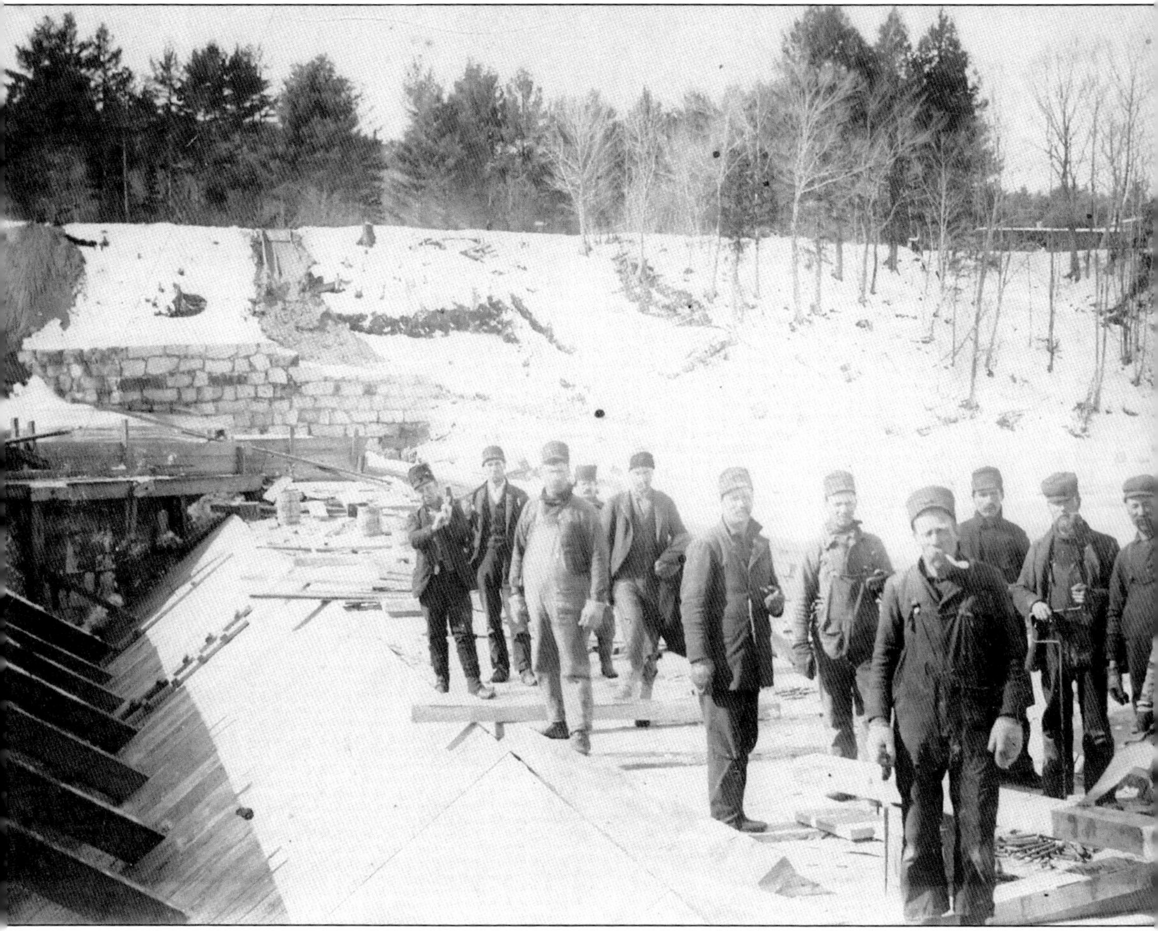

BUILDING THE RILEY DAM. In this photograph from 1908, the Riley Dam is being built.

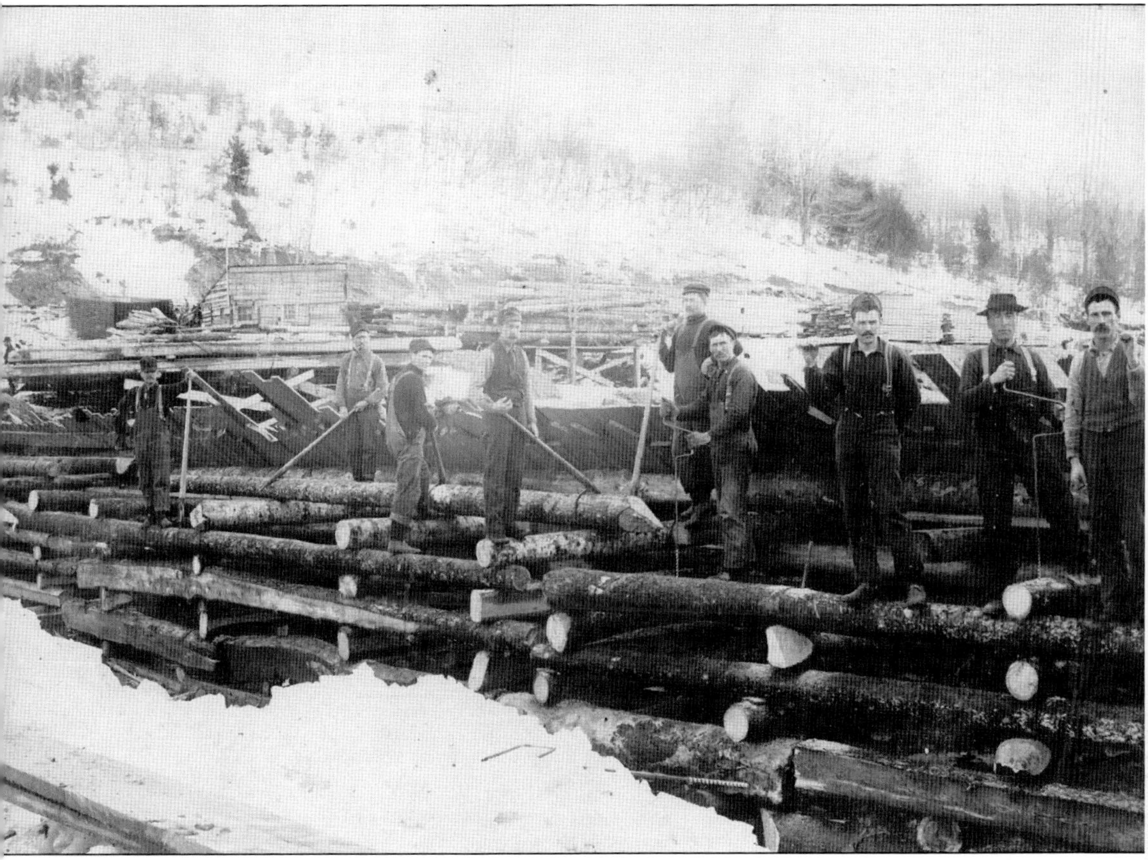

THE RILEY DAM BEING BUILT. As of 1912, the waterpower at Riley was 940 horsepower. This dam provided power for the mill and the surrounding area.

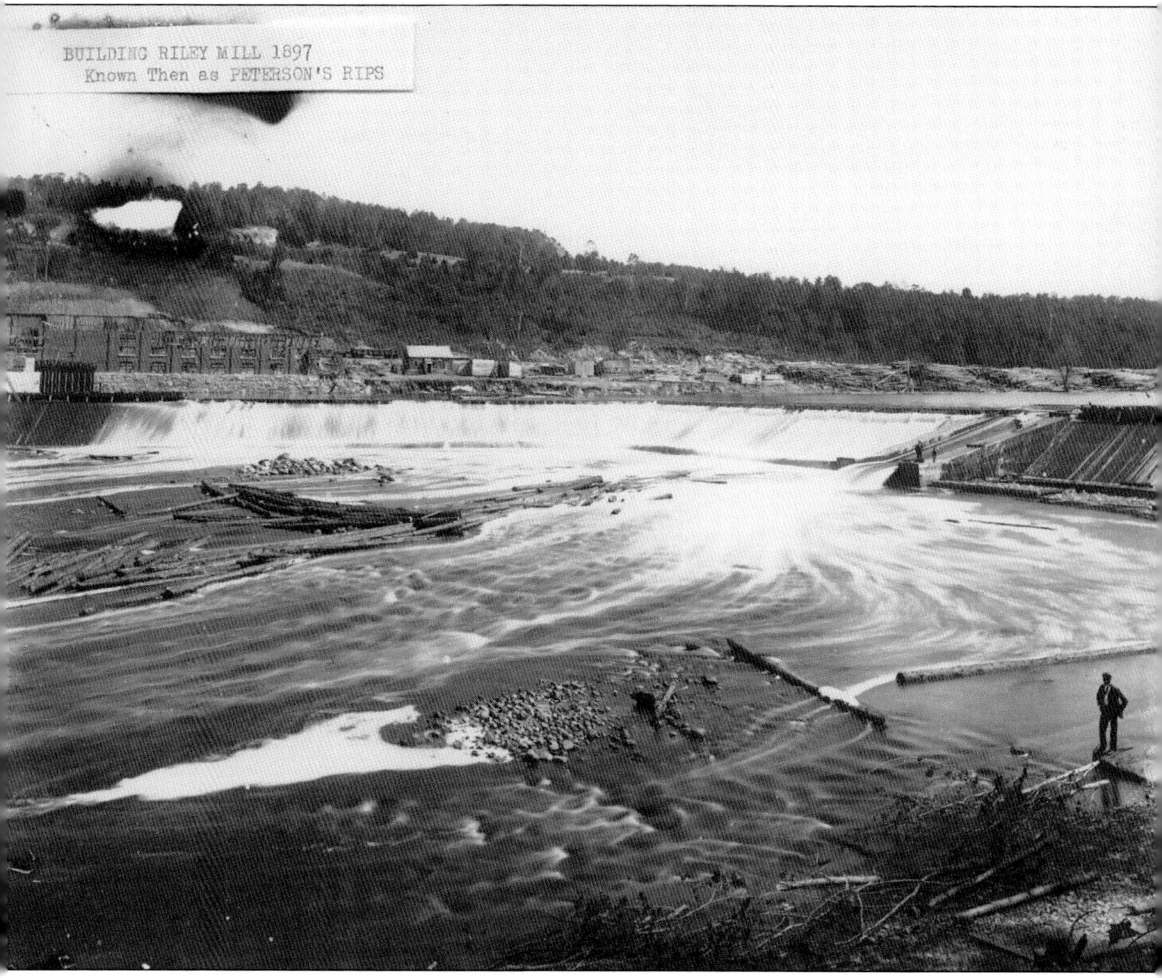

BUILDING THE RILEY MILL, 1897. This area was then known as Peterson's Rips. There are no company houses in the background yet. They were built once immigrants from Italy and other parts of the world came to the mill to work. The Otis Pulp and Paper Company built 13 houses above the mill. Of these houses, 12 contained six rooms. House No. 13 was for the mill manager. It had eight large rooms and was removed from the other houses.

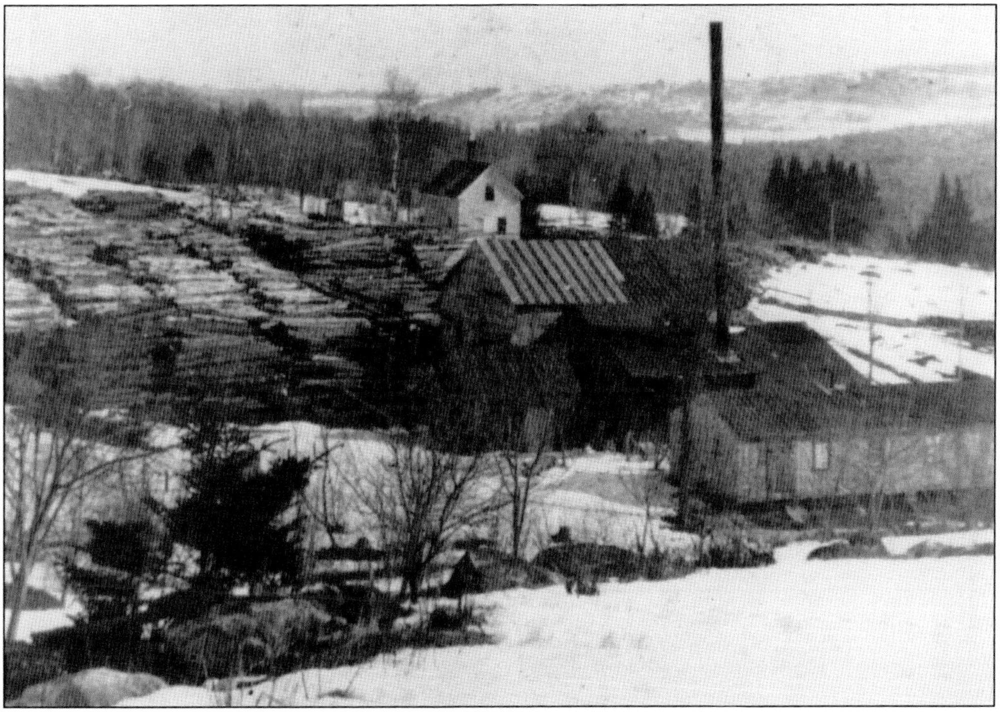

Bean and Hutchinson Barrel Factory. The Bean and Hutchinson Barrel Factory was located on Canton Mountain Road in the early 1900s. Apple barrels were big business at the time.

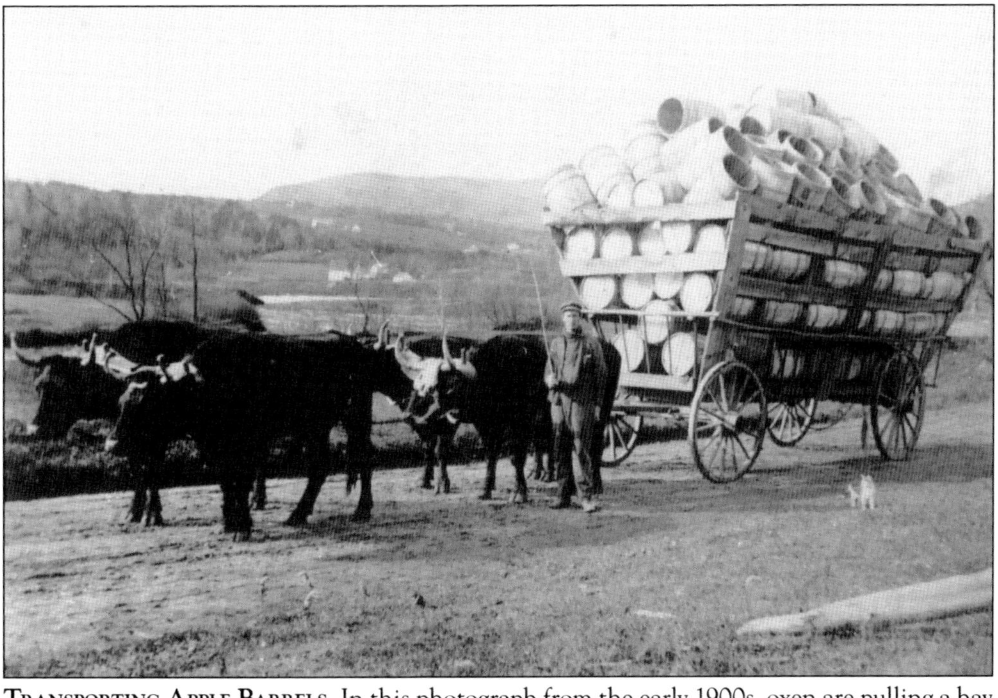

Transporting Apple Barrels. In this photograph from the early 1900s, oxen are pulling a hay cart filled with apple barrels from the Bean and Hutchinson Sawmill and Barrel Factory on the Canton Mountain Road.

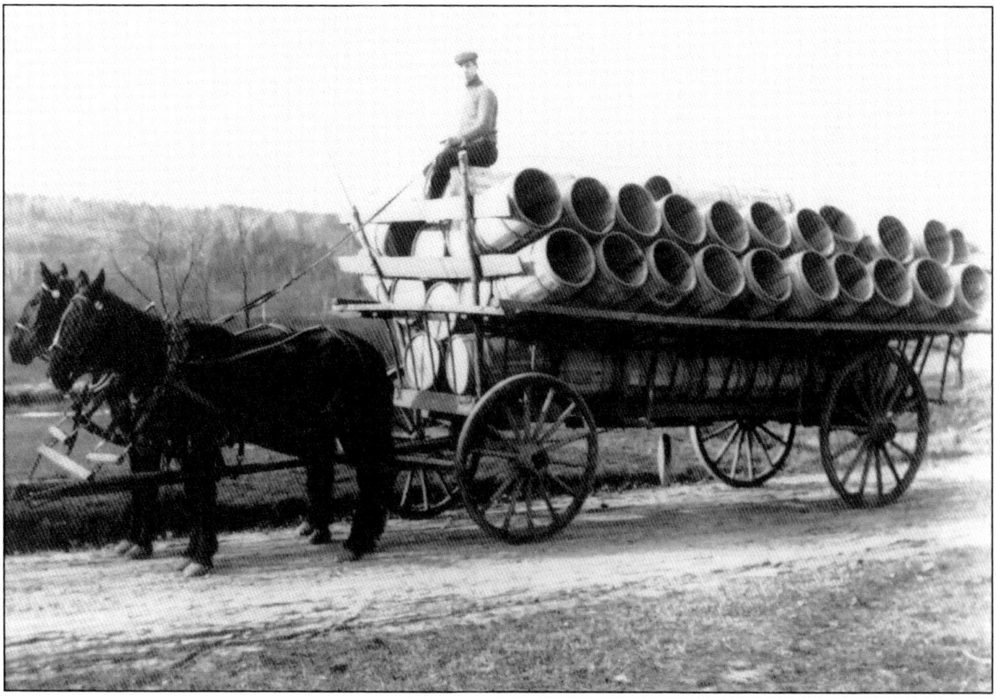

Apple Barrels. Apples are being transported from the Bean and Hutchinson Barrel Factory. In this image, hayracks are being pulled by horses.

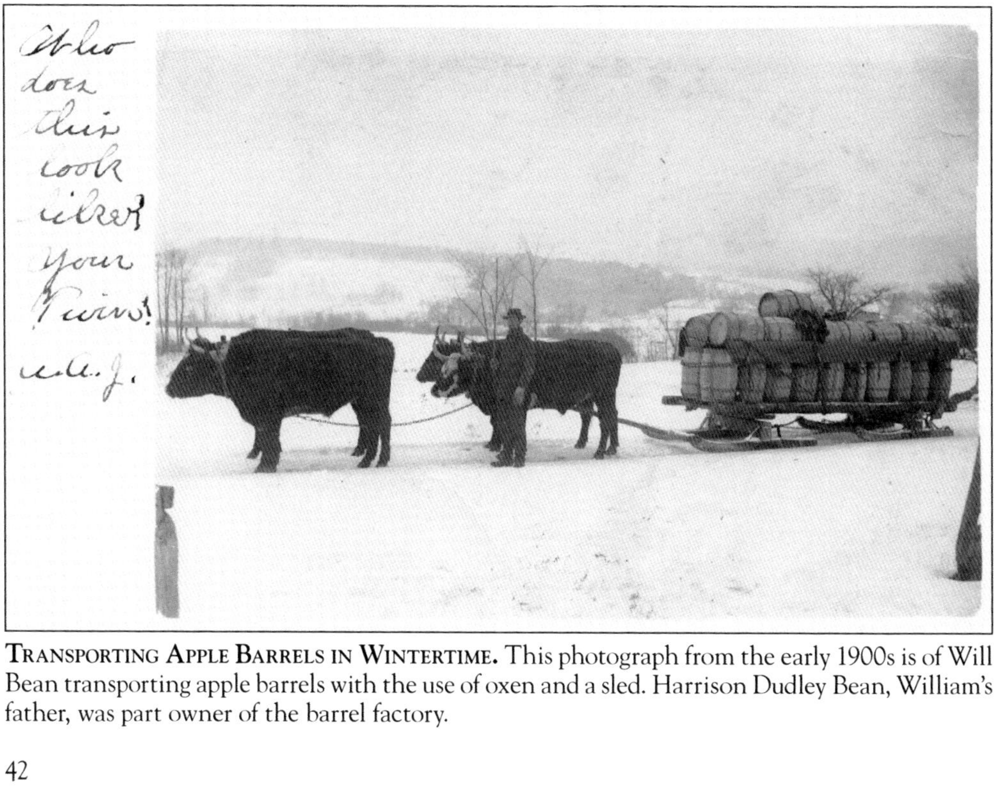

Transporting Apple Barrels in Wintertime. This photograph from the early 1900s is of Will Bean transporting apple barrels with the use of oxen and a sled. Harrison Dudley Bean, William's father, was part owner of the barrel factory.

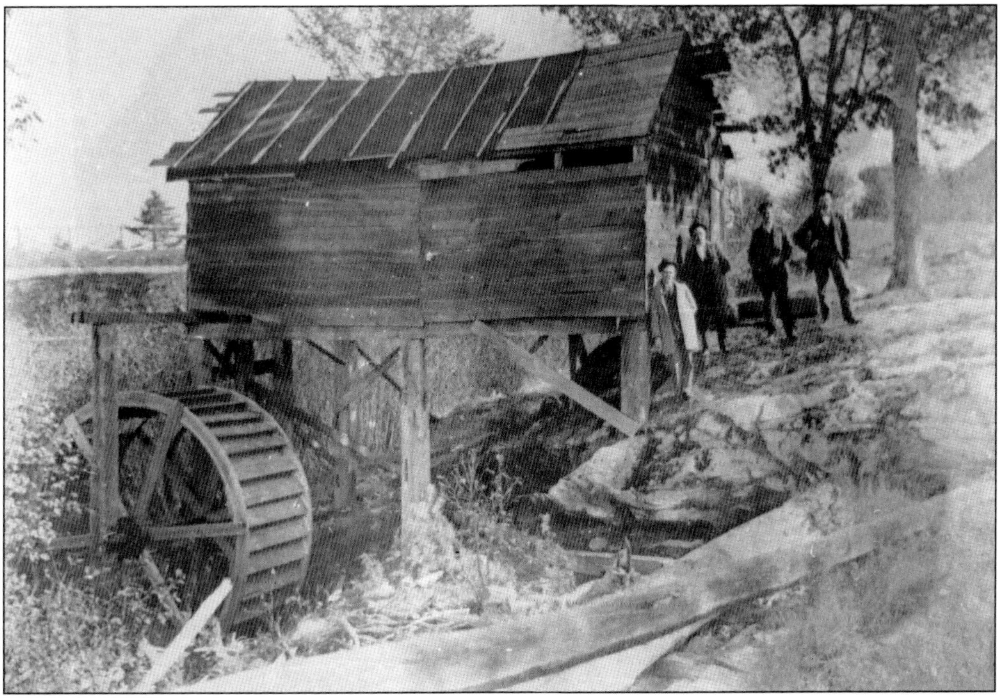

MOSQUITO (SPELLED MUSQUETO) BROOK SAW AND GRISTMILL. Built in 1791 and run by Deacon Livermore, this was the first mill in town. Mills such as this were operated for local custom. They ground the farmer's grist of wheat, rye, or corn. Gristmills provided settlers with grain to make bread and feed their cattle. Sawmills provided lumber to build homes and barns. This mill served both Jay and Livermore. The photograph was taken around 1902.

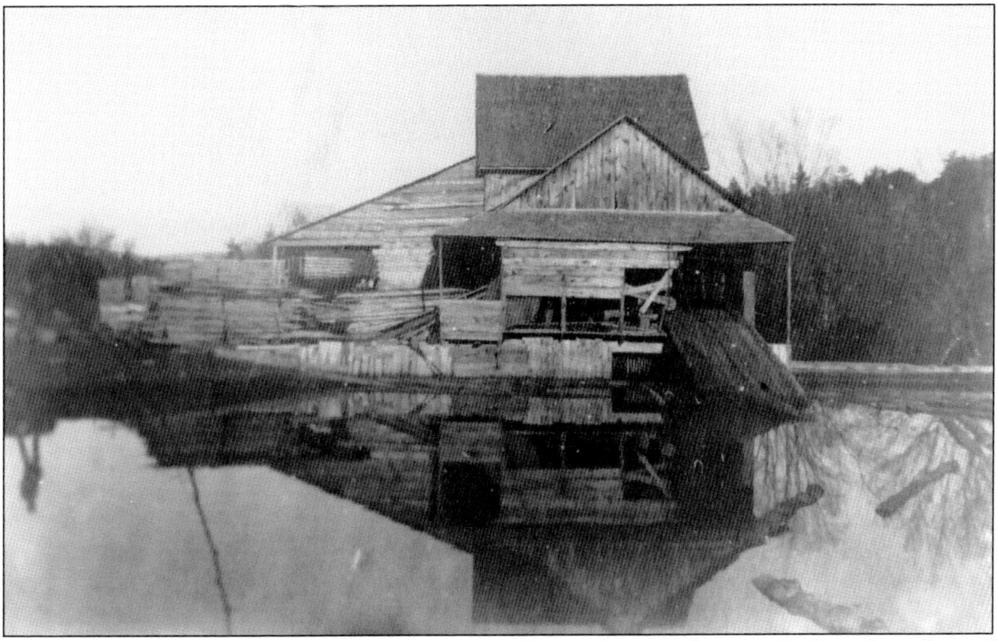

STUBB'S MILL SAWMILL. In this photograph is another early sawmill. It was built in the village of Stubb's Mill around 1897, providing lumber for the early settlers.

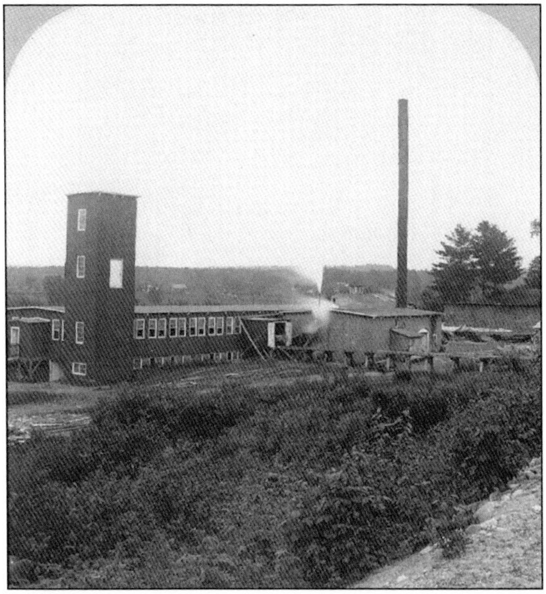

Jay Wood Turning Company's Novelty Works. This corporation was established in 1907 and produced all kinds of wood turning. It was located on the west side of the Androscoggin. When it was in operation, it employed 125 hands in winter and 75 in summer.

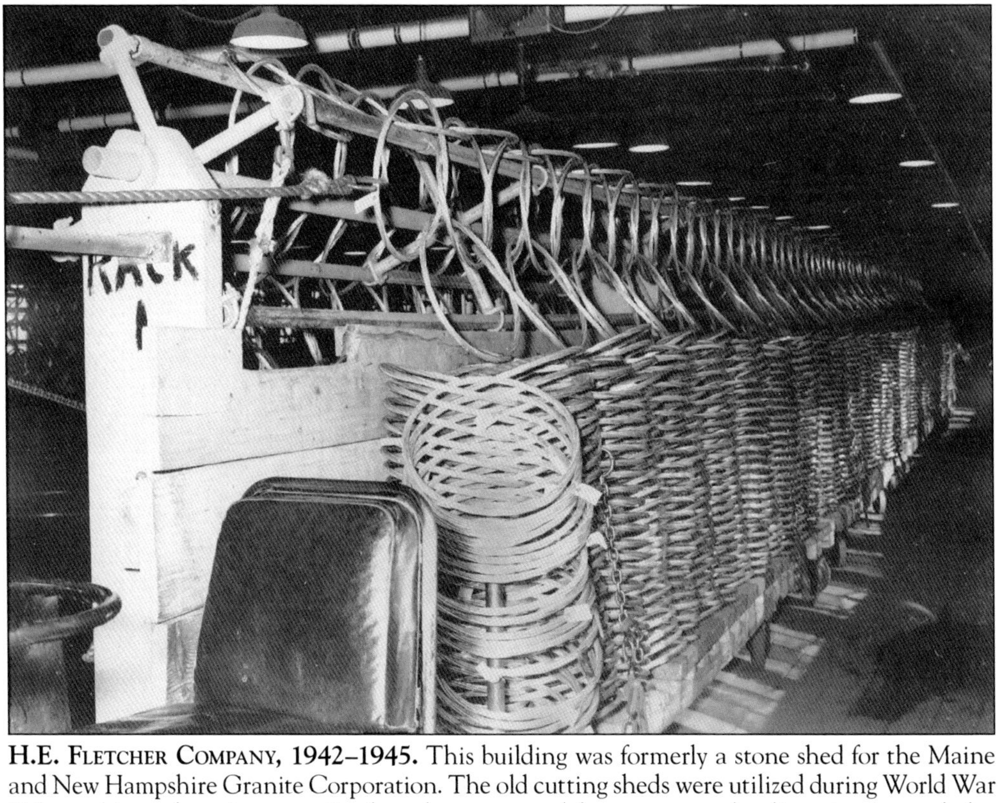

H.E. Fletcher Company, 1942–1945. This building was formerly a stone shed for the Maine and New Hampshire Granite Corporation. The old cutting sheds were utilized during World War II for making submarine nets. Steel mesh was created for emergency landing airstrips and also for beach roadways for amphibious invasion in the pacific. Women worked making these while the men were at war. The Depression had a negative impact on the granite quarry. They closed their doors at North Jay in 1936. This photograph was taken by Harold M. Karkos of Wilton, Maine, in the mid-1940s.

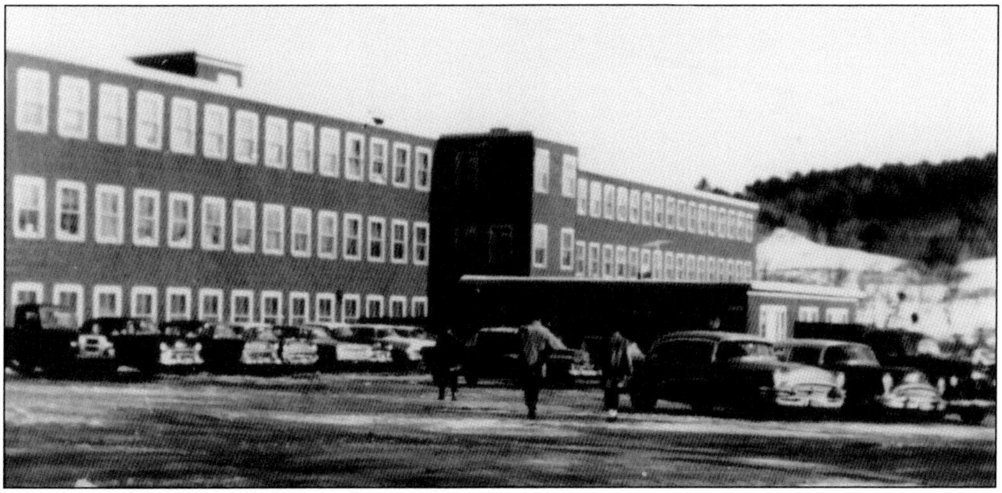

Norrwock Shoe Company, Inc., North Jay, c. 1954. Home offices for Norrwock Shoe Company were in Norridgewock, Maine. This building was constructed after World War II in the village of North Jay. The National Labor Relations Board ruled that employees had been dismissed for union activity in May 1949, and the 11 dismissed workers received back pay. Of the 11 workers, seven requested to return to work. The board ruled that the company had to rehire the workers and reinstate their seniority privileges. The dismissal of these employees followed an attempted strike by the United Mine Workers, District 50, who unsuccessfully attempted to organize the Norrwock shoe workers.

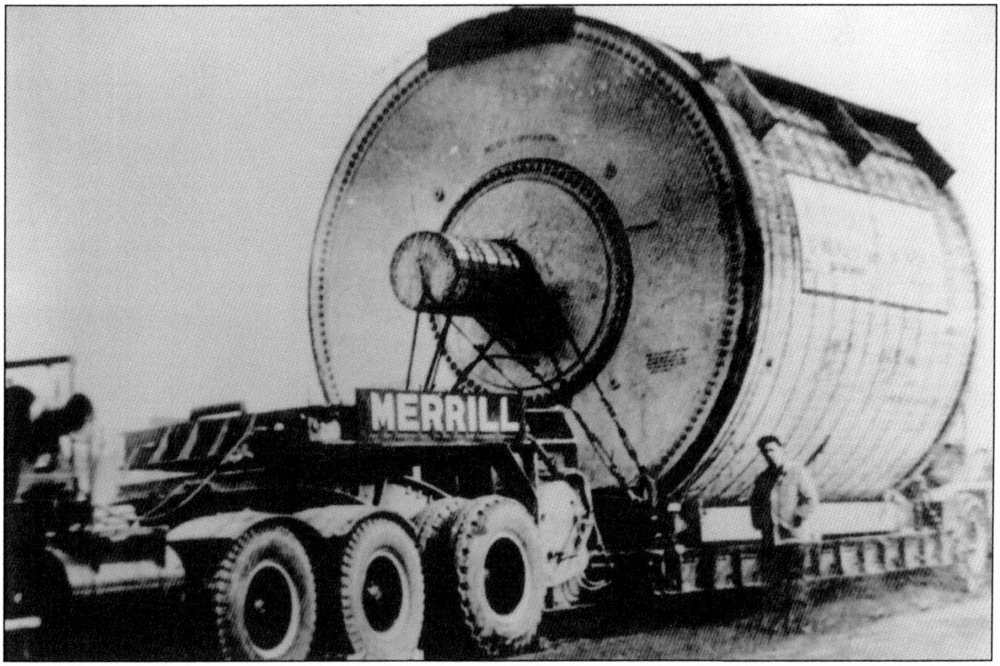

Transporting the Yankee Dryer to the Androscoggin Mill. This is a photograph of the Yankee dryer being hauled to the new International Paper Company's Androscoggin Mill in 1964. The Yankee dryer, which was on the No. 2 machine at the mill, was the largest ever manufactured. Lifted off a barge at Bath Iron Works, it measured 16 feet wide by 20 feet long. From the iron works, it was put on a 1,000-horsepower truck-and-trailer unit and taken to the mill.

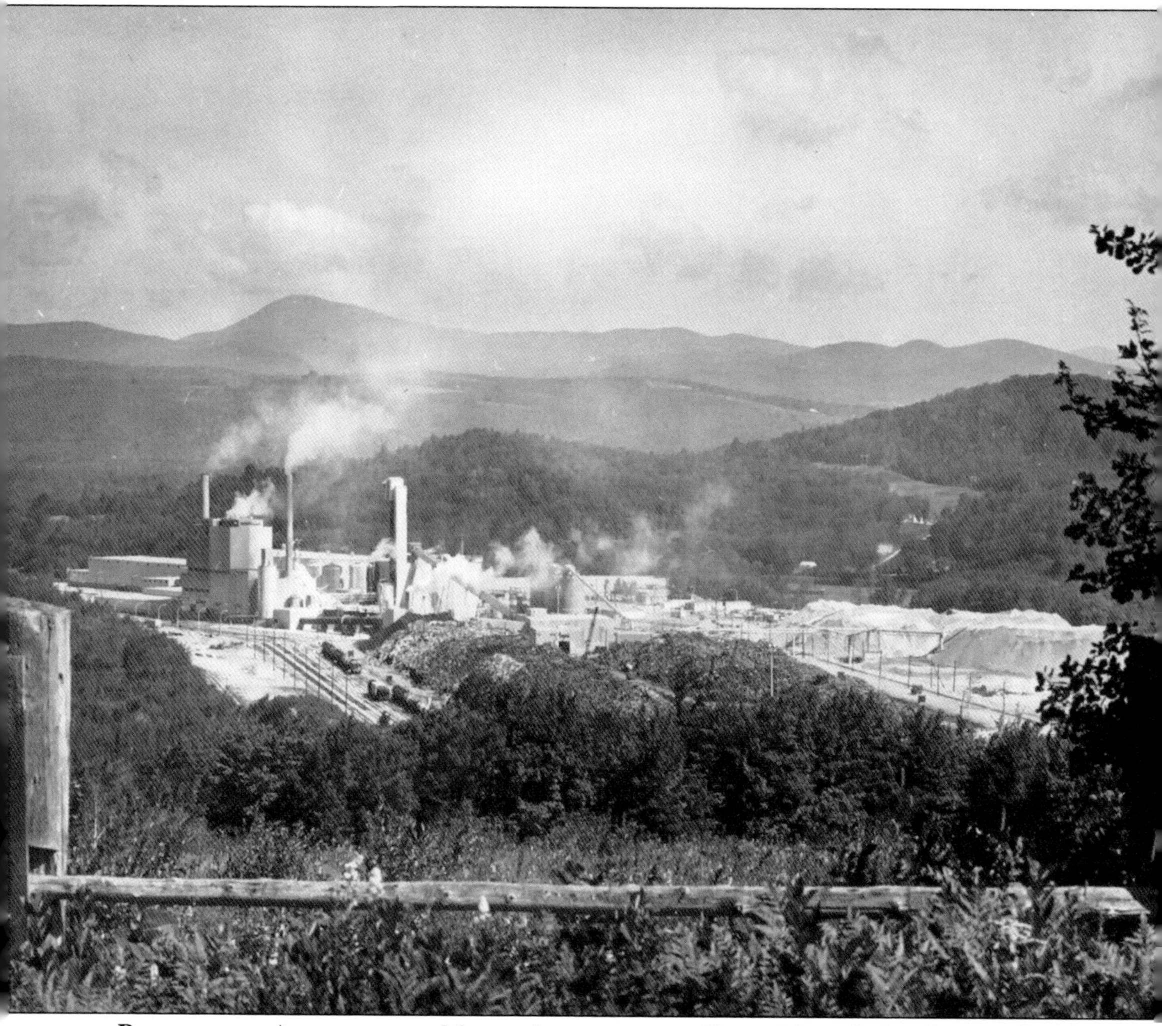

BUILDING THE ANDROSCOGGIN MILL OF INTERNATIONAL PAPER. Named after the river, building commenced on the Androscoggin Mill in 1963. Production began in 1965 on the first of three paper machines. The mill was built less than a mile from its predecessor, the Riley Mill. In 1967, the plant expanded, adding modern air and water pollution control equipment. The mill produced bond paper for a variety of business purposes, coated paper for magazines, and one-time carbonizing tissue paper. The No. 1 and No. 2 paper machines produced rolls of paper up to 210 inches wide.

Three

COMMUNITY

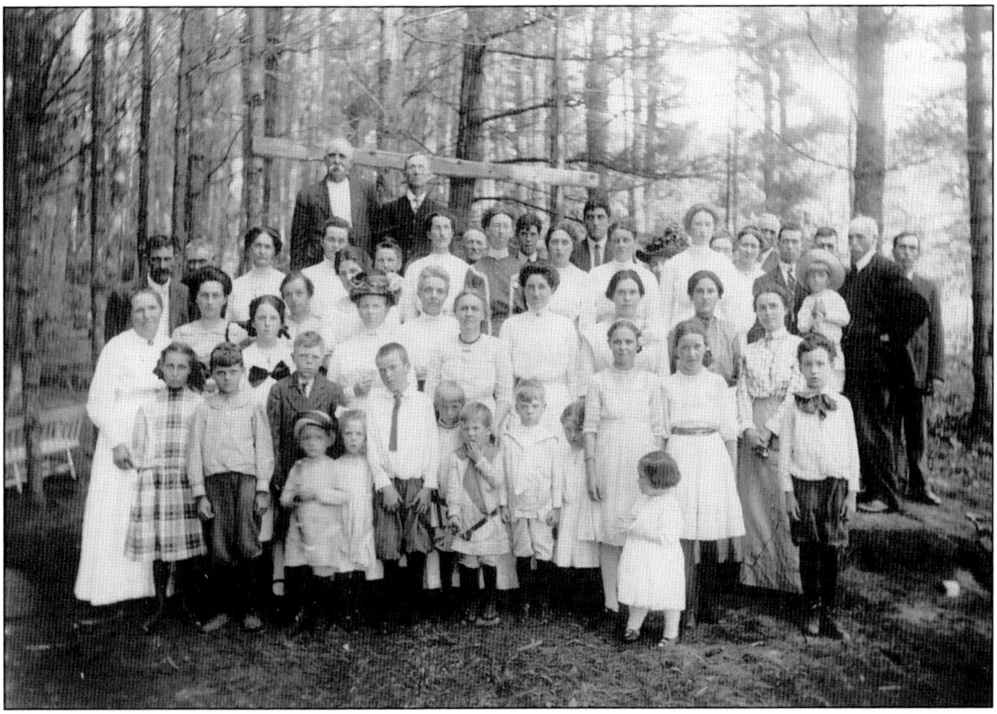

GRANGE PICNIC. North Jay Grange No. 10, Patrons of Husbandry, was once a flourishing fraternal society in the town. It was organized on March 27, 1874, and had 19 members at the time. In this photograph, members and their families gather at a Grange picnic at Jay Bridge around 1900.

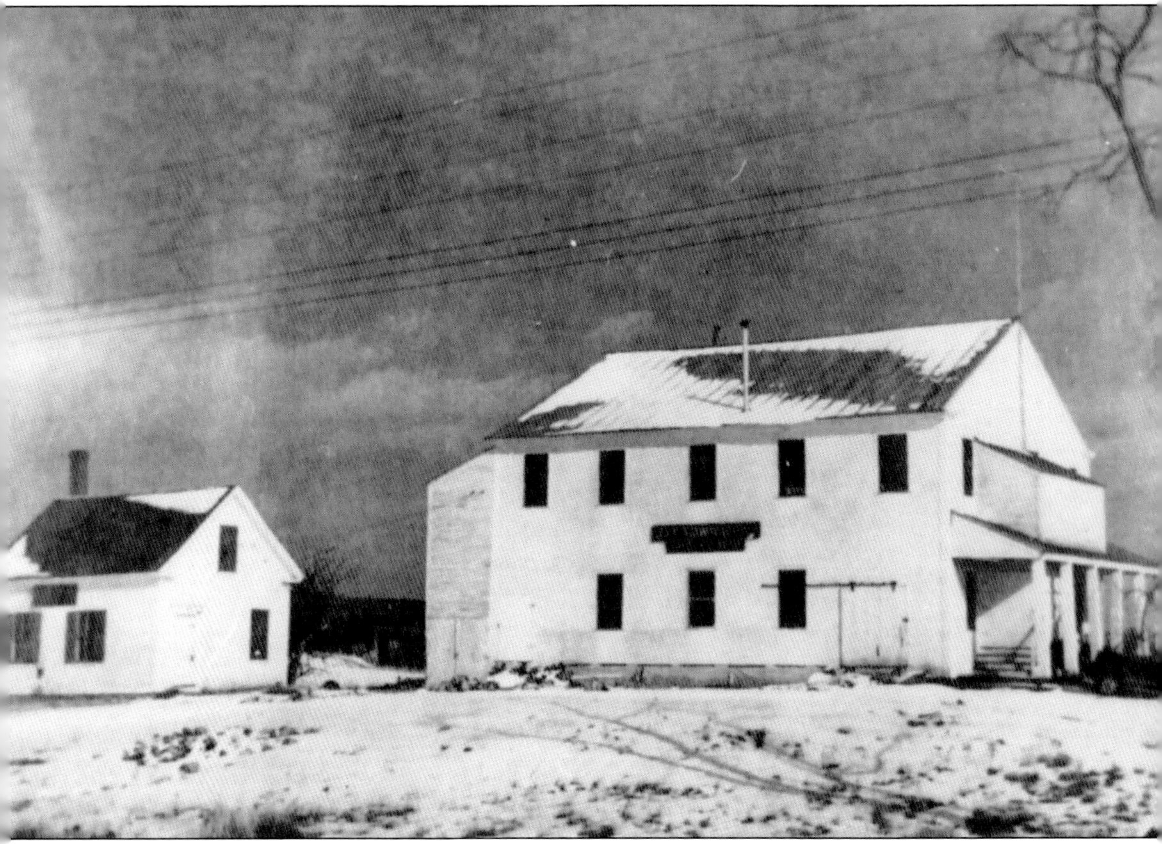

Town Hall. The town hall was originally built in the 1790s as a Baptist church for the settlers of Jay. When it was converted, people voted in the upstairs hall, while on the ground floor were stalls for horses. Large hand-hewn timbers were held in place by long wooden pins. Many boards were nearly two feet in width, sawed with an up-and-down saw.

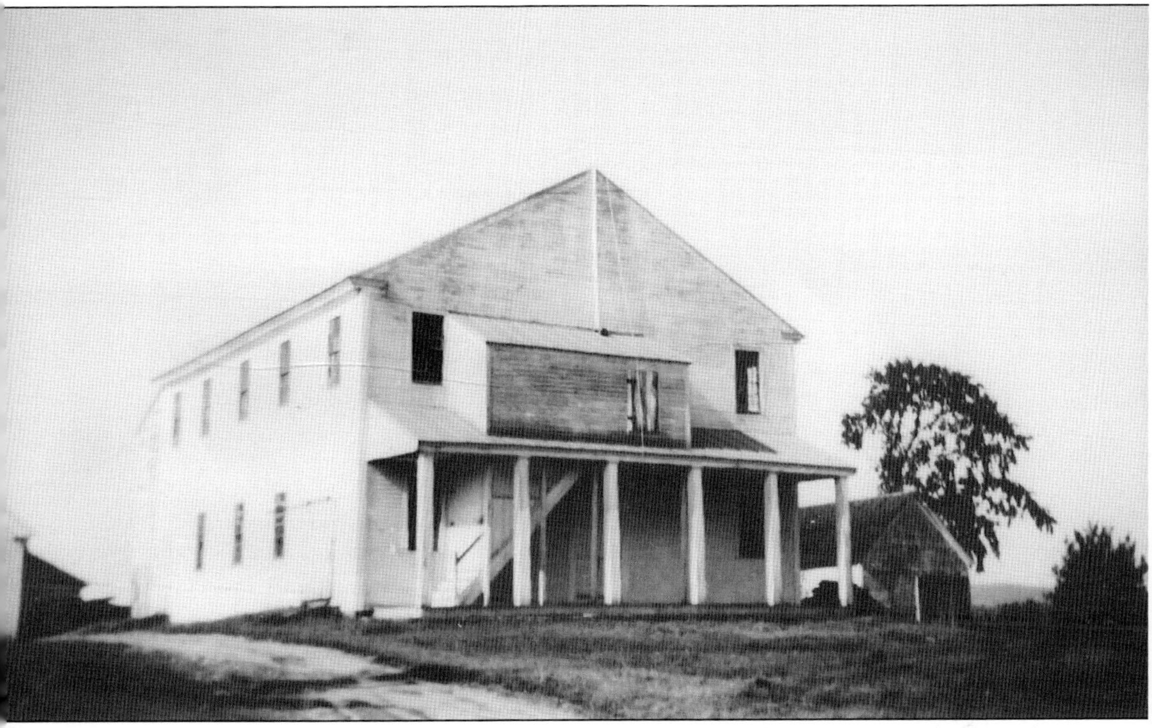

TOWN MEETING DAY, EARLY 1900S. The meetings held in this townhouse were very lively, and only men attended. At this time, there were vendors selling food at the town meeting. Some of the items sold were apples, maple sugar candy with butternuts, a confection made with honey, and most popular of all, gingerbread from the gingerbread cart. This gingerbread came from a baker in Hallowell, Maine. On town meeting days, two stores and the tavern kept open bars, with rum and toddy all day and into the night. The younger people not attending the town meeting assembled outside and held wrestling matches with other young people from different parts of town.

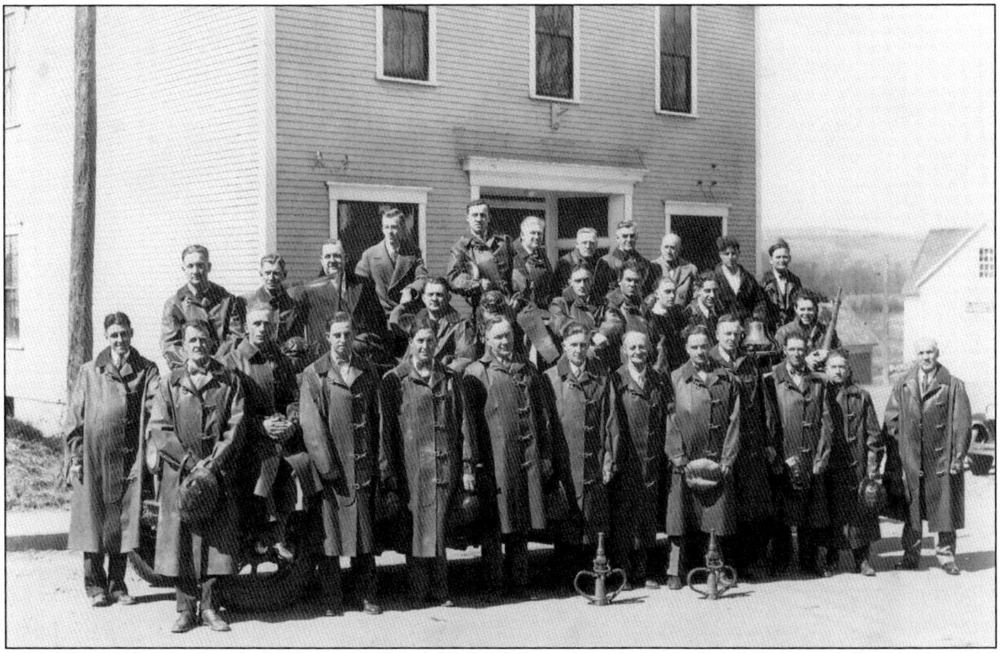

FIRST JAY VOLUNTEER FIRE DEPARTMENT, NORTH JAY. The first interest in a fire department for North Jay was expressed in 1926. At a town meeting on March 14, 1927, voters appropriated $4,000 to purchase a piece of fire apparatus to fight fires in North Jay and vicinity. On July 7, 1927, the new fire truck arrived. The first firemen's meeting was held that night. At this meeting, residents voted to organize the Jay Fire Department. Frank Farnham was named chief and served until 1931.

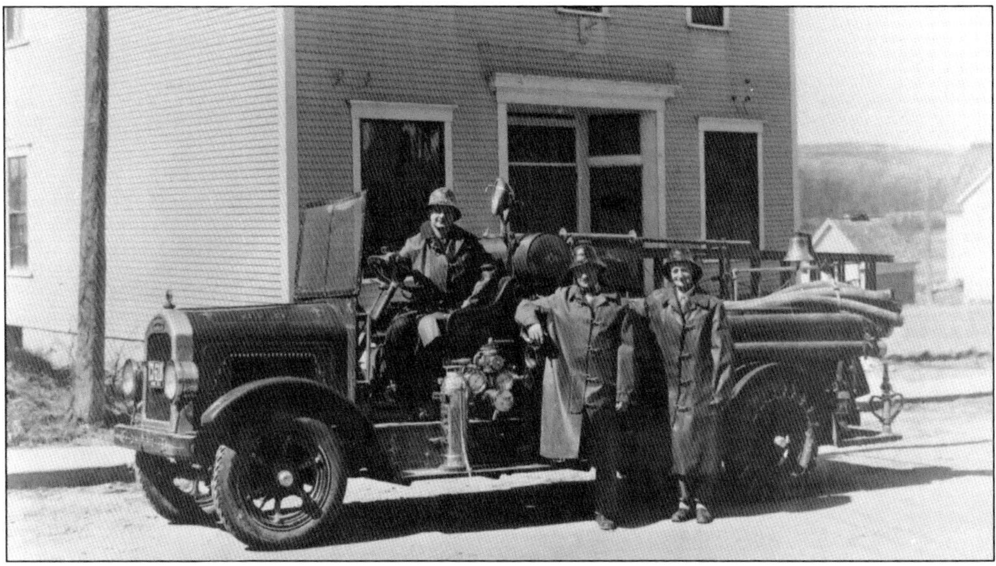

FIRST JAY FIRE TRUCK. The first Jay fire truck is pictured in front of the K.P. Hall in North Jay in 1927. Photographed by the truck are, from left to right, Capt. Cliff Beisaw, Assistant Chief Earl Hawkins, and Chief Frank Farnum. The fire truck is a 1927 McCann. It was powered by a four-cylinder motor and had a three-speed transmission, single wheels with mechanical brakes, a mid-ship pump, and a chemical tank for chimney fires.

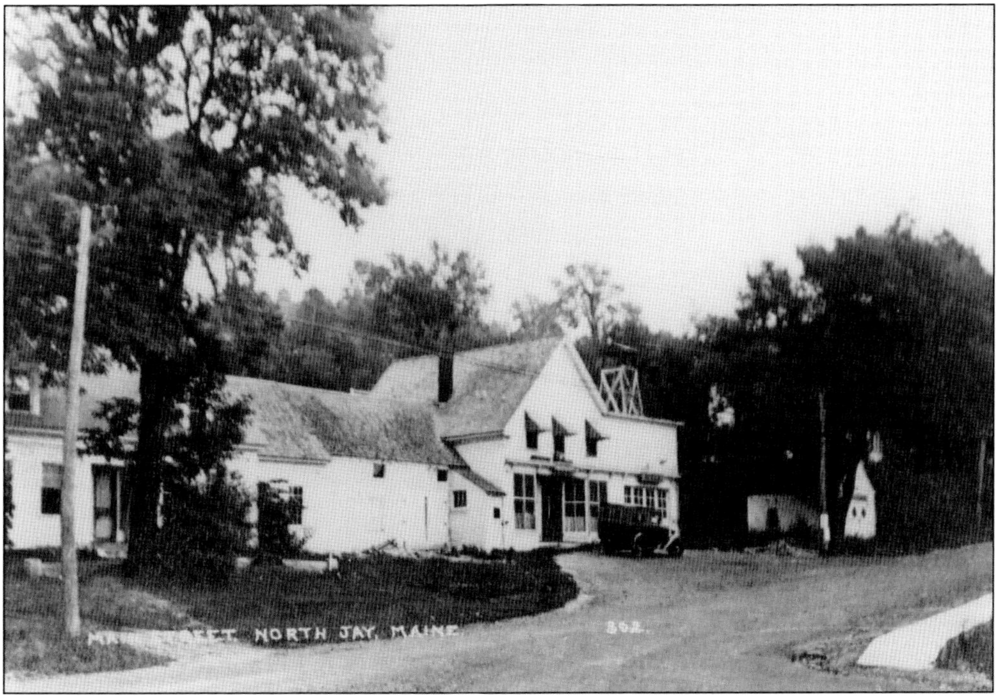

FIRST JAY FIREHOUSE. This was the first Jay firehouse, located in North Jay. The antenna is just visible on the roof.

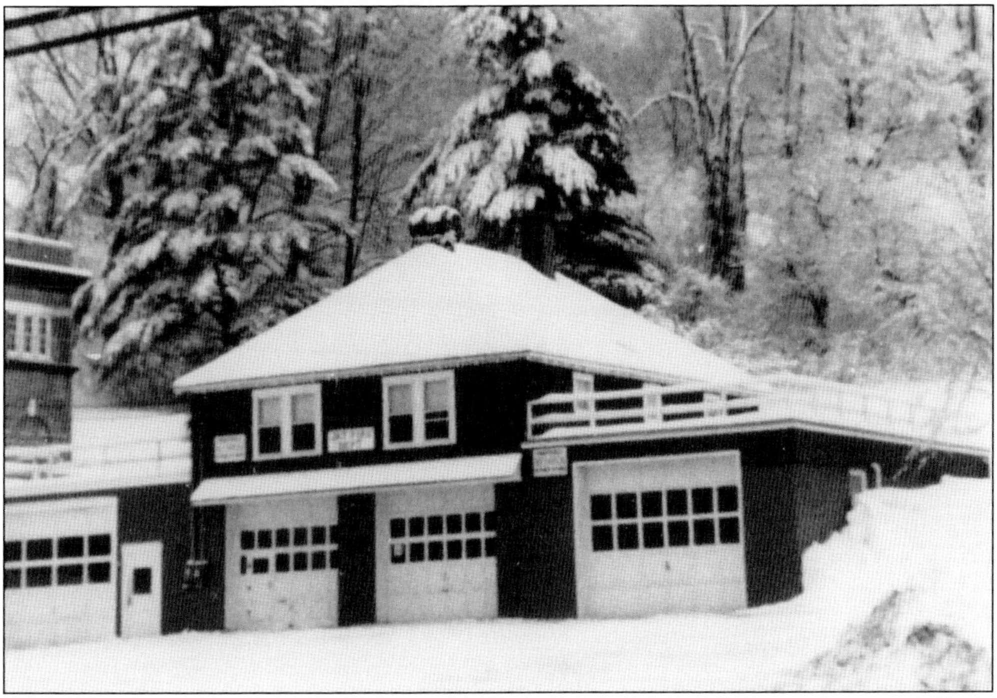

SECOND JAY FIREHOUSE. The second North Jay firehouse was built in the 1940s. It was torn down in the 1970s to build the current structure.

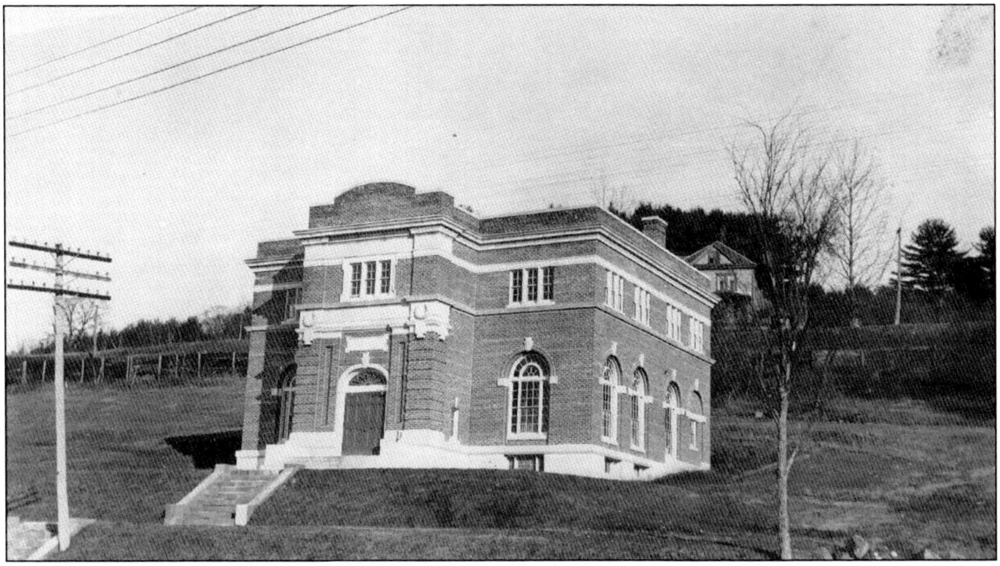

Jay-Niles Memorial Library and Memorial Hall. The library was a gift deeded to the town of Jay on February 21, 1918, from the prominent and successful Niles family siblings of North Jay. It was given in honor and memory of their parents, Veranas and Mehitable Harris Niles. The Niles brothers gave the funds for the library to be built, but the dream of a town library was their sister Eliza's.

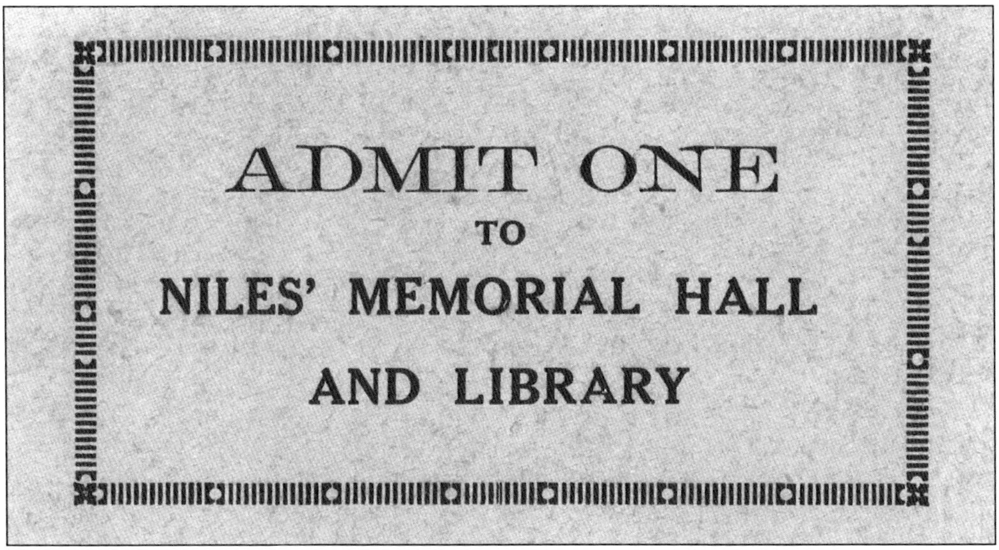

ADMIT ONE
TO
NILES' MEMORIAL HALL
AND LIBRARY

Admit One. This ticket was used for events held in Memorial Hall. Several activities took place in the hall, including plays, Chautauquas, cantatas, Memorial Day services, Christmas celebrations, meetings of the Jay Literary and Pastime Clubs, lectures, and socials. The hall was created in memory of the men who served in the Civil War, and two plaques, one on each side of the stage, commemorate Civil War veterans.

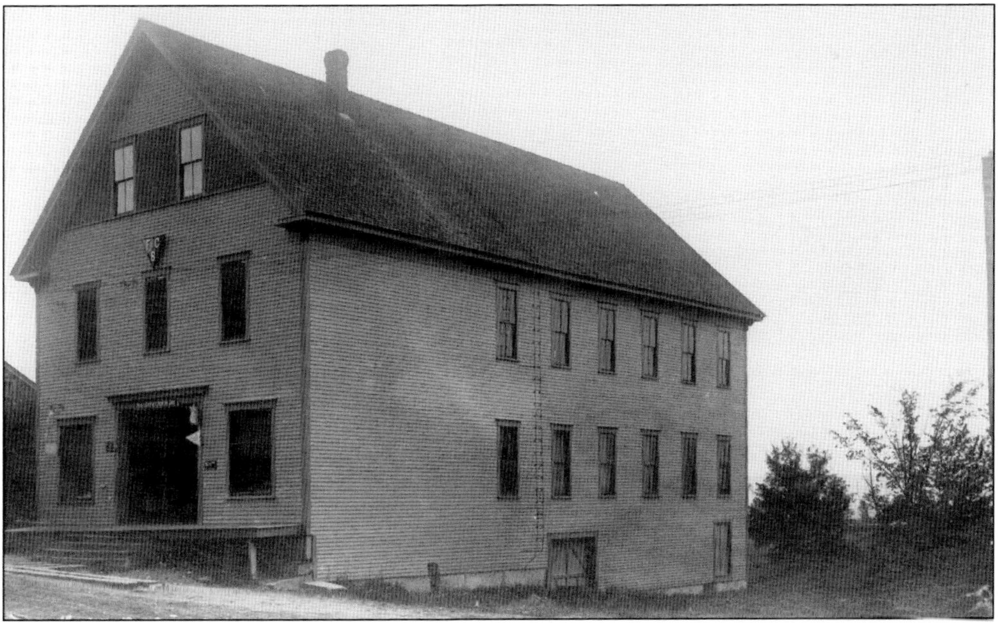

Knights of Pythias and Post Office, North Jay. Dances, stage performances, and even a graduation were held in this hall. A clothing store occupied the front, as did the post office. The Knights of Pythias was a nonsectarian fraternal organization dedicated to universal peace. Notice the F, C, and B on the front of the building. They stand for the distinguishing principles of the Order of Knights of Pythias: "Friendship, charity, and benevolence."

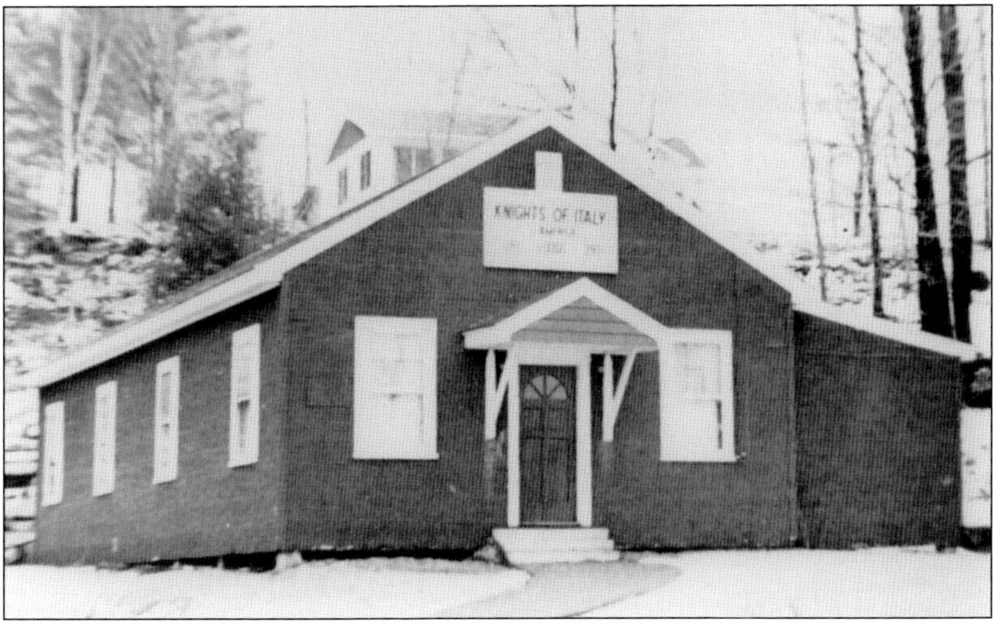

Knights of Italy Hall, 1940. This was also known as the Sons of Italy Lodge. The Order of the Sons of Italy is the largest and oldest Italian American fraternal society in the United States. There were many Italian immigrants who came to Jay to work, and this lodge gave them a place to belong. Gathering sites such as this one were created in America to help Italian immigrants assimilate into American society.

6

INMATES OF ALMSHOUSE.

Sarah J. Childs,	aged 57,	No. of weeks, 52
Bert Bryant,	" 37,	" " 52
Mrs. Simeon Foye,	" 78,	" " 52
John Martin,	" 80,	" " 42
John Pease,	" 26,	" " 52
Total number of weeks,		250

Total expenditures of Almshouse,	$3,963 82
Total receipts of Almshouse,	3,439 91
Expense above receipts,	$523 91

EXPENSE OF POOR OUT OF ALMSHOUSE.

Paid D. B. Macomber, aid to Betsey Macomber,	$ 100 00
Mary A. Chase, aid to Lelia Bowley,	52 00
J. F. Jefferds, casket for Philip Gurney's child,	7 00
Maine Insane Hospital for support of Carrie L. Brown,	138 66
C. L. Macomber, supplies to Mrs. J. B. Ouilette,	114 71
Town of Farmington, aid to G. R. Bean's family,	35 46
A. C. Allen, board of tramps,	2 50
G. P. Butterfield, " "	3 00
S. B. Farnum, " "	5 00
Town of E. Livermore, aid to Ida Knowles,	13 79
French Hospital, support and car fare of John Hennessey and Peter Shea,	61 27
O. S. Waite, aid to Bert Grose,	3 00
Frank Butler, car fare to Augusta,	2 95
S. R. Leland, aid to Mrs. McGraw and family,	23 60
	$562 94
Balance against Almshouse,	523 91
Total pauper expense,	$1,086 85

Town Farm. There was a town farm in Jay for many years, built in 1793 by Revolutionary soldier Isaac West. The town put an addition on the building in 1870. It had 17 rooms. The property was sold in 1816 to Joseph Adams, and the town of Jay bought part of the parcel in 1849. Between 1857 and 1864, they bought the entire property. While the town farm was in operation, the destitute became inmates there and had to work for their keep. They made cheese and butter to sell. They also had eggs, dried apples, and stock. In later years, this building was a private residence. Inmates were listed in the town report, as can be seen here.

Four

Transportation

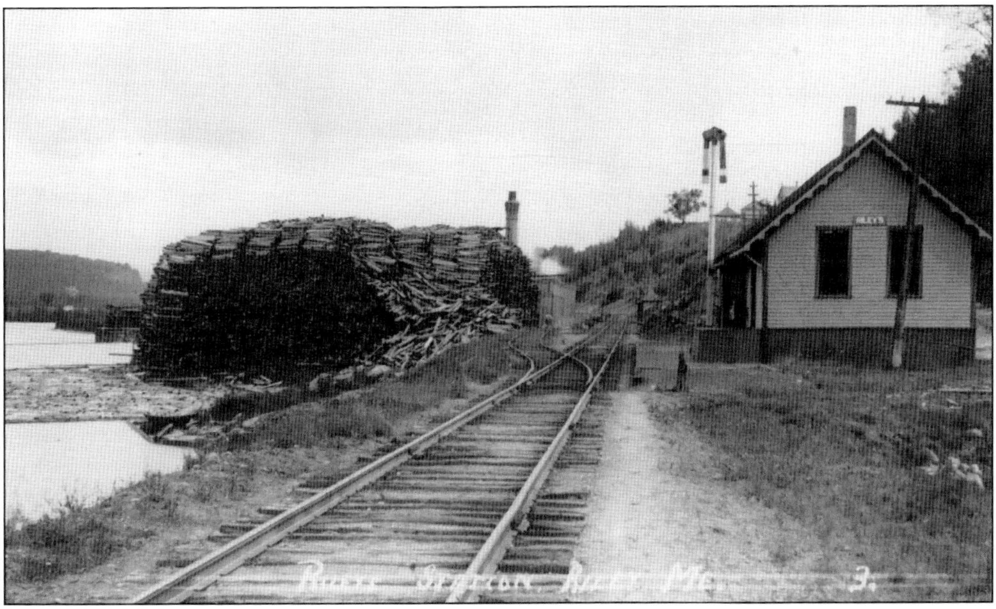

Riley's Railroad Station, c. 1903. The station was built near the Riley Mill and Petersons Rips in 1897. The pulp pile can be seen in this photograph. This station was located 4.6 miles out of Livermore, on the branch to Gilbertville. Hugh Chisholm was involved in running a branch railroad line through Riley and Canton to Rumford. The railway was used to supply raw products and to ship finished goods.

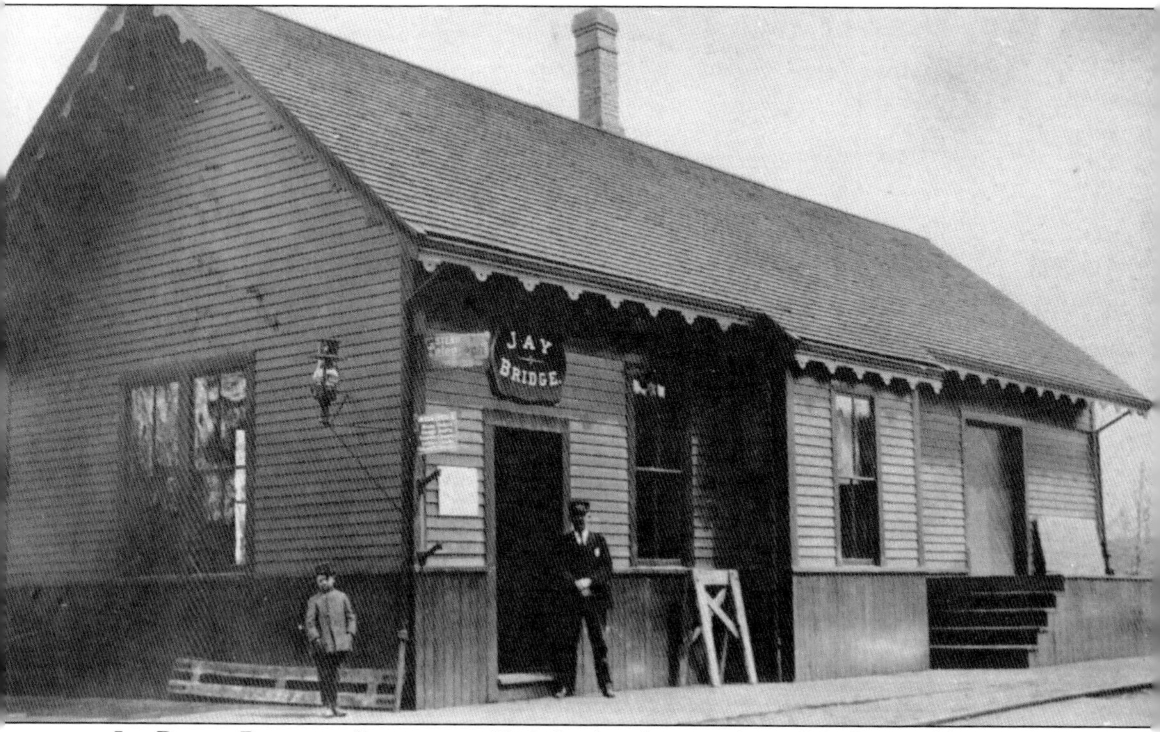

Jay Bridge Railroad Station, c. 1903. In this photograph are D.L. Day and his son Danny. This was part of the Maine Central Railroad's Livermore Falls to Rumford branch. The station, built in 1897, was located on the west side of the Androscoggin River and was on the line to Riley and Canton. Railroad agents for this station were as follows: C.H. Randall in 1898, D.L. Day from 1901 to 1908, R.H. Palmer in 1910, E.L. Gordon in 1911, Frank E. Otis in 1913, and E.L. Gordon from 1914 to 1918.

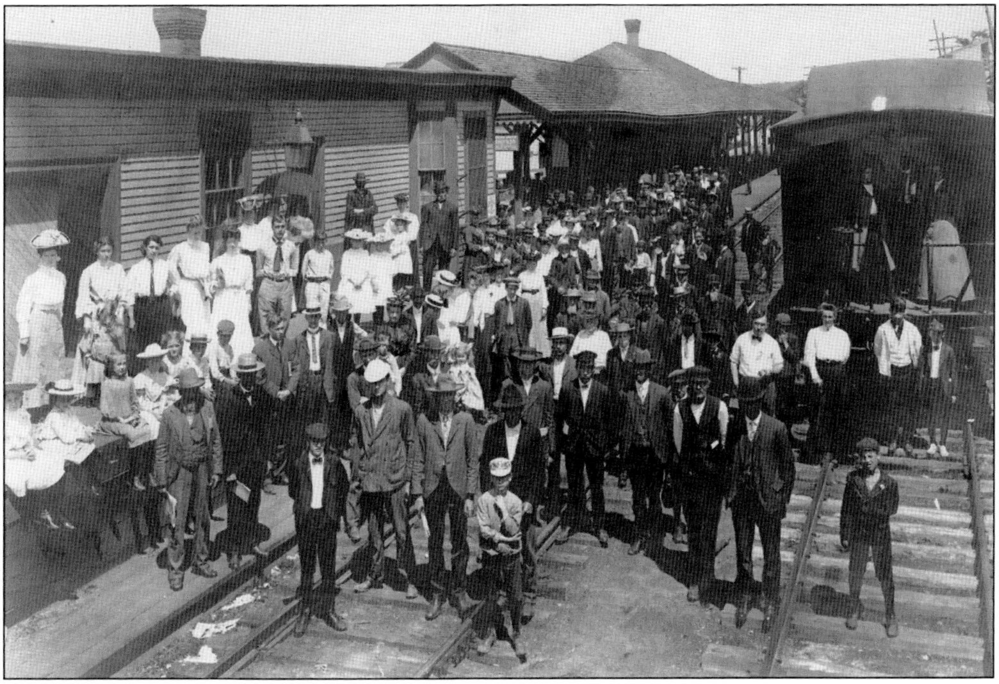

North Jay Railroad Station on the Maine Central Rail Road. In this photograph from 1910, a number of passengers wait for the train. The tracks were laid in 1857. At one point, there were three passenger trains a day here.

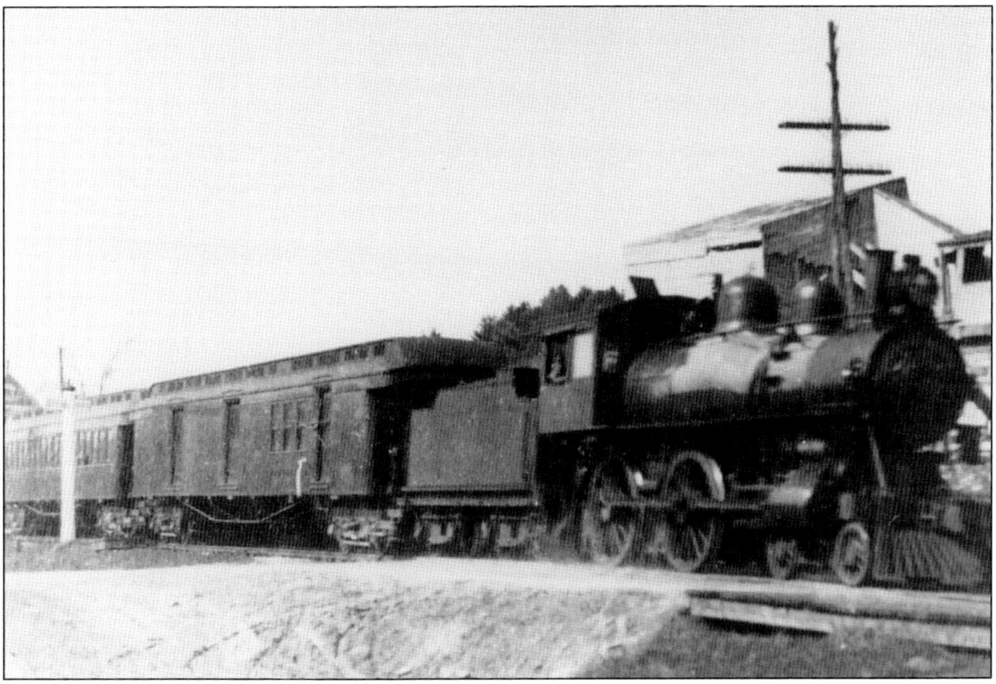

All Aboard. In this photograph from 1910, a passenger train pulls into the North Jay station.

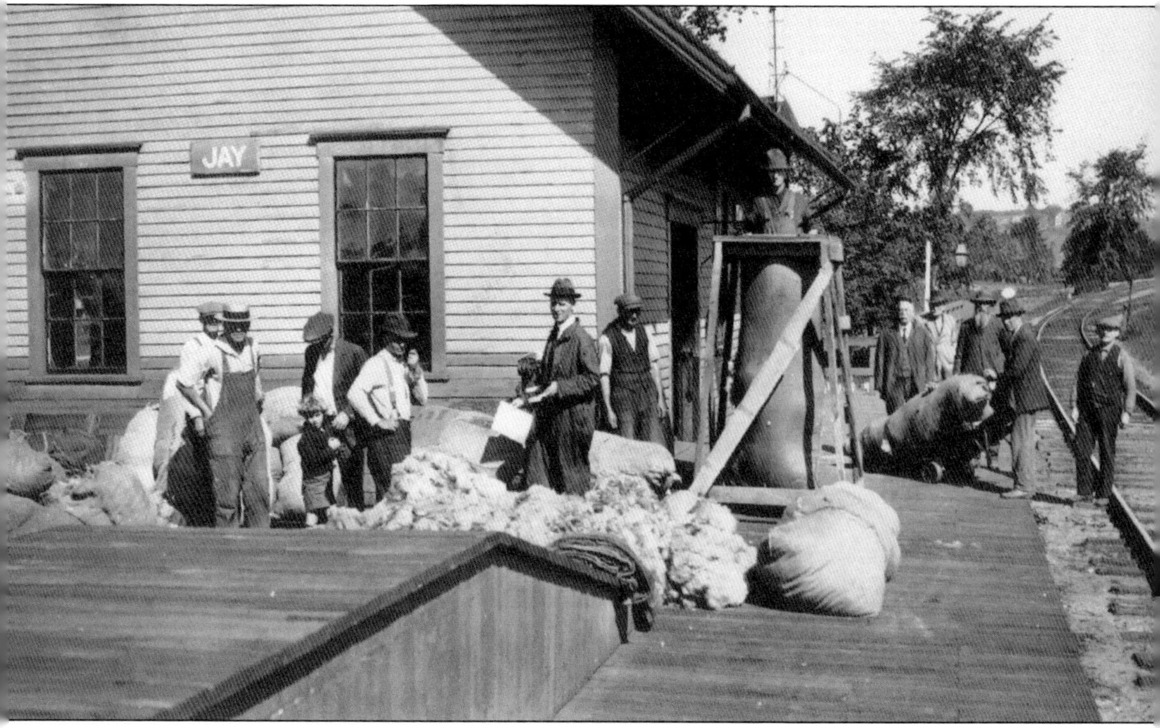

Depot Flat. The railroad station in Jay at Depot Flat was built around 1857. It was important to early commerce and trade in the town. The men in this picture are weighing wool at the depot. This railroad line ran from Farmington to Portland. Several of the railroad station agents for this area were J.E. Snell, B.E. DeLong, Frank Gray, and Thomas J. Mullen.

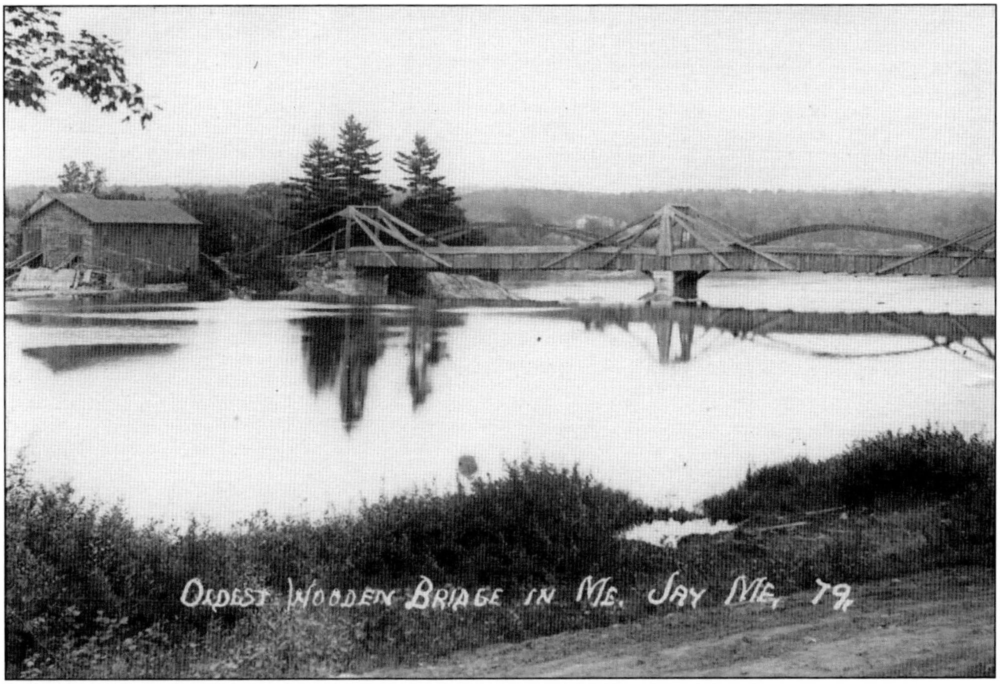

OLDEST WOODEN BRIDGE IN MAINE. This bridge was erected in 1835 and used as a toll bridge until 1846. Prior to it being built, folks were only able to cross the river by fords and ferries. The tolls were as follows: 2¢ for foot passengers; 6¢ for person and a horse; 10¢ for a horse with a cart, sled, or sleigh with a driver and a passenger within; 12.5¢ for a team of two beasts with a driver, cart, wagon, or sleigh; 16¢ for a horse and chaise, chair, or sulky with one or two passengers; and 35¢ for a pleasure carriage drawn by two horses. Military personnel, those attending funerals, persons traveling to and from church on Sunday, and ministers were allowed free passage.

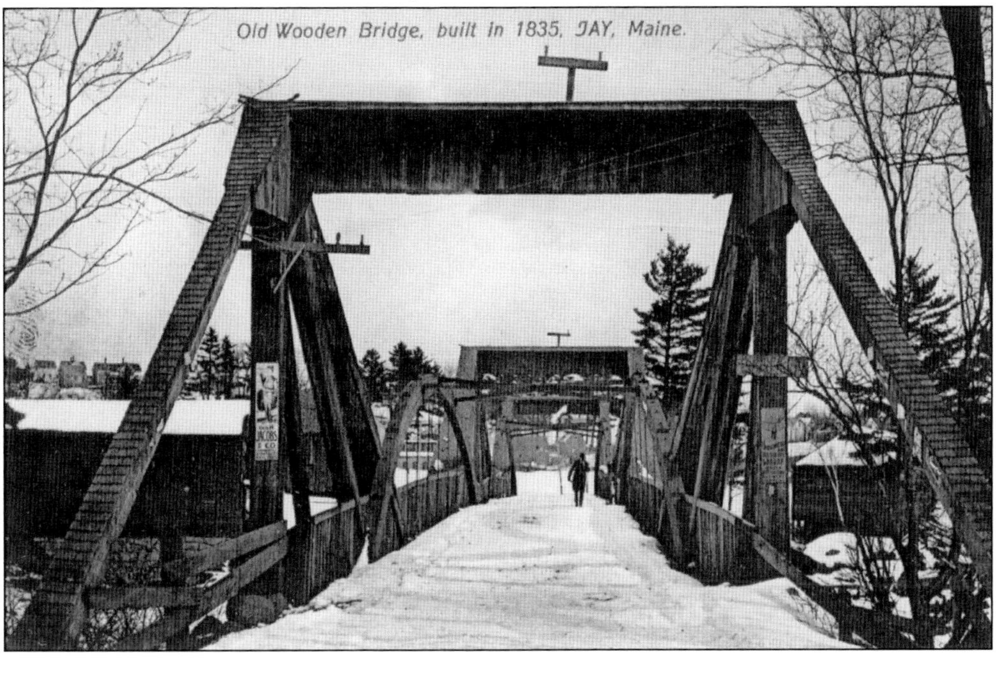

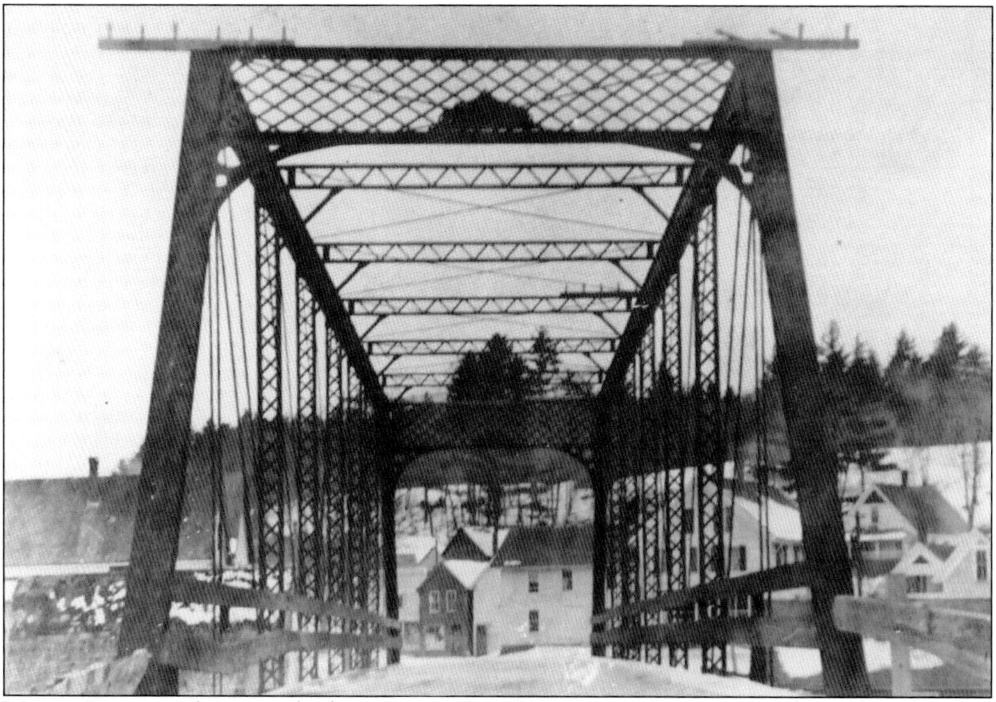

Metal Bridge. This view, looking east to Jay Village, is of the completed metal bridge that replaced the covered bridge.

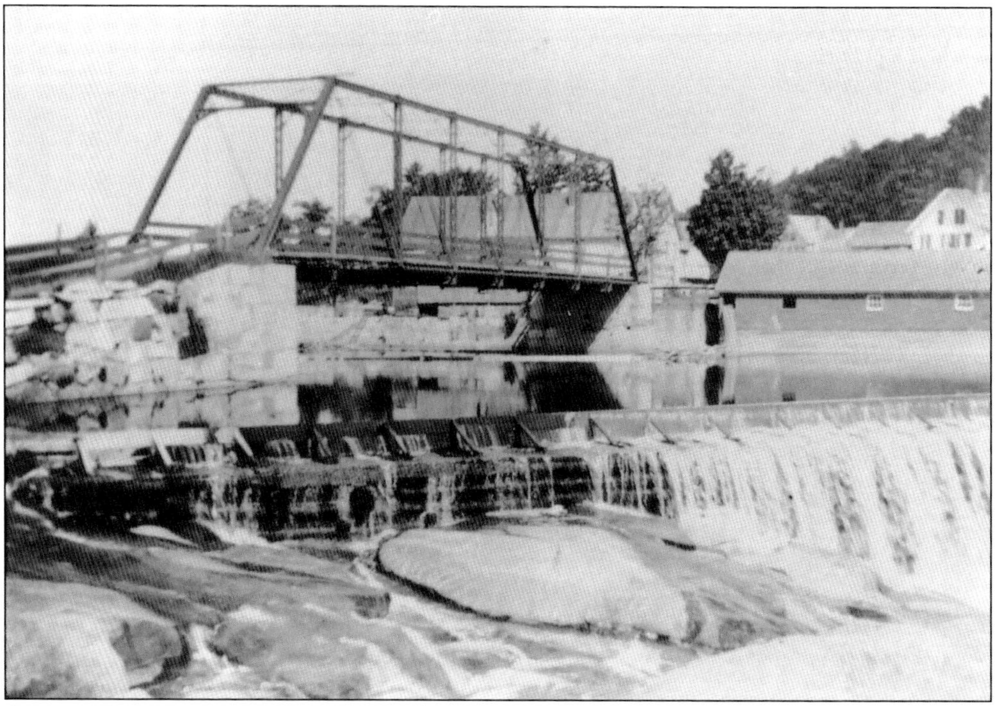

Another View of the Metal Bridge. This shows the bridge when it was still under construction. It went from the Falmouth Mill on the island to the mainland.

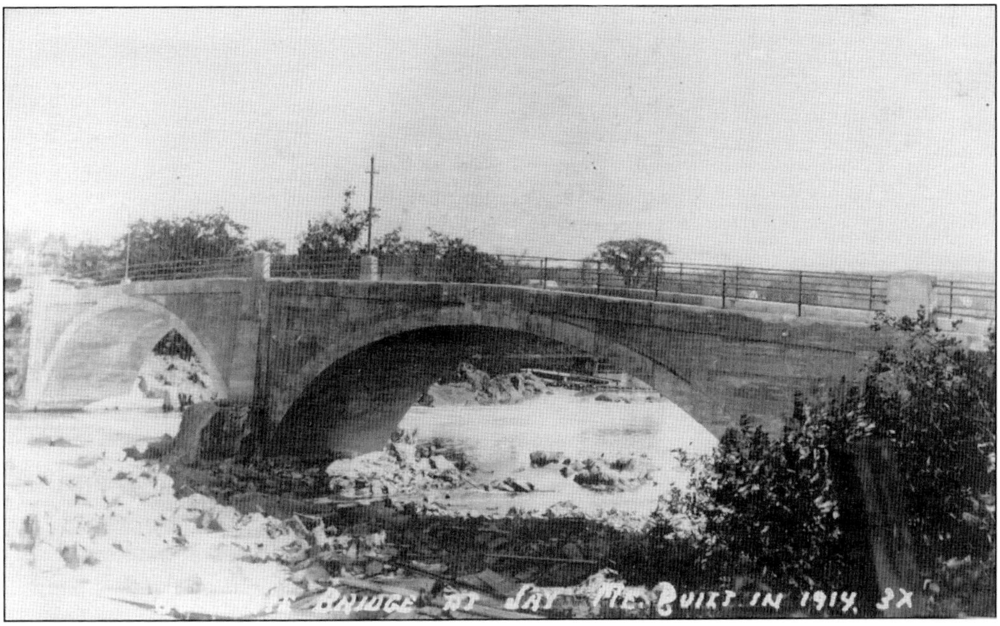

Cement Bridge. This bridge replaced the old toll bridge in 1914.

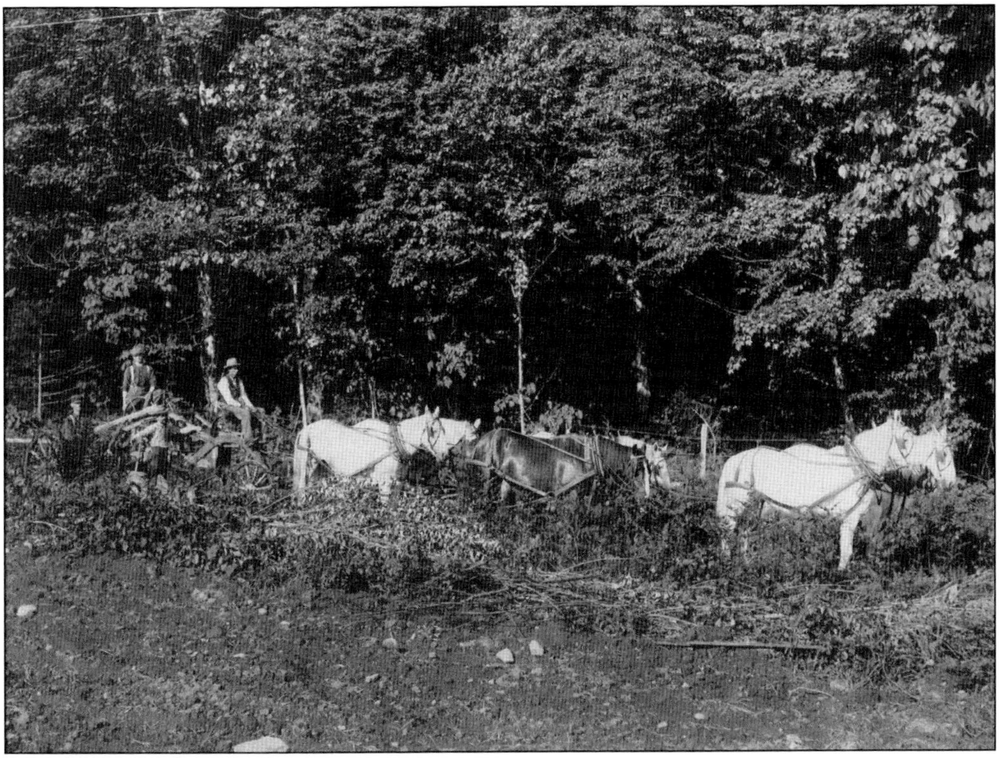

Road Crew on Davenport Hill. In this photograph, one can see land being cleared by horses and nonmotorized equipment. They did not have the heavy equipment available today, so the work had to be done with a team of horses, six in this case. In the foreground, one can see where the land has already been cleared. This photograph was taken in 1920.

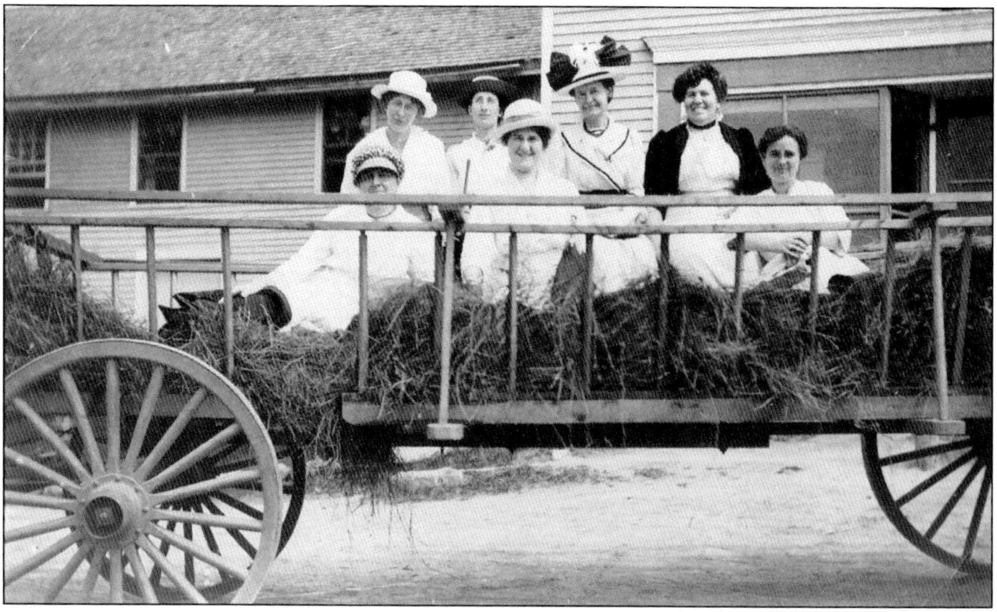

Traveling by Hay Wagon. This group of women is going for a ride in a hay wagon in North Jay. In the photograph are Maude Hobbs, Minnie Allen, Myrtie Holman, Eva Kyes, Jessie Merritt, Carrie Spaulding, and Grace Fawcett. Apparently, these horse-drawn wagons were not used only on the farm, but also for leisurely rides on country roads. This photograph was taken in the late 1800s or early 1900s.

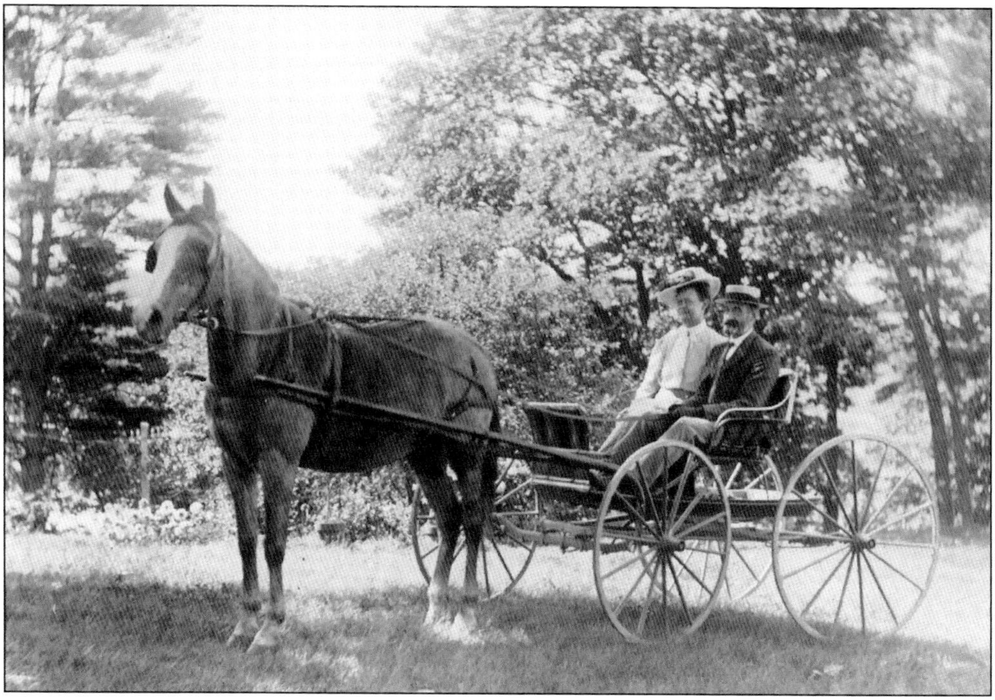

Dr. and Mrs. Frank W. Merritt with Horse and Buggy. Dr. Merritt practiced as a physician and surgeon in the Jay area from 1894 to 1918. He married Celia S. Hartley. Horse and buggy was the primary mode of short distance personal transportation from 1815 to 1915.

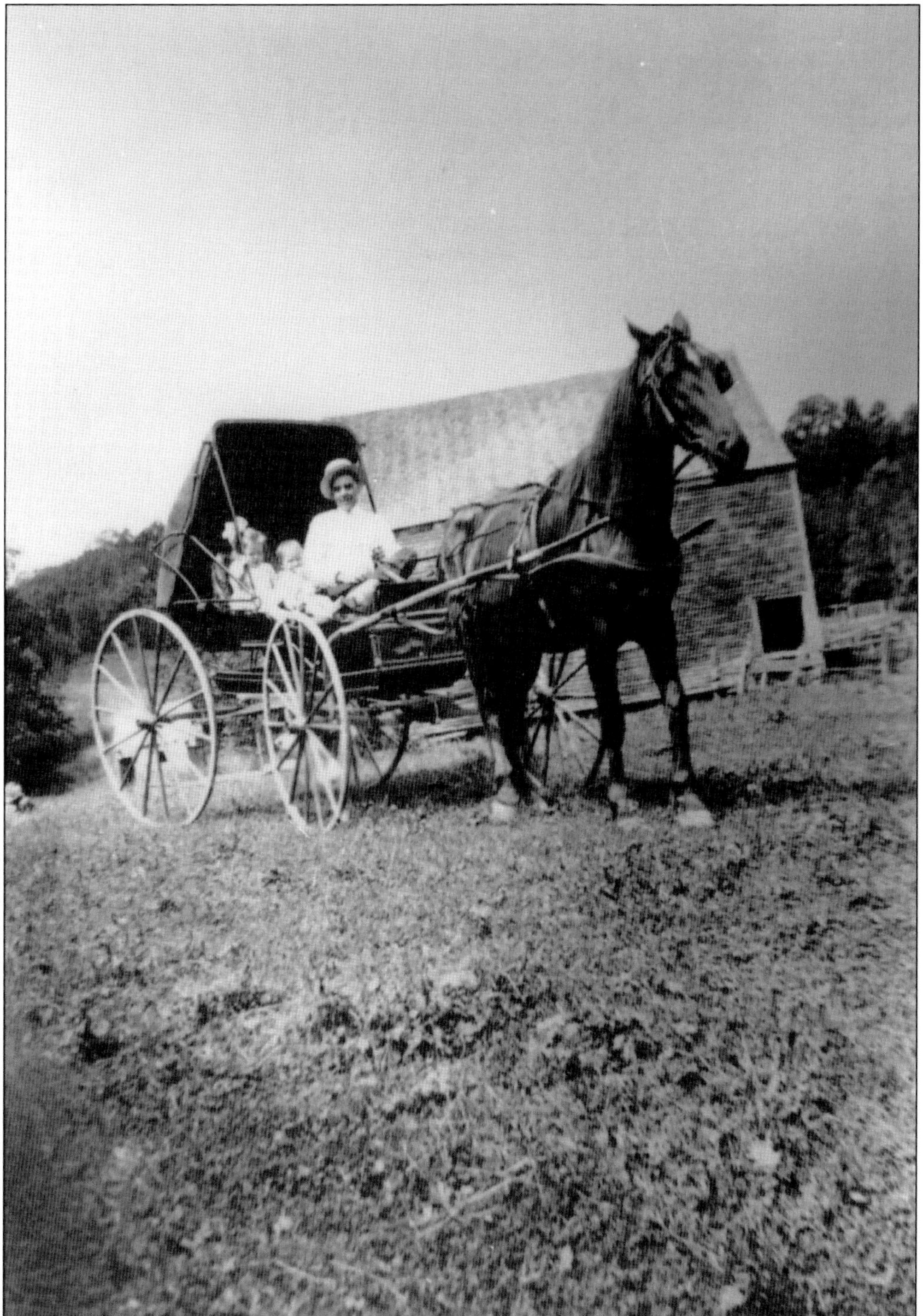

Traveling by Horse and Carriage on the Latham Farm. The family is getting ready for a ride in the carriage. The Latham barn is in the background. This photograph was likely taken in the early 1900s.

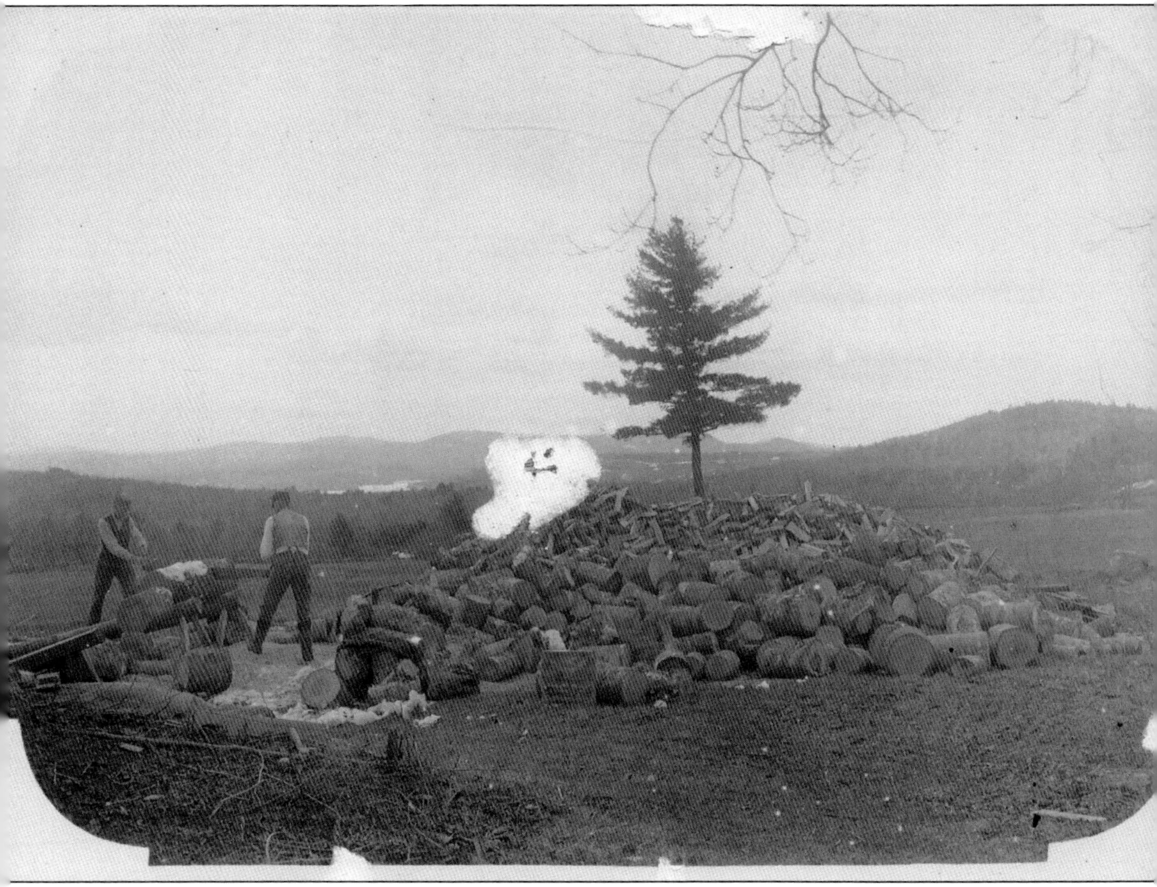

Harvesting Wood in the Early 1900s. This photograph was likely taken on Jay Hill. One can see what was probably the Androscoggin River in the background. Harvesting wood was difficult during this time. The most advanced tool was a saw.

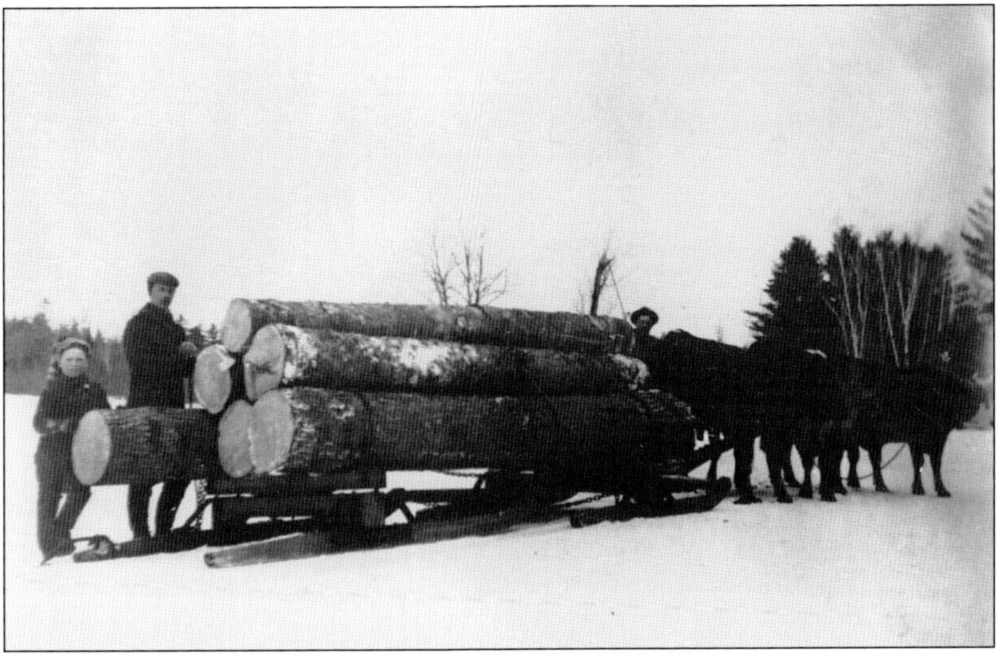

Oxen Hauling Logs during the Winter on Jay Hill. Many farmers logged during the winter to make a little extra money. During the colder months, it was often easier to haul heavy loads by sled rather than by wheeled apparatuses.

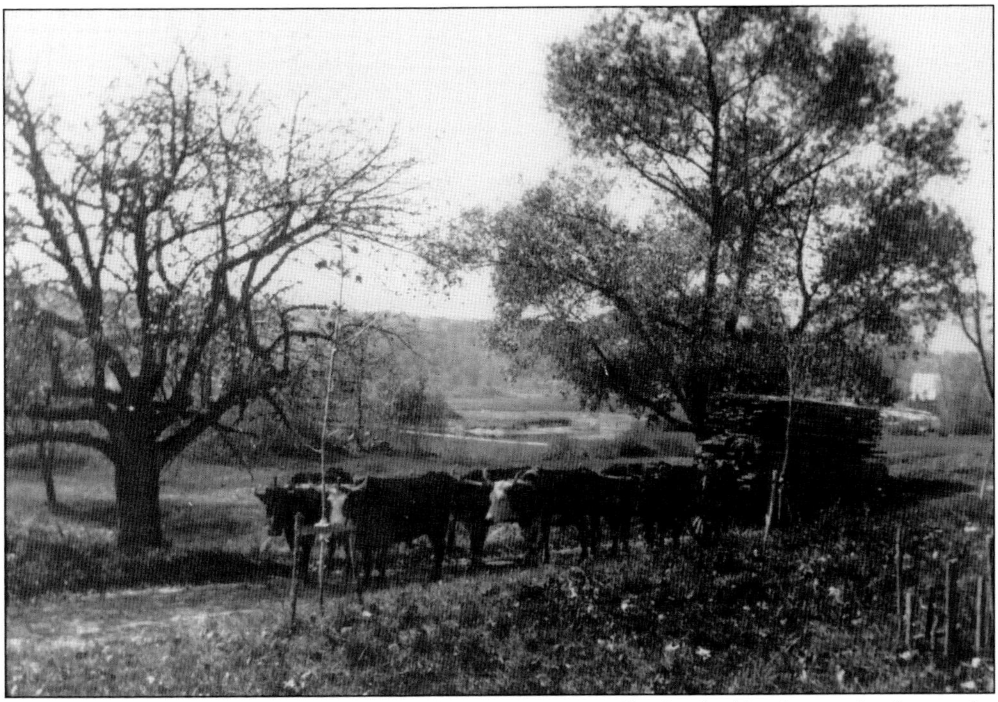

Oxen Hauling Lumber. In the image above, six oxen pull a load of lumber on Jay Intervale. This lumber most likely came from the closest sawmill.

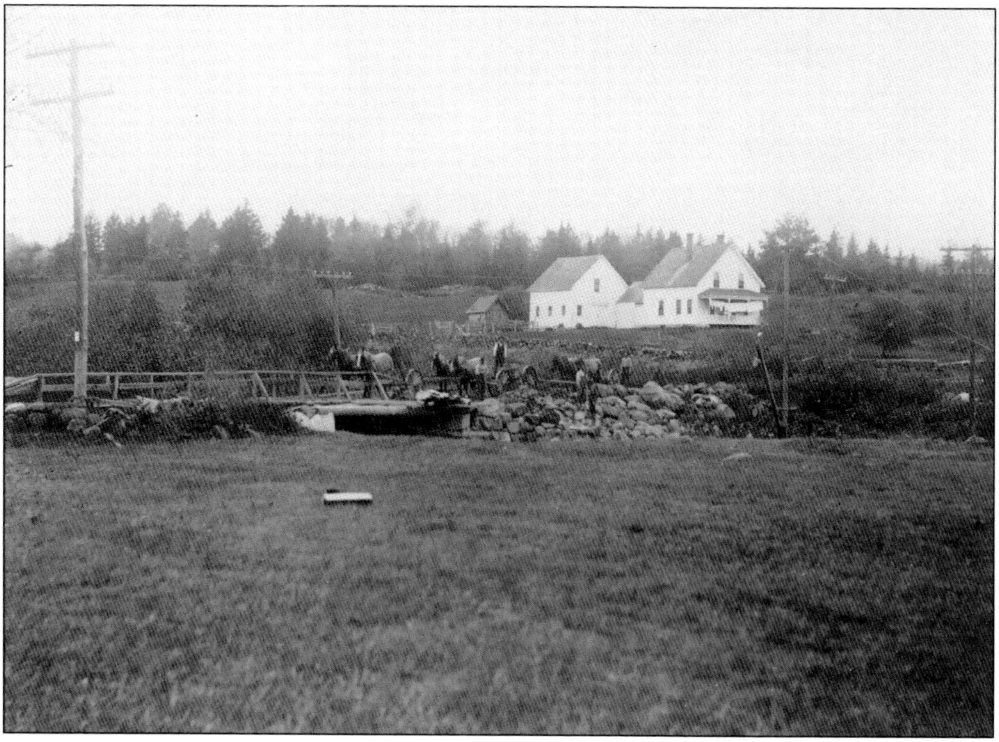

Board Commissioner Elmer Bryant and Crew Widening Bridge near Macomber Hill Road in North Jay. Elmer Bryant was also a farmer and quarryman who delivered milk in his spare time. He lived on Macomber Hill Road in Jay with his wife, Sarah Marcella. They had 11 children.

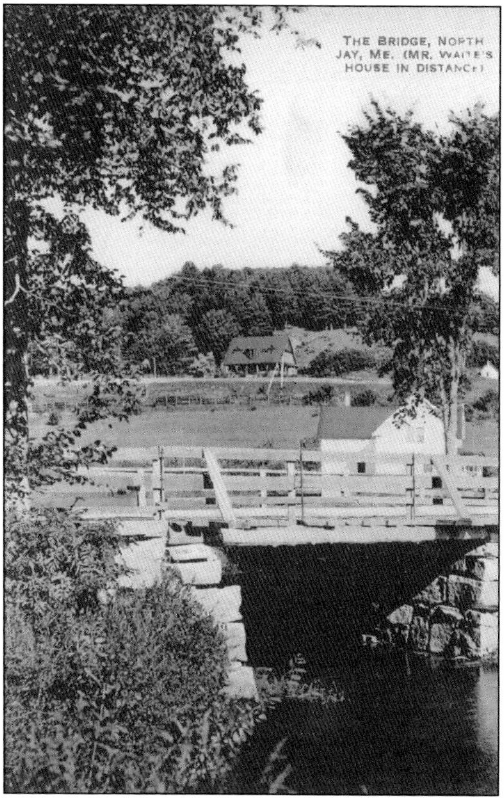

Bridge in North Jay. This photograph of the bridge in North Jay was taken in the early 1900s. O.S. Waite's house is visible in the distance. Carriages with horses used this bridge, as did sleds and sleighs in the wintertime.

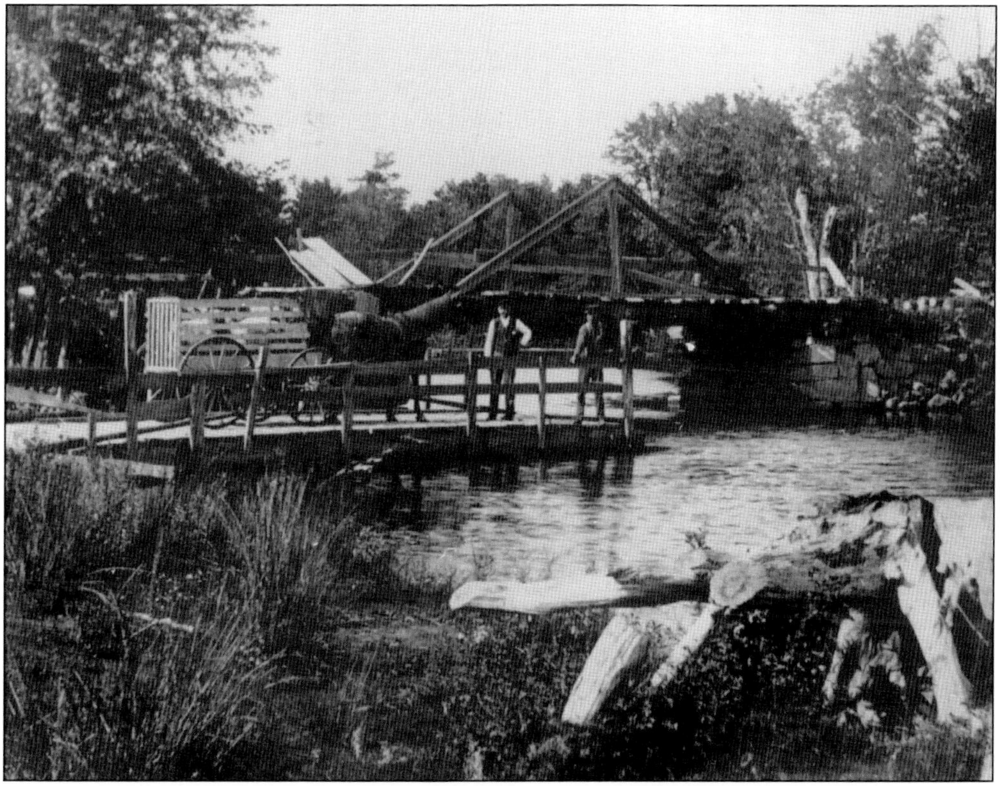

Lothrop Bridge. This is the old Lothrop Bridge on Jay Intervale, most likely on the Seven Mile Stream. Clint Gray and Henry Clark are standing on the ferry in the foreground.

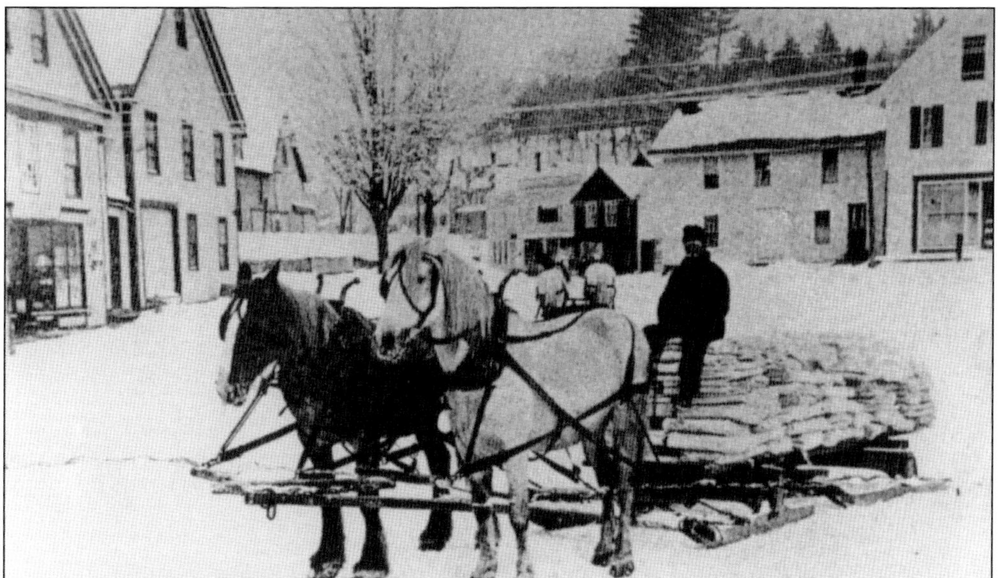

Transporting Pulp. Thomas Hickey sits on a load of ground wood pulp from a pulp and paper mill in Jay Village in 1904. The pulp is being hauled on a horse-drawn sled of sorts, probably on the way to the Otis Mill to be made into paper.

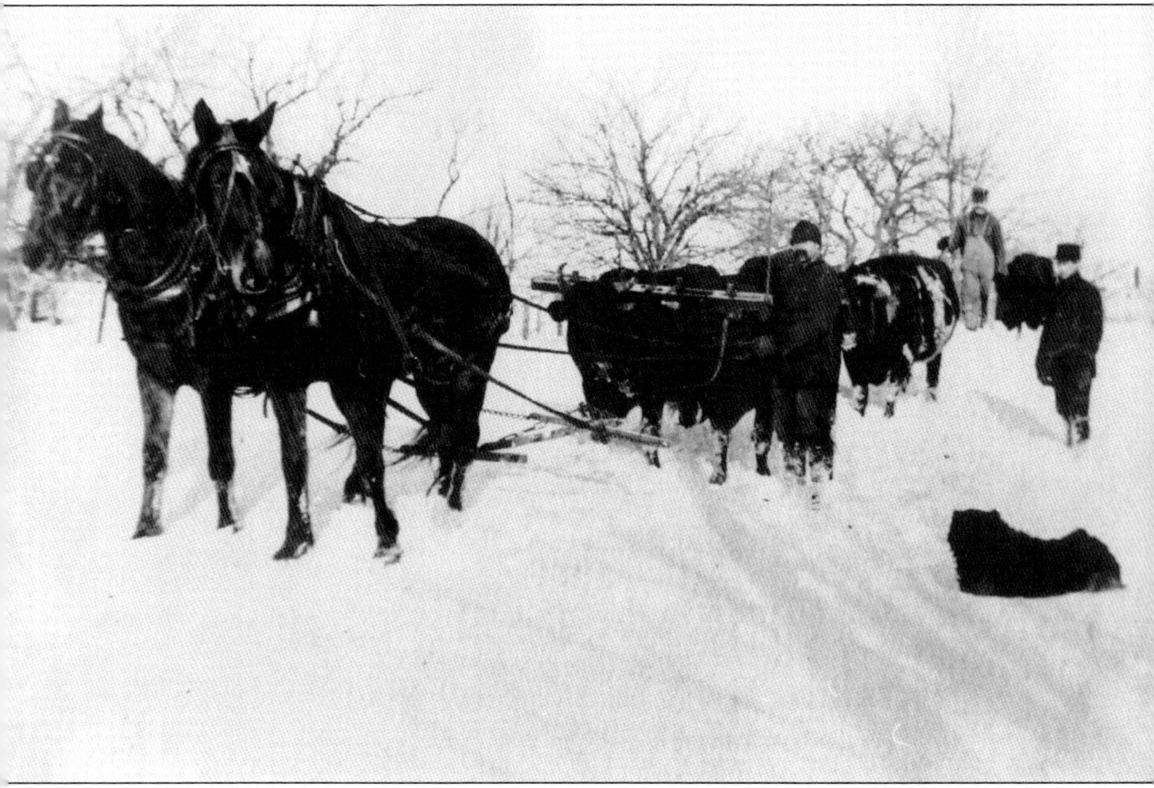

Breaking Road. These animals, horses and oxen, are breaking road on the top of Jay Hill during the wintertime. It is unusual to see oxen and horses hitched together. This was probably taken in the late 1800s, before the arrival of the automobile to the area. The roads were "rolled" to make it easier for other vehicles to get through after a storm.

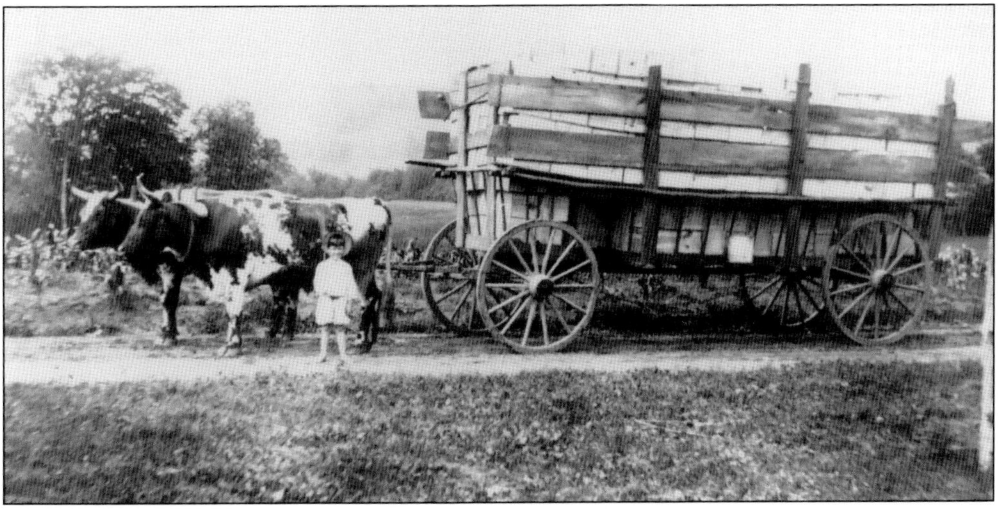

The Box Business. In this image, a team of oxen pulls a cart with boxes on it that were probably being hauled from the local box shop. They may have come from the Jay Wood Turning Company, which made many novelty items and also had a box shop attached.

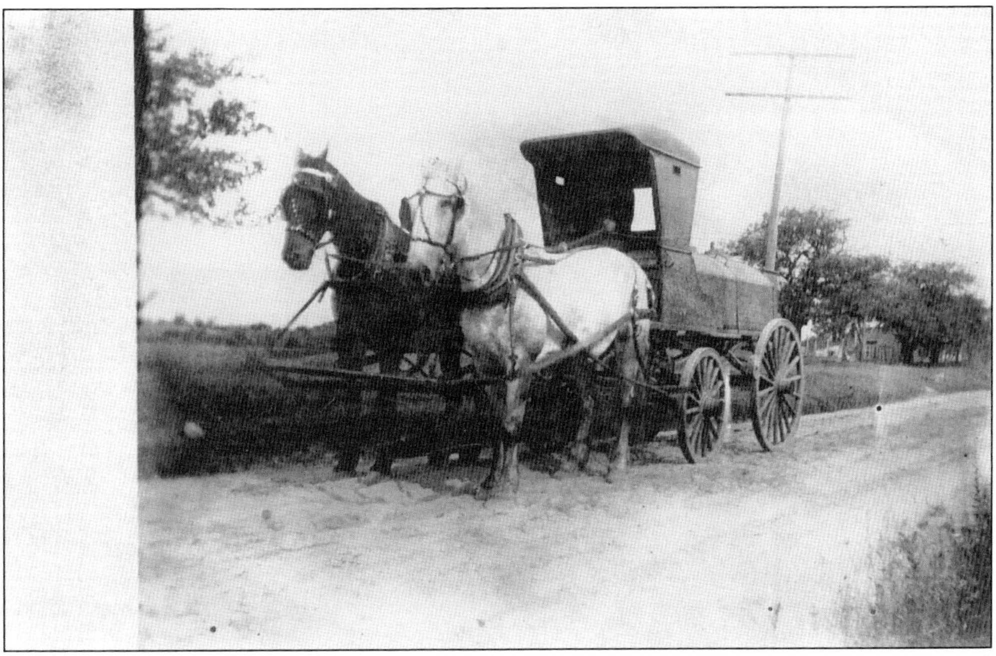

Oil Tank Used for Delivery of Kerosene. Wilfred Frank Holt (in the photograph above) lived in North Jay and delivered oil for the Standard Oil Company. He was also a livery man and farmer.

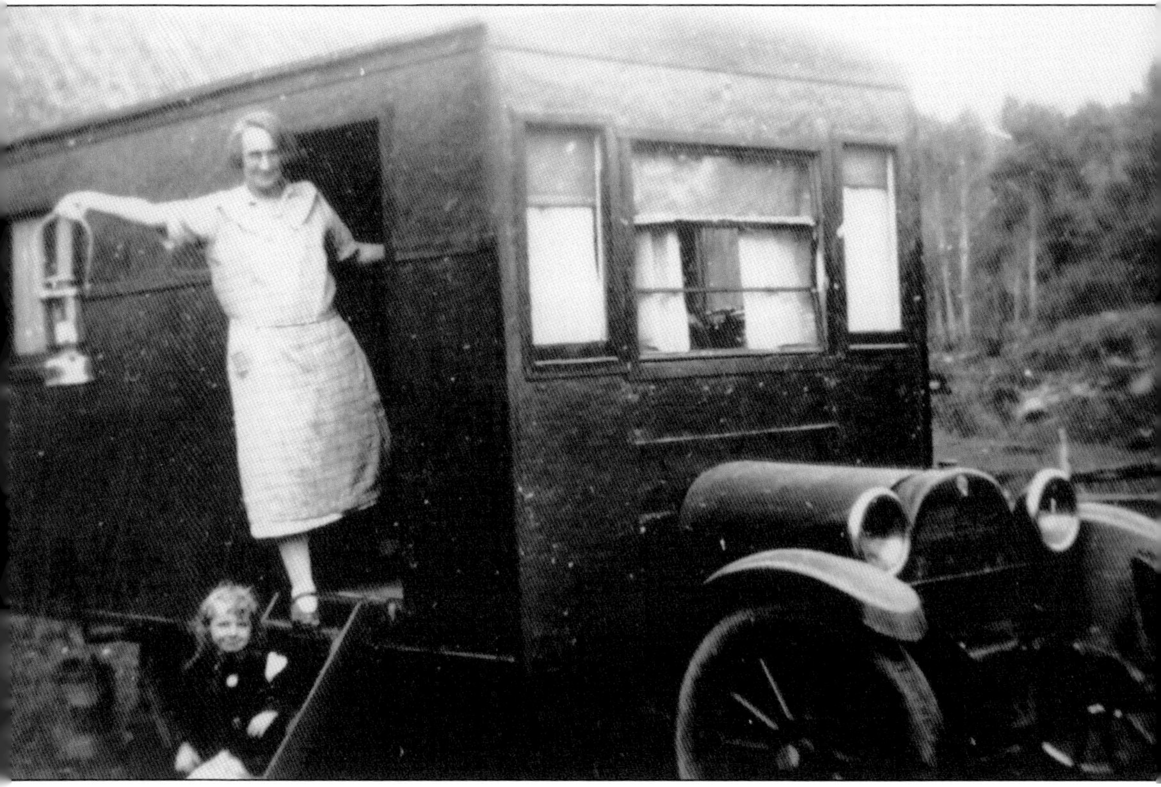

Travel Vehicles in the Early Days of the Automobile. In this photograph from 1920, Daisy Latham is swinging her lantern from the family vehicle. Martha Latham, her daughter, is in the foreground. The family barn is visible in the background. The advent of the automobile lessened the isolation of those in rural communities.

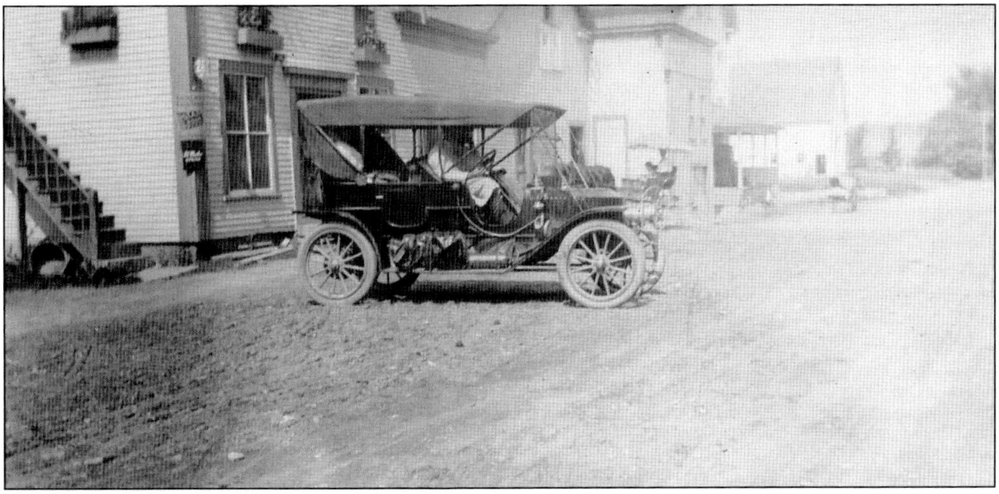

THE AUTOMOBILE. When automobiles started to be mass produced, prices came down, and they became more accessible. In this photograph, Mr. and Mrs. Bryant and Annie Williams start on a trip to Old Town. A trip much longer than 10 to 15 miles was unthinkable before the advent of the automobile.

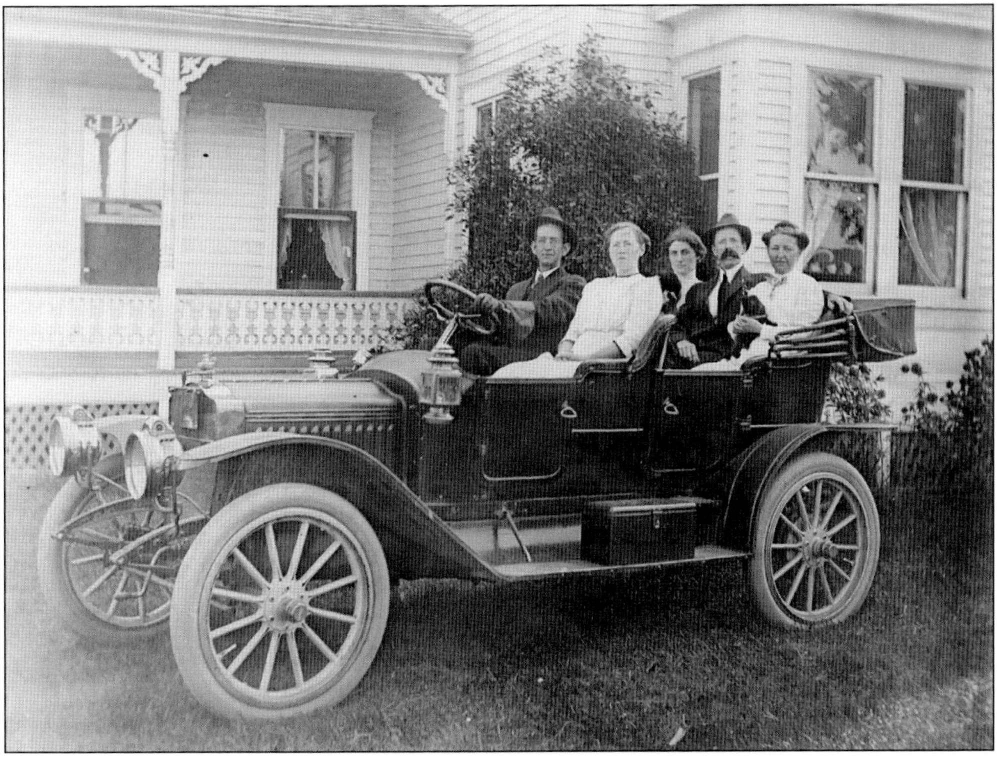

DAY TRIP. This family appears to be going on a trip. One of the women in the back seat is holding a kitten. The name Marion Hinkley is written on the back of this photograph, so some of the passengers may be members of the Hinkley family. This appears to be a Stanley Steamer. The Stanley Motor Carriage Company was founded in 1902 and went defunct in 1924. The Stanley Steamer was more expensive than the Model T. This might have led to the Steamer's demise, as most people could not afford them.

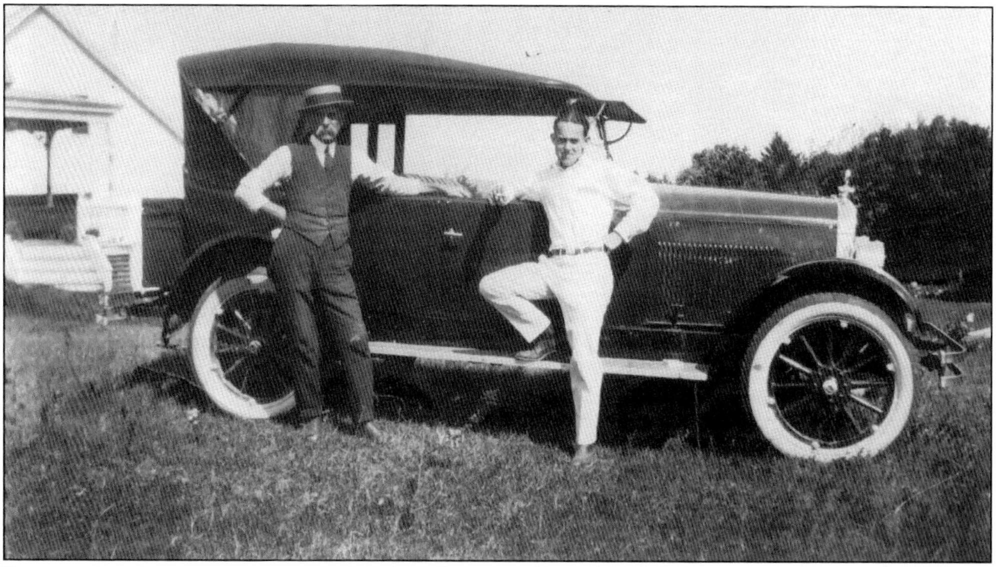

SHOWING OFF THEIR AUTOMOBILE. In this photograph, two men stand in front of a vehicle in Jay. Judging from their clothing, the image was taken in the late 1920s or early 1930s.

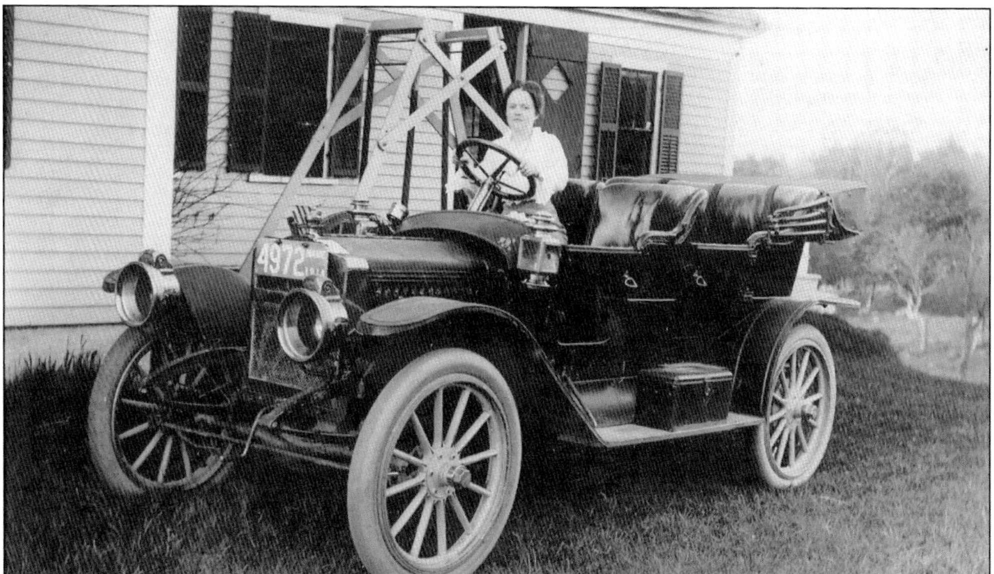

GETTING WOMEN BEHIND THE WHEEL. In the late 1920s, automobile manufacturers started to target women drivers by advertising in women's magazines and by making cars more appealing to women. They began offering a broader range of colors for vehicles, improved the quality of the upholstery and interior linings, and made the cars easier to drive and maintain. In this photograph from the 1920s is Annie Clark.

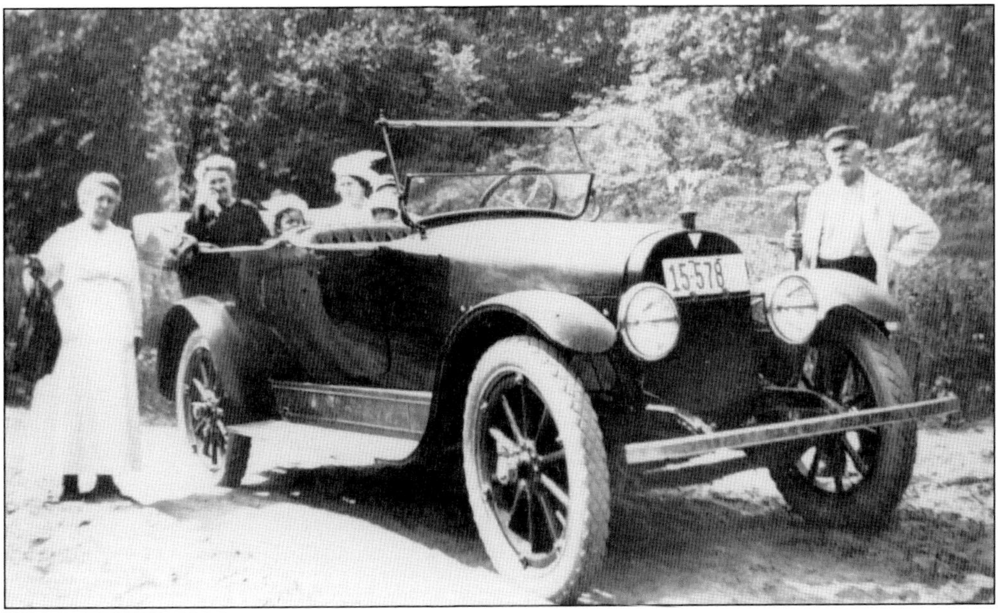

Getting Ready for a Day Trip. George W. Latham and his family prepare for a drive in this photograph. Automobiles eased isolation as individuals were no longer bound so close to home. They could reach their destinations in a fraction of the time it would have taken with a horse and buggy.

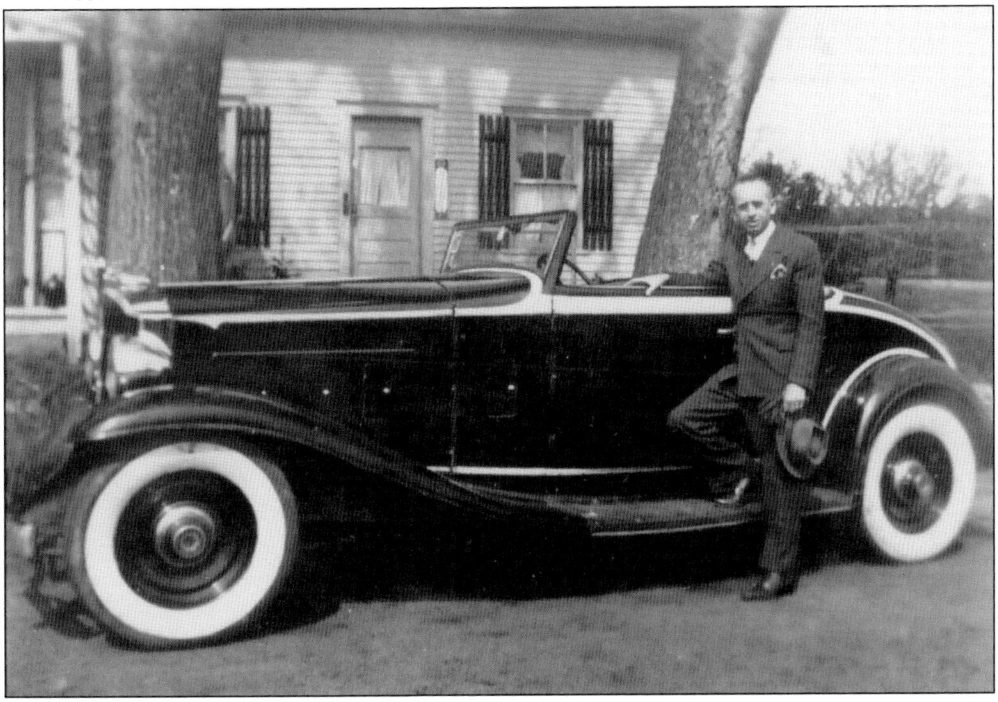

Maurice Latham in front of His 1945 Packard. Maurice was the son of Frank and Daisy Latham. Packard started production of the Clipper again after World War II. After producing only 16,600 cars in 1941 and a few thousand in 1942, Detroit stopped building civilian automobiles and concentrated on defense production. In 1945, Detroit got back into the business of building automobiles.

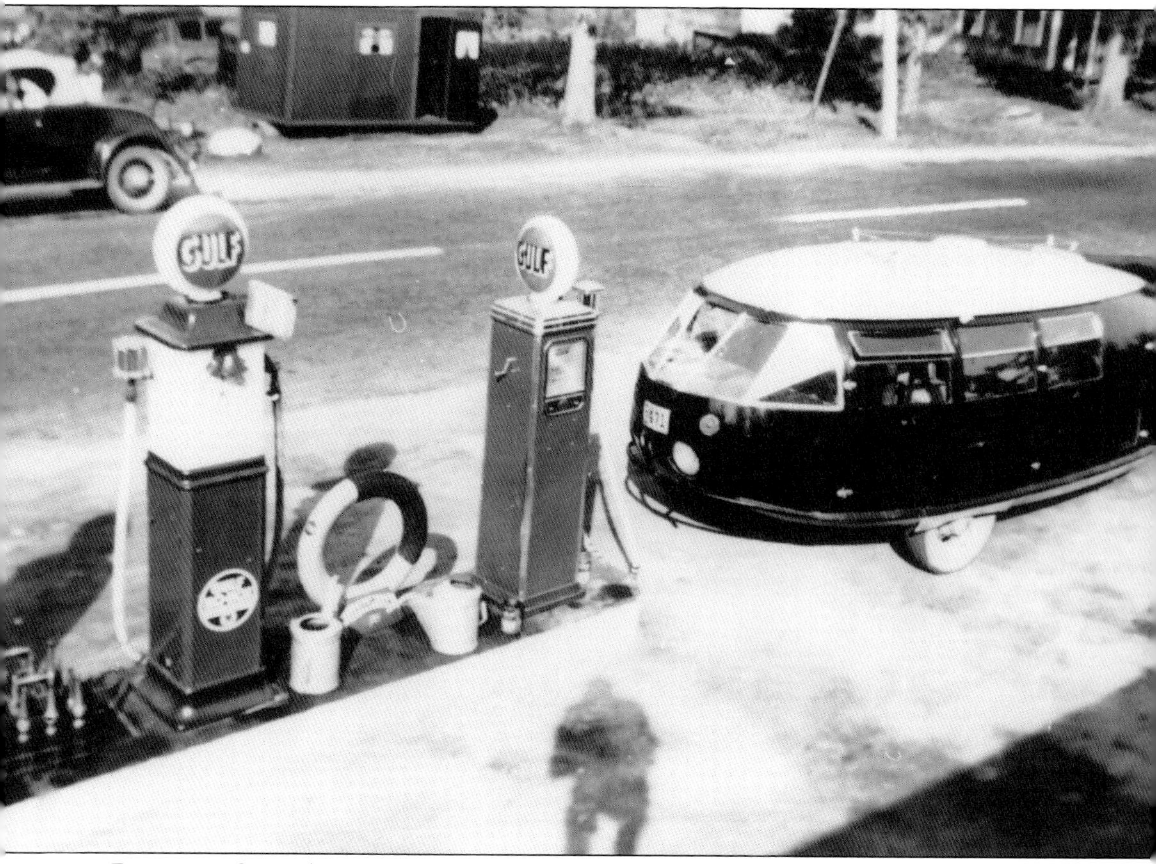

DYMAXION CAR. The arrival of this vehicle at Latham's Filling Station caused quite a stir. This vehicle appears to be what was called a Dymaxion, a 20-foot-long three-wheeled vehicle with rear-wheel (single) steering; it seated a driver and about 10 passengers. This aluminum-bodied auto was designed by Buckminster Fuller in 1933. It was about six feet tall, weighed about 1,600 pounds, went 120 miles per hour, and got as much as 30 miles per gallon. Imagine the effect this unusual vehicle had on this small, rural town. This photograph was probably taken in the 1930s.

Five

WORSHIP

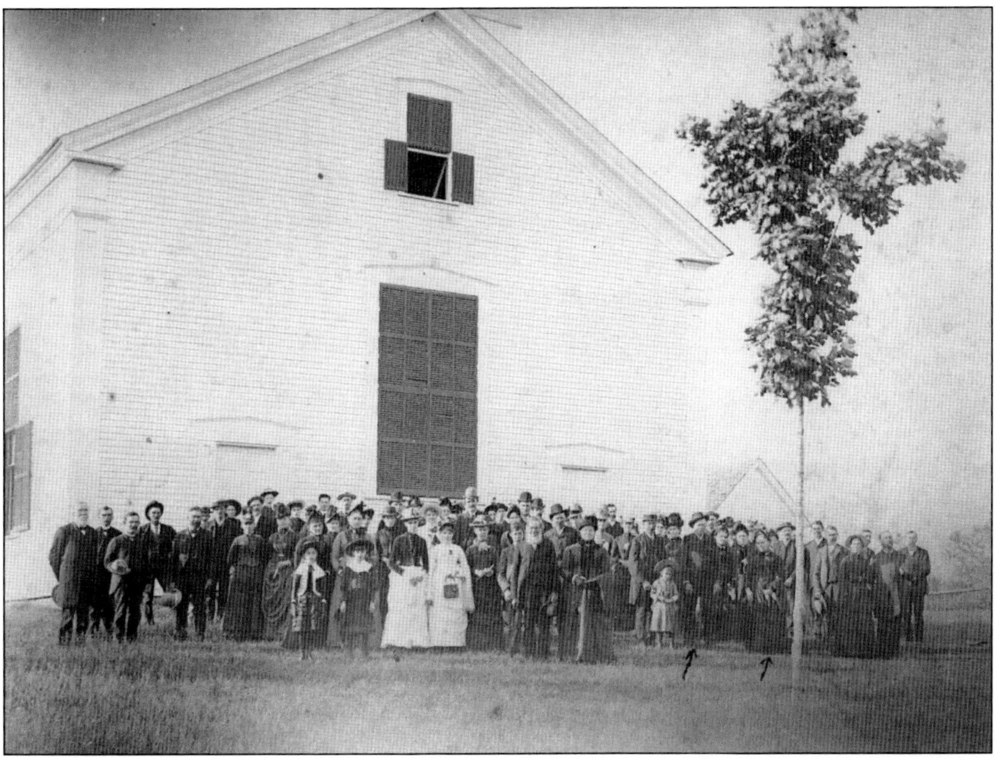

FIRST BAPTIST CHURCH ON JAY HILL, C. 1890. The first meetinghouse was built in 1799 and was made of logs, but it was never finished. In 1806, this building was constructed in the old English style, with a large vestibule surmounted by a bell deck and steeple. It had broad galleries on three sides and an elevated pulpit. As it was not heated, churchgoers brought their own foot stoves to stay warm.

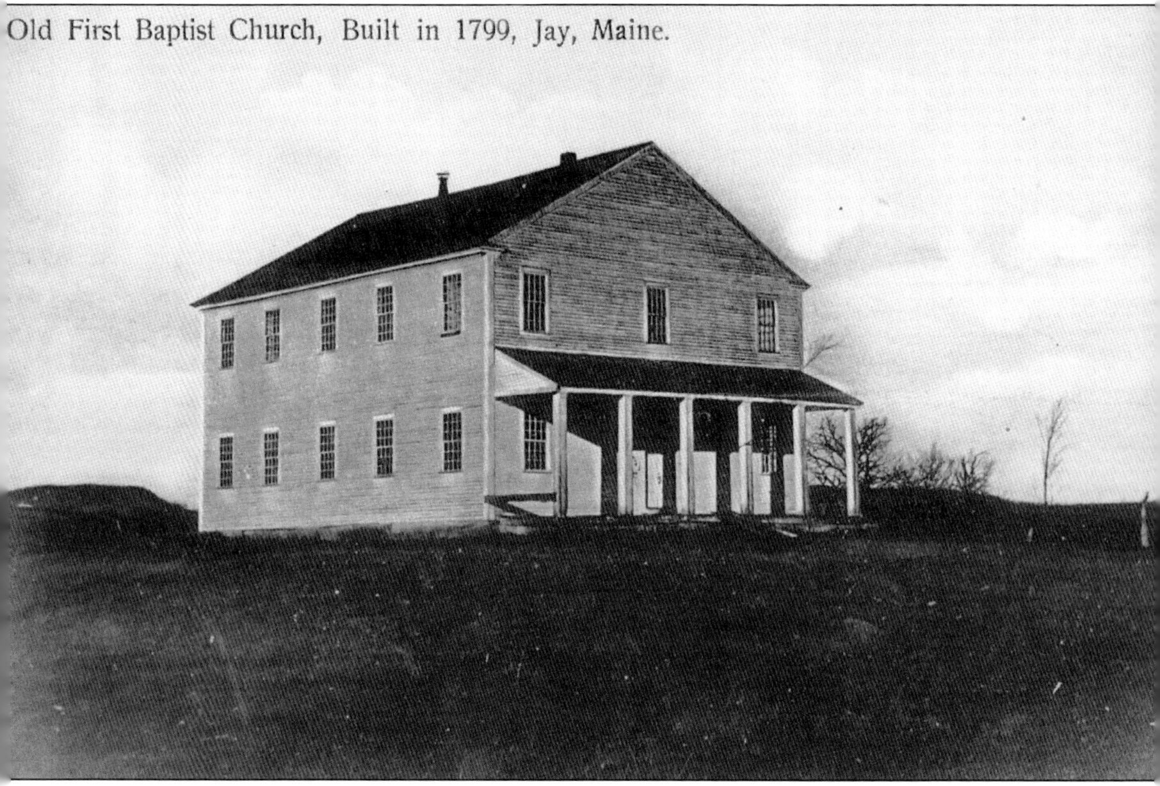

JAY BAPTIST CHURCH. This photograph is of the Jay Baptist Church after some renovations were done. The building was sold to the town of Jay in the late 1800s and used solely as a meetinghouse. The pews were removed in 1924. However, when the town was first settled, one of the conditions of settlement was to erect a house of worship. This was the first church building completed for this purpose.

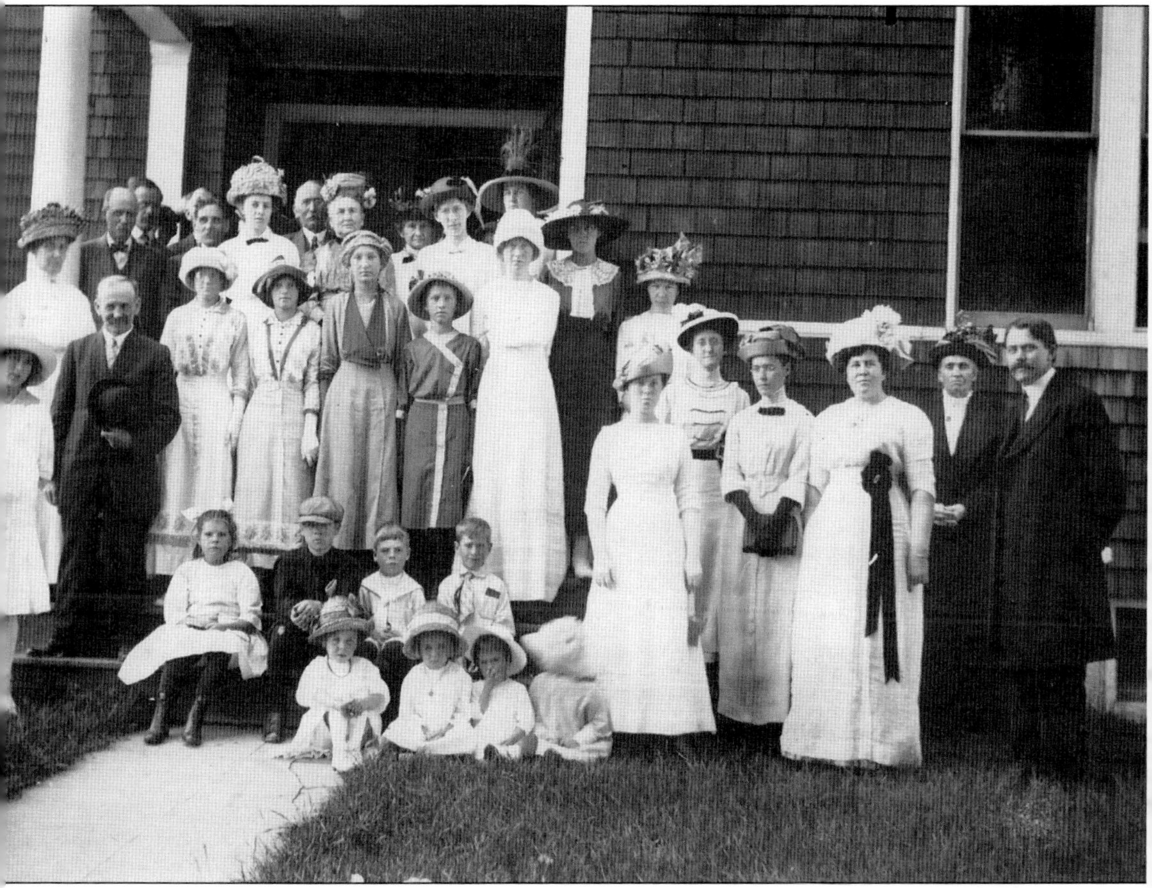

SUNDAY SERVICE AT JAY BAPTIST CHURCH. Built in 1893 and opened in 1894, this is the third Jay Baptist Church to be constructed. This photograph was taken after Sunday service around 1913 and includes, from left to right, (first row, on ground) Harriet Thompson, Helen Ayles, Marian Macomber, and Rachel Thompson; (second row, on first step) Clifford Thompson, Sadie Tinnen, Freddie McSweeney, Oakes Thompson, and Clyde Thomas; (standing on ground) Arline Maxwell, Bertha Macomber, Rebecca Spaulding, Hattie Thompson, and Rev. George Cook; (on second step) Lizzie Spoffard, Lena Spoffard, Lucile Thomas, Geneva Thomas, Ilda Thomas, and Grace Ayles; (third step) Mabel Thompson, Will Greenleaf, Ella Lee, Julia Parsons, Myrtie Holman, Mildred Muller, and Annie Thompson; (fourth row) Mr. Gordon, Payson Adams, E. Knight, Patience Paine, and Eva Macomber.

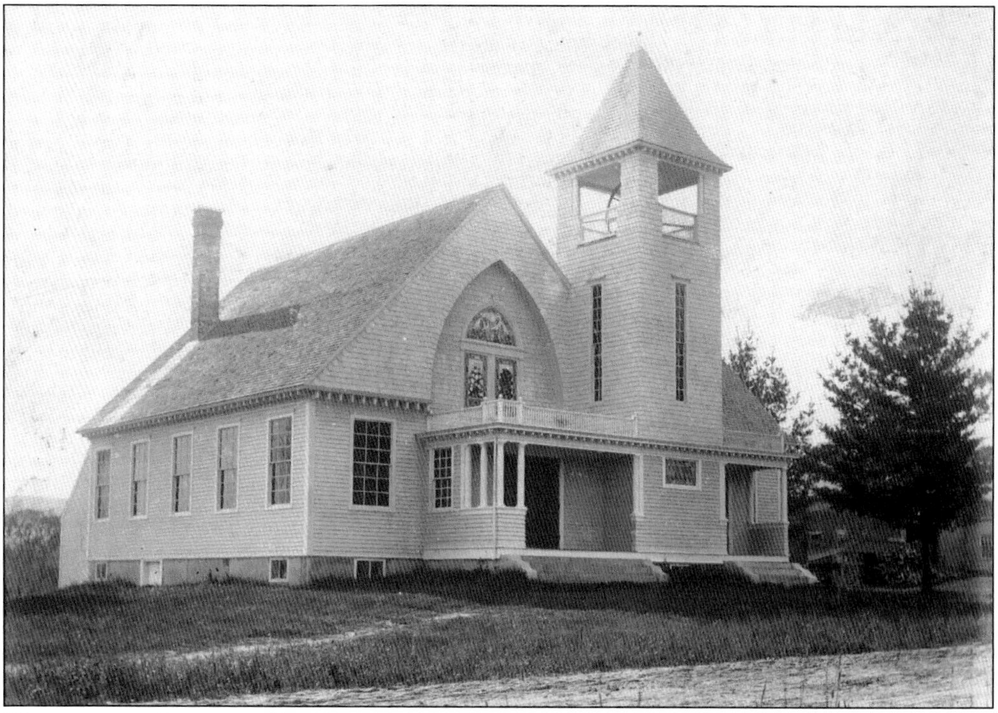

UNIVERSALIST CHURCH. This church was built in 1898. A stained glass window designed by the J.R. Lamb Company of New York in 1898 is still a fixture in what is now the Regular Baptist Church. The Universalist church was built by subscription, in part with generous donations from the Niles brothers of Boston and Payson Tucker of the Maine Central Railroad. The Niles family was quite prominent in North Jay. The early pastors of this church were Rev. Blanche A. Wright, Rev. Hannah J. Powell, Rev. H.S. Fiske, and Rev. S.M. Nieveen. The photograph above was likely taken in the early 1900s. The image below, *In the Maine Woods*, is a sepia watercolor by H.S. Fiske, who served as the Universalist minister in North Jay.

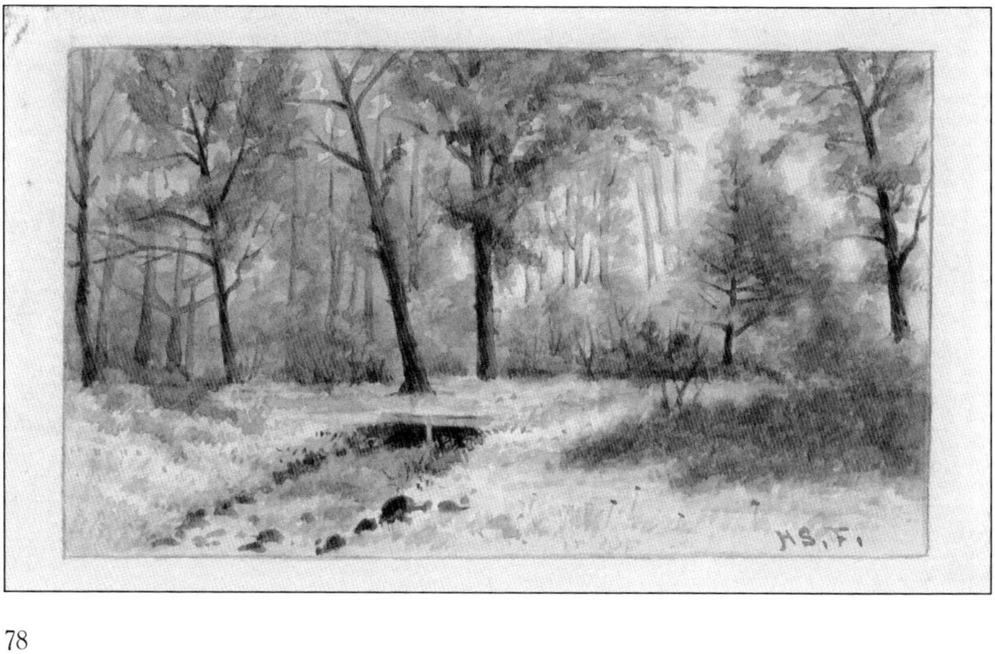

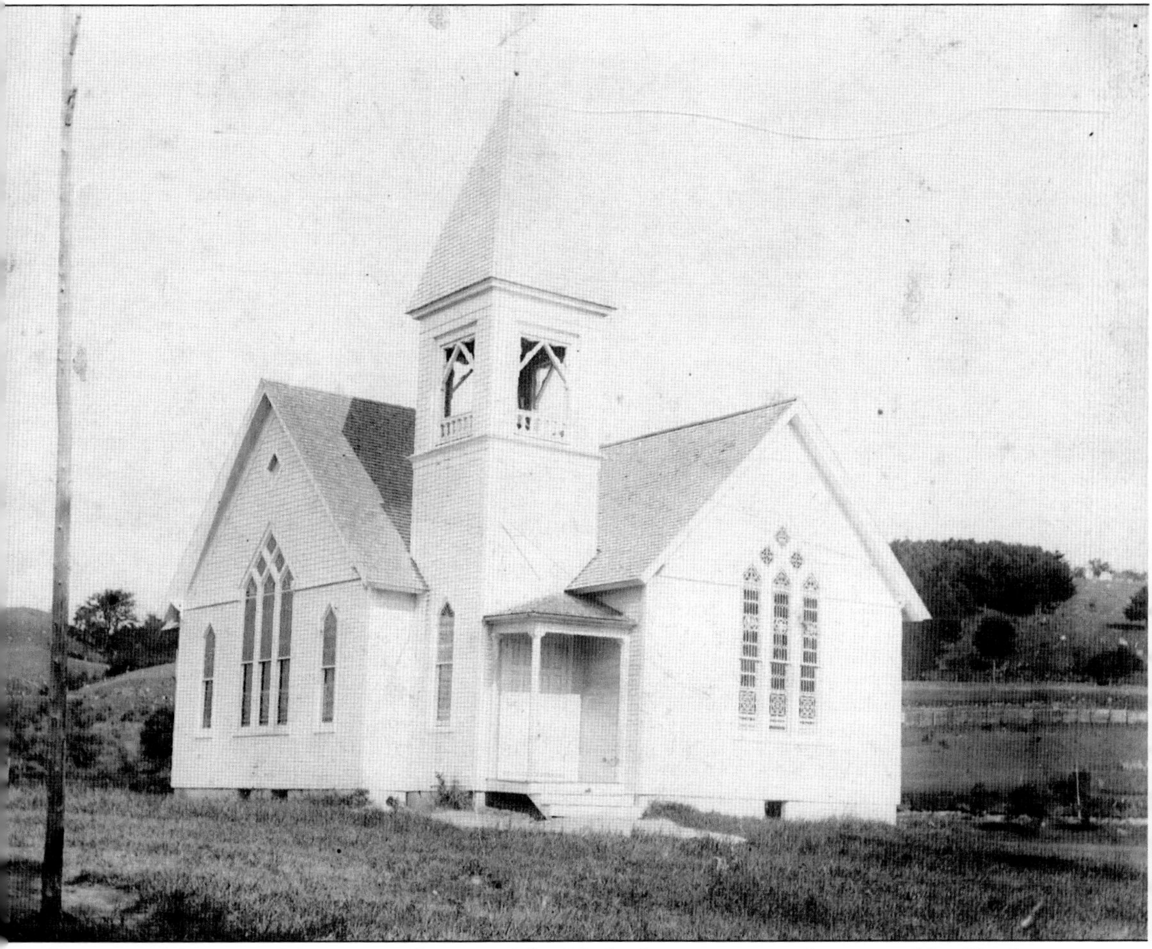

Bartlett Memorial Methodist Church. The Methodist society was first started by Charles Williams, a stonecutter. The first meetings were held in the Grange hall. This church was built in 1897 at a cost of $3,500. Reverend Fickett was the first minister at the new church. This photograph likely dates in the late 19th or early 20th century, as there are no power lines yet. The exact date is not known. This photograph was taken before Emerson School was built.

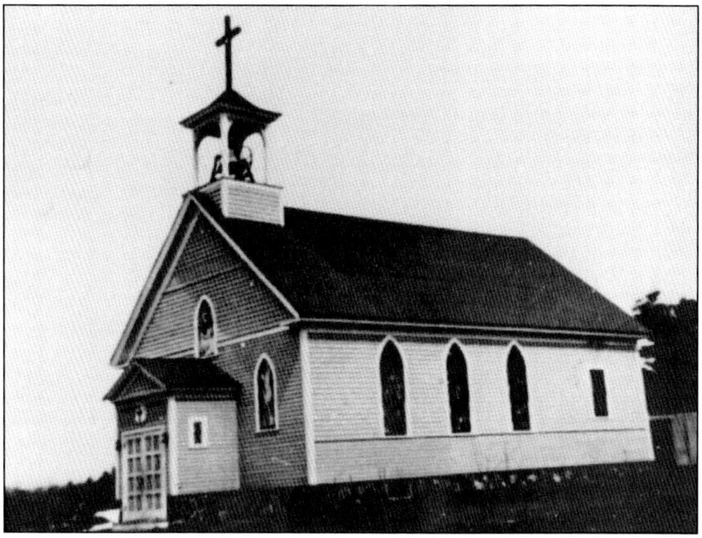

ST. MARY'S CHURCH OF THE ASSUMPTION, RILEY. Construction started in 1913 and cost $1,500. The chapel was of wood frame construction. The main body of the chapel had nine arched windows of cathedral glass. The last item added was a 750-pound steel-alloy bell purchased from C.S. Foundry Company of Hillsboro, Ohio. It was used to call villagers to church and announce that the priest had arrived to celebrate Mass.

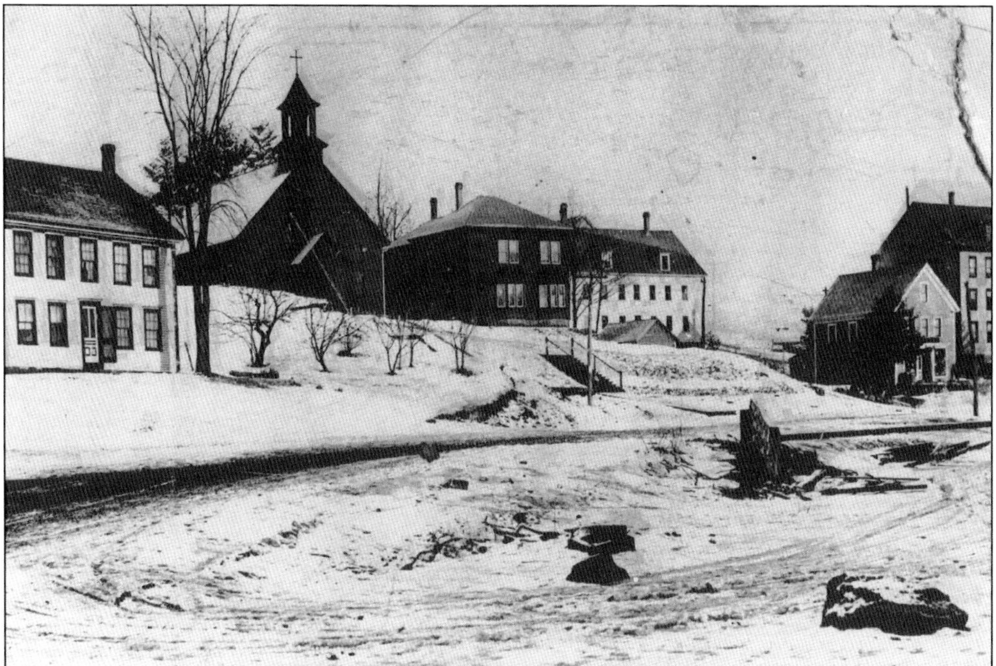

ST. ROSE CATHOLIC CHURCH, BUILT IN 1894. The school and pastor's house were erected soon after the church. Although attempts to establish Catholicism in Jay date back to the 1700s, it took hold in the late 1800s, about the time many immigrants from Quebec, Ireland, Italy, and Czechoslovakia moved to the area to work in the paper mills of Riley and Chisholm. This church was destroyed by fire in 1948.

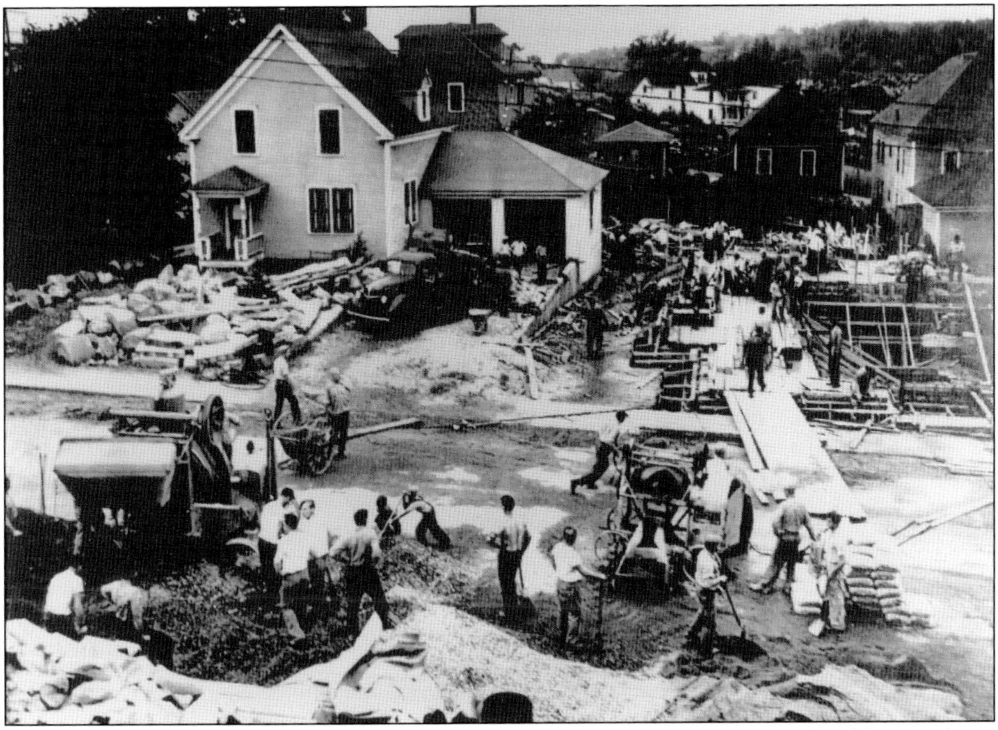

The Second St. Rose Catholic Church Construction Site, 1948. Several parishioners built the new church. According to Rev. Julius N. Boucher, "Fine churches are not built and paid for with inspiring speeches, lofty intentions, enthusiastic promises, not even prayers alone." This building cost $200,000. Construction was accomplished by the 625 families of wage earners who made up the parish of St. Rose of Lima in 1948 and 1949.

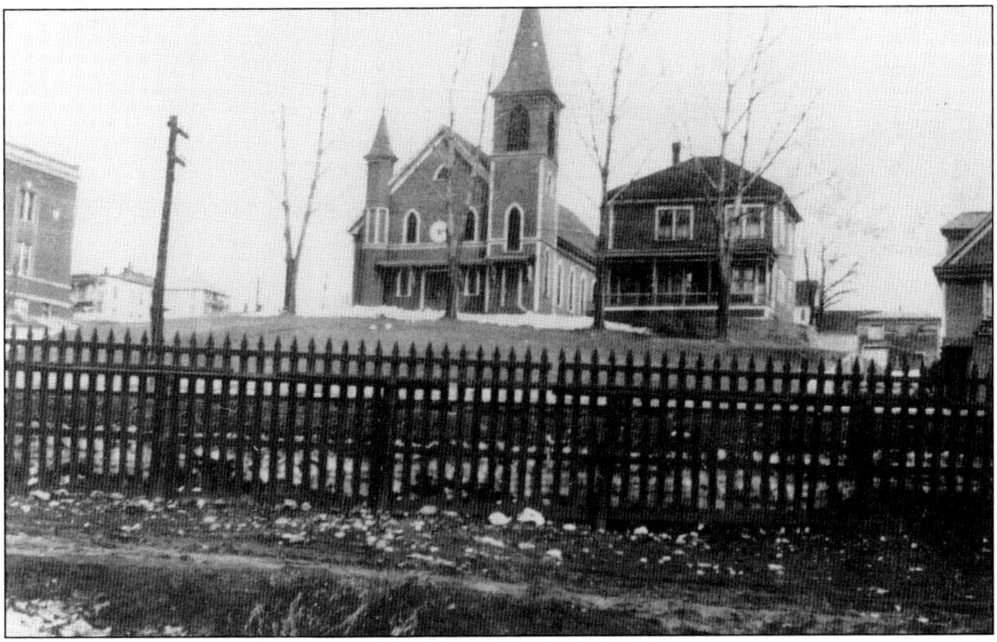

St. Rose Catholic Church. In this photograph is the finished church.

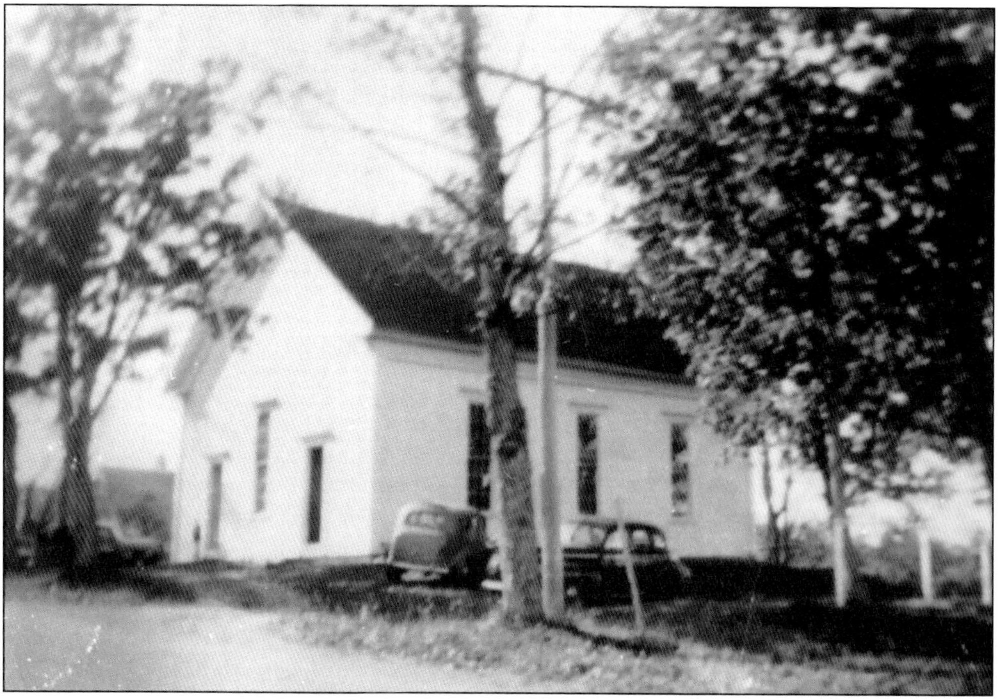

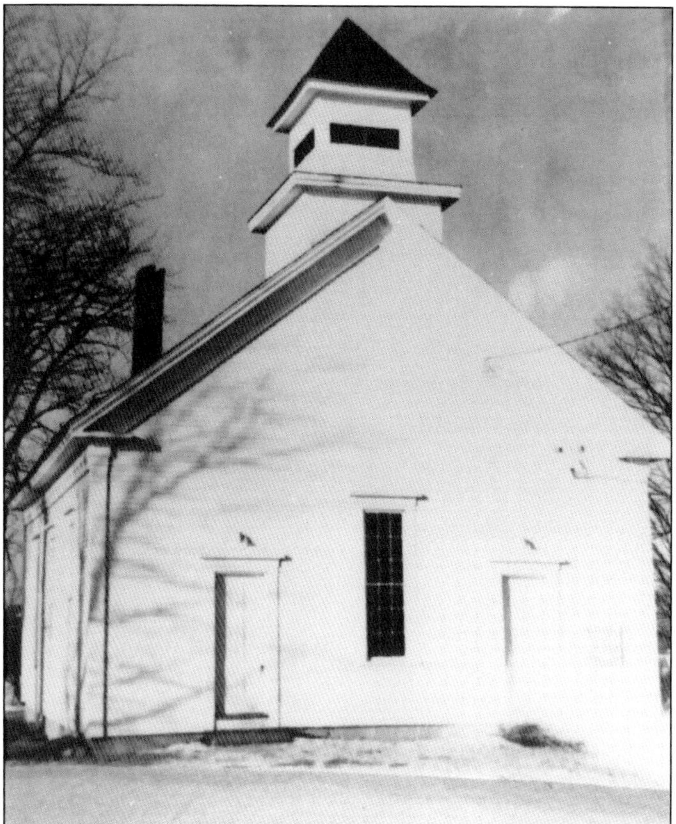

Bean's Corner Baptist Church at Its Original Location. First Baptist Church on Bean's Corner is pictured here. Later, it was moved to the other side of the road and a steeple was added.

The Baptist Church on Bean's Corner. This photograph is of the church after it was moved and the steeple erected. Before a church was built in 1865, services were held in the schoolhouse of District No. 4. The early pastors included Revs. John Foster, John Cheney, Hubbard Chandler, William Badger, S.P. Morrell, Roger Ela, Henry Preble, and J.S. Swift.

Six

BUSINESS

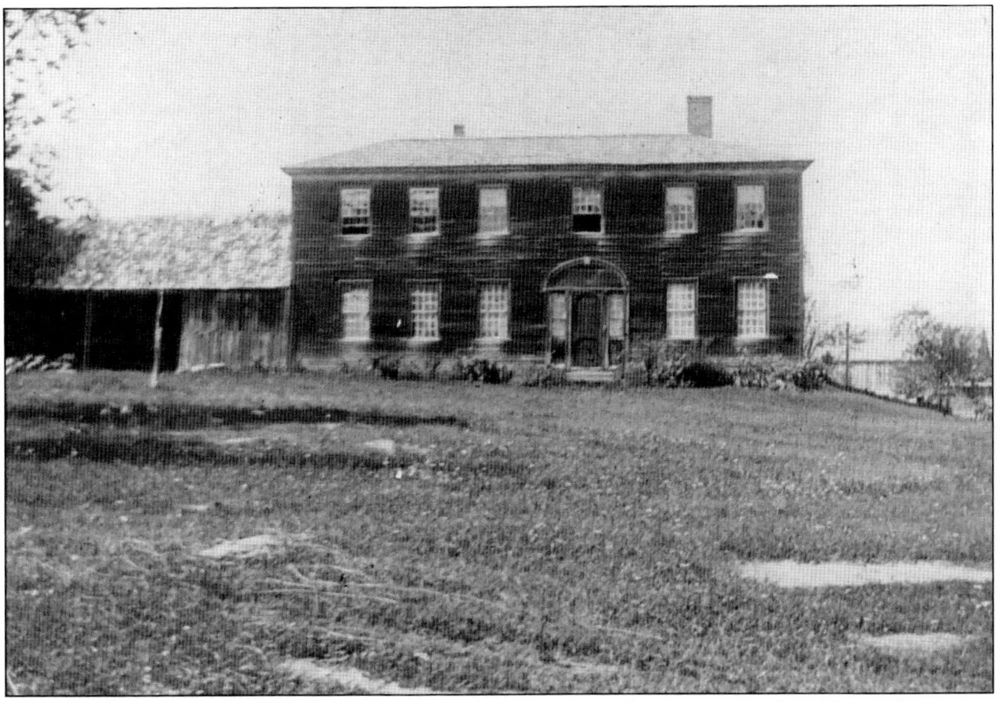

JAY TAVERN, C. 1895–1898. The tavern was built in 1793 by Moses Crafts. The timbers were hand hewn, put together with pegs and hand-wrought nails. It was a popular stopping place for stagecoaches passing through. People came from miles around to dance in the elegant ballroom. Many would come for the night and leave in the early morning on the stage going north to Farmington or south to Hallowell.

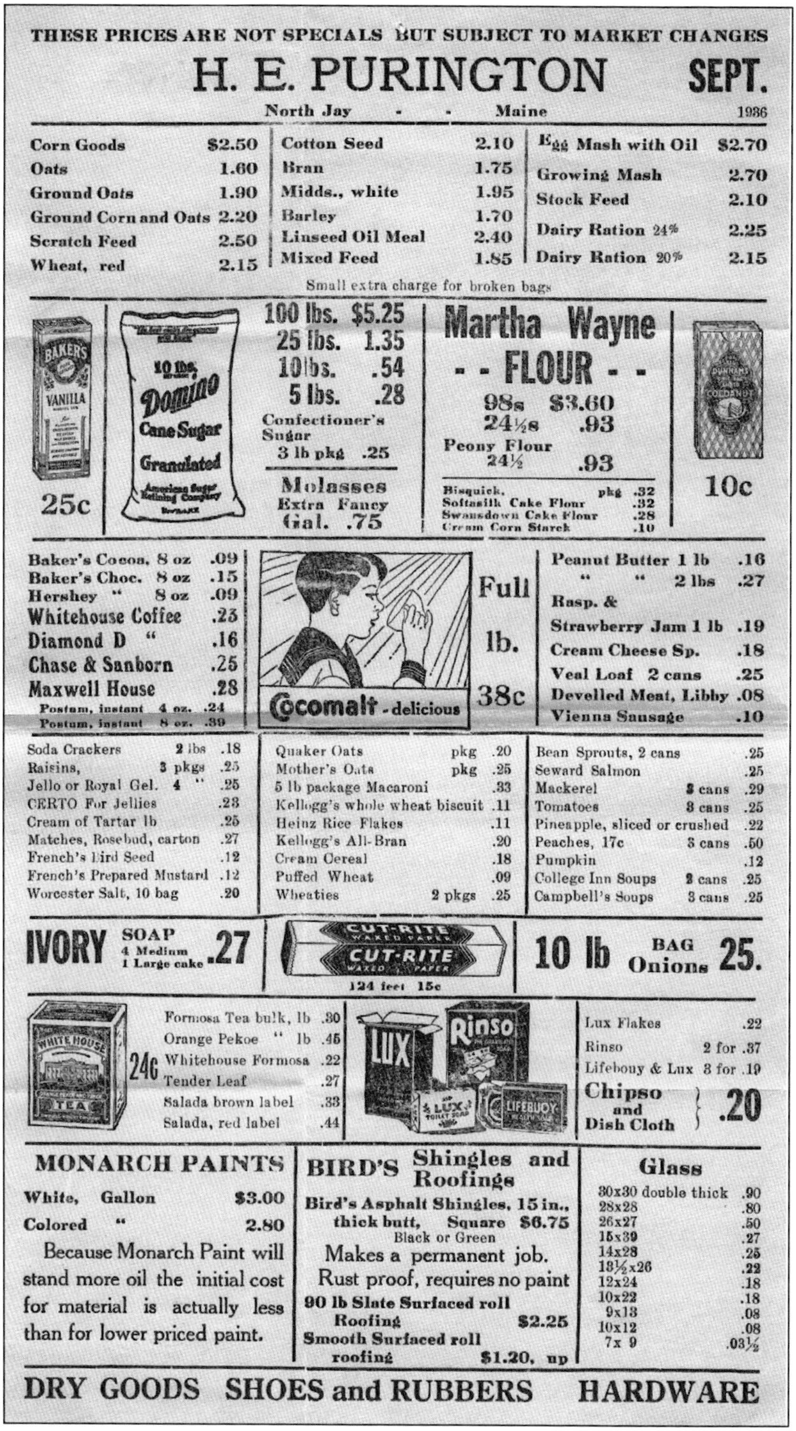

THESE PRICES ARE NOT SPECIALS BUT SUBJECT TO MARKET CHANGES

H. E. PURINGTON **SEPT.**

North Jay - - Maine 1936

Corn Goods	$2.50	Cotton Seed	2.10	Egg Mash with Oil	$2.70
Oats	1.60	Bran	1.75	Growing Mash	2.70
Ground Oats	1.90	Midds., white	1.95	Stock Feed	2.10
Ground Corn and Oats	2.20	Barley	1.70	Dairy Ration 24%	2.25
Scratch Feed	2.50	Linseed Oil Meal	2.40	Dairy Ration 20%	2.15
Wheat, red	2.15	Mixed Feed	1.85		

Small extra charge for broken bags

25c

100 lbs. $5.25
25 lbs. 1.35
10 lbs. .54
5 lbs. .28

Confectioner's Sugar
3 lb pkg .25

Molasses
Extra Fancy
Gal. .75

Martha Wayne - - FLOUR - -

98s $3.60
24½s .93

Peony Flour
24½ .93

Bisquick,	pkg	.32
Softasilk Cake Flour		.32
Swansdown Cake Flour		.28
Cream Corn Starch		.10

10c

Baker's Cocoa, 8 oz	.09
Baker's Choc. 8 oz	.15
Hershey " 8 oz	.09
Whitehouse Coffee	.25
Diamond D "	.16
Chase & Sanborn	.25
Maxwell House	.28
Postum, instant 4 oz.	.24
Postum, instant 8 oz.	.39

Cocomalt - delicious

Full lb. 38c

Peanut Butter 1 lb	.16
" " 2 lbs	.27
Rasp. & Strawberry Jam 1 lb	.19
Cream Cheese Sp.	.18
Veal Loaf 2 cans	.25
Develled Meat, Libby	.08
Vienna Sausage	.10

Soda Crackers	2 lbs	.18
Raisins,	3 pkgs	.25
Jello or Royal Gel.	4 "	.25
CERTO For Jellies		.23
Cream of Tartar lb		.25
Matches, Rosebud, carton		.27
French's Bird Seed		.12
French's Prepared Mustard		.12
Worcester Salt, 10 bag		.20

Quaker Oats	pkg	.20
Mother's Oats	pkg	.25
5 lb package Macaroni		.33
Kellogg's whole wheat biscuit		.11
Heinz Rice Flakes		.11
Kellogg's All-Bran		.20
Cream Cereal		.18
Puffed Wheat		.09
Wheaties	2 pkgs	.25

Bean Sprouts, 2 cans		.25
Seward Salmon		.25
Mackerel	3 cans	.29
Tomatoes	3 cans	.25
Pineapple, sliced or crushed		.22
Peaches, 17c	3 cans	.50
Pumpkin		.12
College Inn Soups	2 cans	.25
Campbell's Soups	3 cans	.25

IVORY SOAP 4 Medium 1 Large cake .27

124 feet 15c

10 lb BAG Onions **25.**

24c

Formosa Tea bulk, lb		.30
Orange Pekoe	" lb	.45
Whitehouse Formosa		.22
Tender Leaf		.27
Salada brown label		.33
Salada, red label		.44

Lux Flakes	.22
Rinso	2 for .37
Lifebouy & Lux	3 for .19
Chipso and Dish Cloth	.20

MONARCH PAINTS

White, Gallon	$3.00
Colored "	2.80

Because Monarch Paint will stand more oil the initial cost for material is actually less than for lower priced paint.

BIRD'S Shingles and Roofings

Bird's Asphalt Shingles, 15 in., thick butt, Square $6.75
Black or Green

Makes a permanent job.
Rust proof, requires no paint

90 lb Slate Surfaced roll Roofing $2.25
Smooth Surfaced roll roofing $1.20, up

Glass

30x30 double thick	.90
28x28	.80
26x27	.50
15x39	.27
14x28	.25
13½x26	.22
12x24	.18
10x22	.18
9x13	.08
10x12	.08
7x 9	.03½

DRY GOODS SHOES and RUBBERS HARDWARE

H.E. Purington's Store. This was a grocery, grain store, and eventually a filling station in North Jay. After many years of being the agent at the Grange store, Henry Evert Purington decided to open his own store. The advertisements on this page and the next were from his establishment in the 1930s.

H.E. PURINGTON STORE FLYER. Purington was a merchant and teacher. Some prices taken from his 1906 account book are as follows: a barrel of flour cost $4.50, coffee cost 30¢ per pound, beef cost 5¢ per pound, a pitchfork cost 40¢, a hoe cost 35¢, five gallons of kerosene cost 60¢, one dozen eggs cost 15¢, a broom cost 28¢, and ticking cost 14¢ a yard. These are examples of the varied items available in a general store.

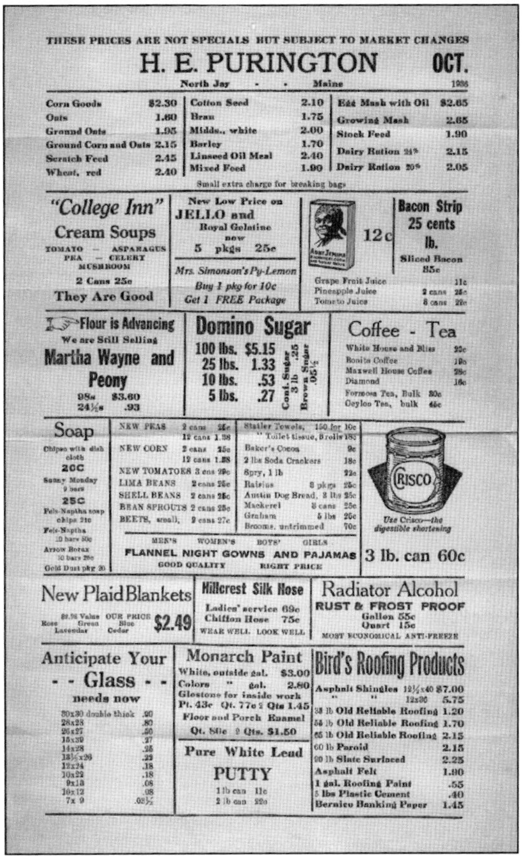
THESE PRICES ARE NOT SPECIALS BUT SUBJECT TO MARKET CHANGES

H. E. PURINGTON OCT.

North Jay - - Maine 1936

Corn Goods	$2.30	Cotton Seed	2.10	Egg Mash with Oil	$2.65
Oats	1.60	Bran	1.75	Growing Mash	2.65
Ground Oats	1.95	Midds., white	2.00	Stock Feed	1.90
Ground Corn and Oats	2.15	Barley	1.70	Dairy Ration 24%	2.15
Scratch Feed	2.45	Linseed Oil Meal	2.40	Dairy Ration 20%	2.05
Wheat, red	2.40	Mixed Feed	1.90		

Small extra charge for breaking bags

"College Inn" Cream Soups
TOMATO — ASPARAGUS
PEA — CELERY
MUSHROOM
2 Cans 25c
They Are Good

New Low Price on JELLO and Royal Gelatine now 5 pkgs 25c

Mrs. Simonson's Py-Lemon
Buy 1 pkg for 10c
Get 1 FREE Package

12c

Bacon Strip 25 cents lb.
Sliced Bacon 35c

Grape Fruit Juice 11c
Pineapple Juice 2 cans 25c
Tomato Juice 3 cans 22c

Flour is Advancing
We are Still Selling
Martha Wayne and Peony
98s $3.60
24½s .93

Domino Sugar
100 lbs. $5.15
25 lbs. 1.33
10 lbs. .53
5 lbs. .27
Conf. Sugar 3 lb .25
Brown Sugar .05½

Coffee - Tea
White House and Bliss 29c
Bonita Coffee 19c
Maxwell House Coffee 28c
Diamond 16c
Formosa Tea, Bulk 30c
Ceylon Tea, bulk 45c

Soap
Chipso with dish cloth 20C
Sunny Monday 9 bars 25C
Fels-Naptha soap chips 21c
Fels-Naptha 10 bars 50c
Arrow Borax 10 bars 29c
Gold Dust pkg 20

NEW PEAS 2 cans 25c
12 cans 1.38
NEW CORN 2 cans 25c
12 cans 1.38
NEW TOMATOES 3 cns 29c
LIMA BEANS 2 cans 25c
SHELL BEANS 2 cans 25c
BEAN SPROUTS 2 cans 25c
BEETS, small, 2 cans 27c

Statler Towels, 150 for 10c
" Toilet tissue, 3 rolls 18c
Baker's Cocoa 9c
2 lbs Soda Crackers 18c
Spry, 1 lb 22c
Raisins 3 pkgs 25c
Austin Dog Bread, 3 lbs 25c
Mackerel 3 cans 25c
Graham 5 lbs 25c
Brooms, untrimmed 70c

MEN'S WOMEN'S BOYS' GIRLS
FLANNEL NIGHT GOWNS AND PAJAMAS
GOOD QUALITY RIGHT PRICE

CRISCO
Use Crisco—the digestible shortening
3 lb. can 60c

New Plaid Blankets
$2.98 Value OUR PRICE $2.49
Rose Green Blue
Lavendar Cedar

Hillcrest Silk Hose
Ladies' service 69c
Chiffon Hose 75c
WEAR WELL LOOK WELL

Radiator Alcohol
RUST & FROST PROOF
Gallon 55c
Quart 15c
MOST ECONOMICAL ANTI-FREEZE

Anticipate Your - - Glass - - needs now

30x30 double thick	.90
28x28	.80
26x27	.50
15x39	.27
14x28	.25
13½x26	.22
12x24	.18
10x22	.18
9x13	.08
10x12	.08
7x 9	.03½

Monarch Paint
White, outside gal. $3.00
Colors " gal. 2.80
Glostone for inside work
Pt. 43c Qt. 77c 2 Qts 1.45
Floor and Porch Enamel
Qt. 80c 2 Qts. $1.50

Pure White Lead

PUTTY
1 lb can 11c
2 lb can 22c

Bird's Roofing Products

Asphalt Shingles 12½x40	$7.00
" " 12x36	5.75
35 lb Old Reliable Roofing	1.20
55 lb Old Reliable Roofing	1.70
65 lb Old Reliable Roofing	2.15
60 lb Paroid	2.15
90 lb Slate Surfaced	2.25
Asphalt Felt	1.90
1 gal. Roofing Paint	.55
5 lbs Plastic Cement	.40
Bernico Banking Paper	1.45

MAURICE PURINGTON'S STORE IN NORTH JAY. H.E. Purington was Maurice's father. Judging from the vehicles parked here, this photograph was probably taken in the 1940s. Although it is not certain when Maurice took over his father's store, it appears to have been in the mid-1940s.

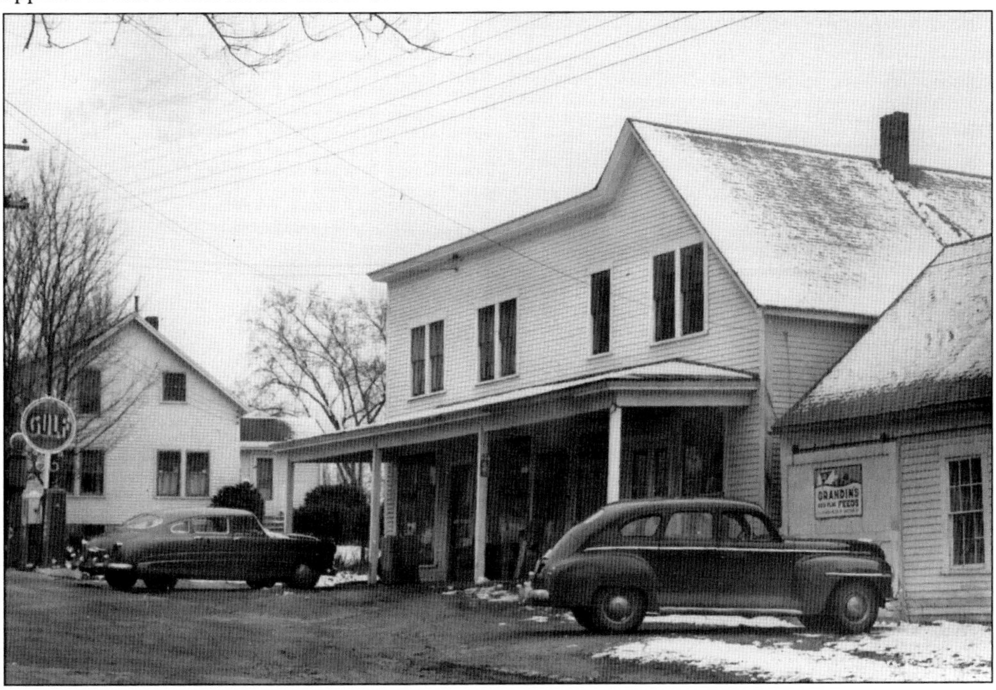

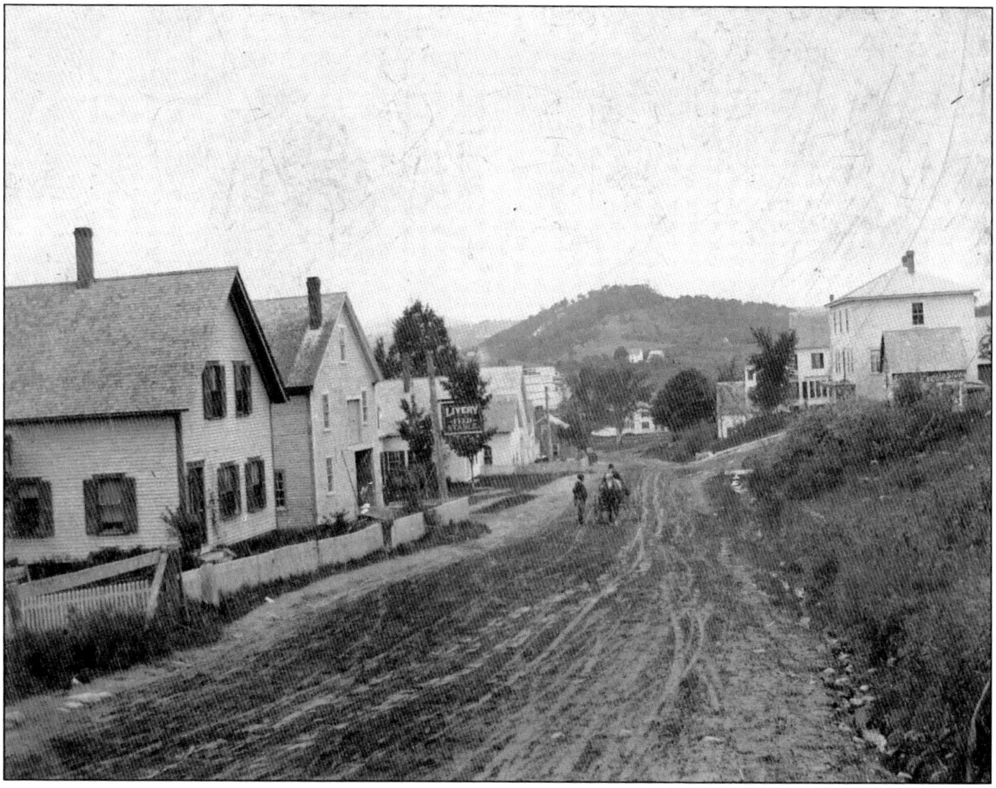

Mountain View House. North Jay's only hotel was photographed in 1899. It had a livery and feed stable connected. J.A. Cascadden was the proprietor, and he ran the hotel from 1899 to 1901. Having a livery meant that when people came to town, they would have a place to stable their horses during their stay. Many livery stables attached to hotels at this time had horses and carriages to hire as well. Below is the card for the Mountain View House.

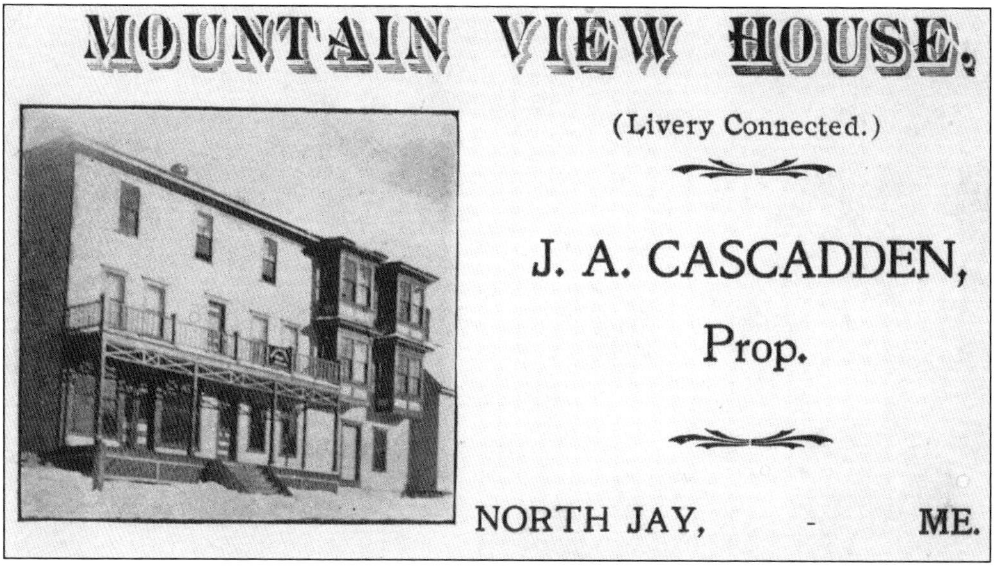

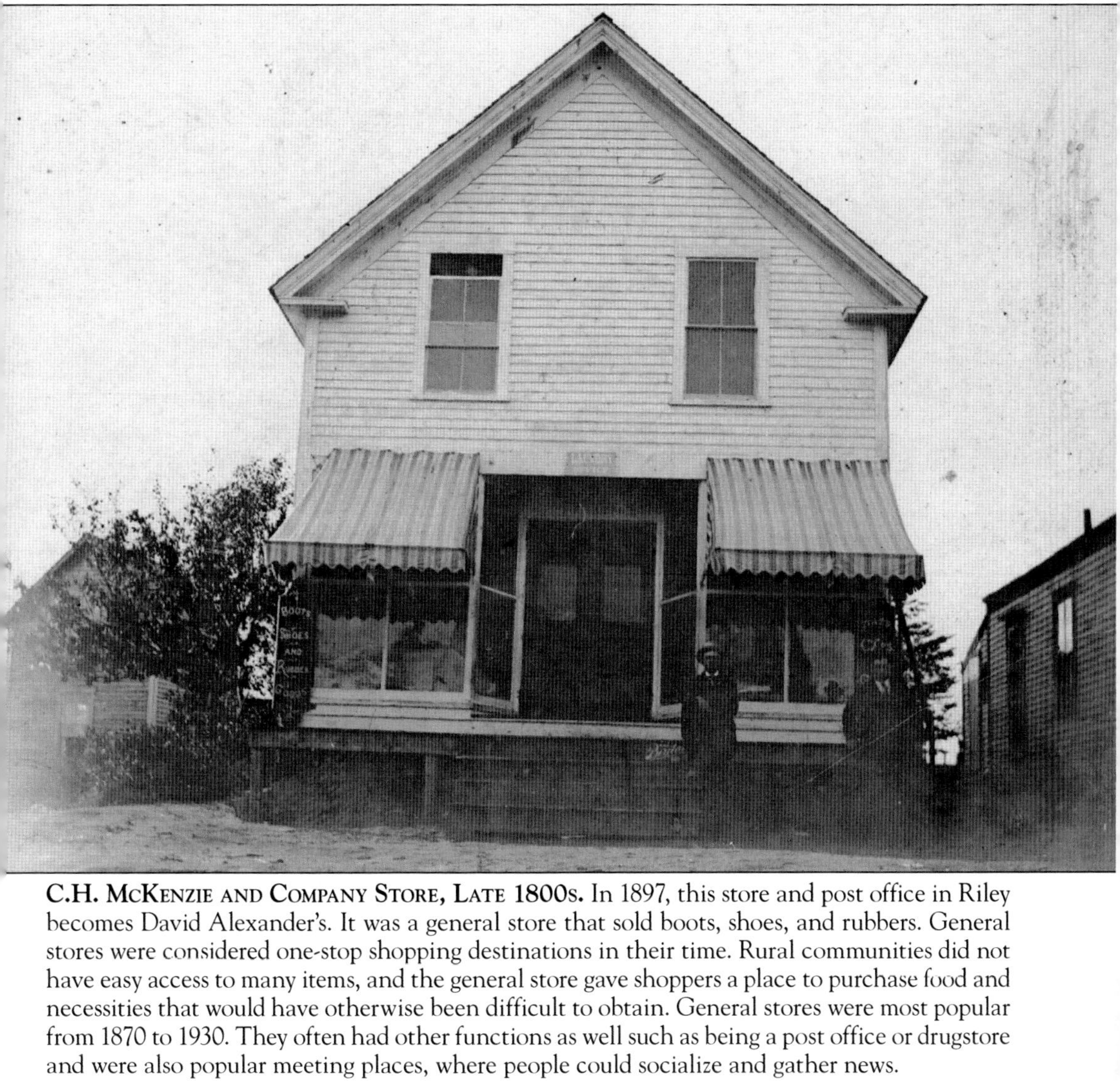

C.H. McKenzie and Company Store, Late 1800s. In 1897, this store and post office in Riley becomes David Alexander's. It was a general store that sold boots, shoes, and rubbers. General stores were considered one-stop shopping destinations in their time. Rural communities did not have easy access to many items, and the general store gave shoppers a place to purchase food and necessities that would have otherwise been difficult to obtain. General stores were most popular from 1870 to 1930. They often had other functions as well such as being a post office or drugstore and were also popular meeting places, where people could socialize and gather news.

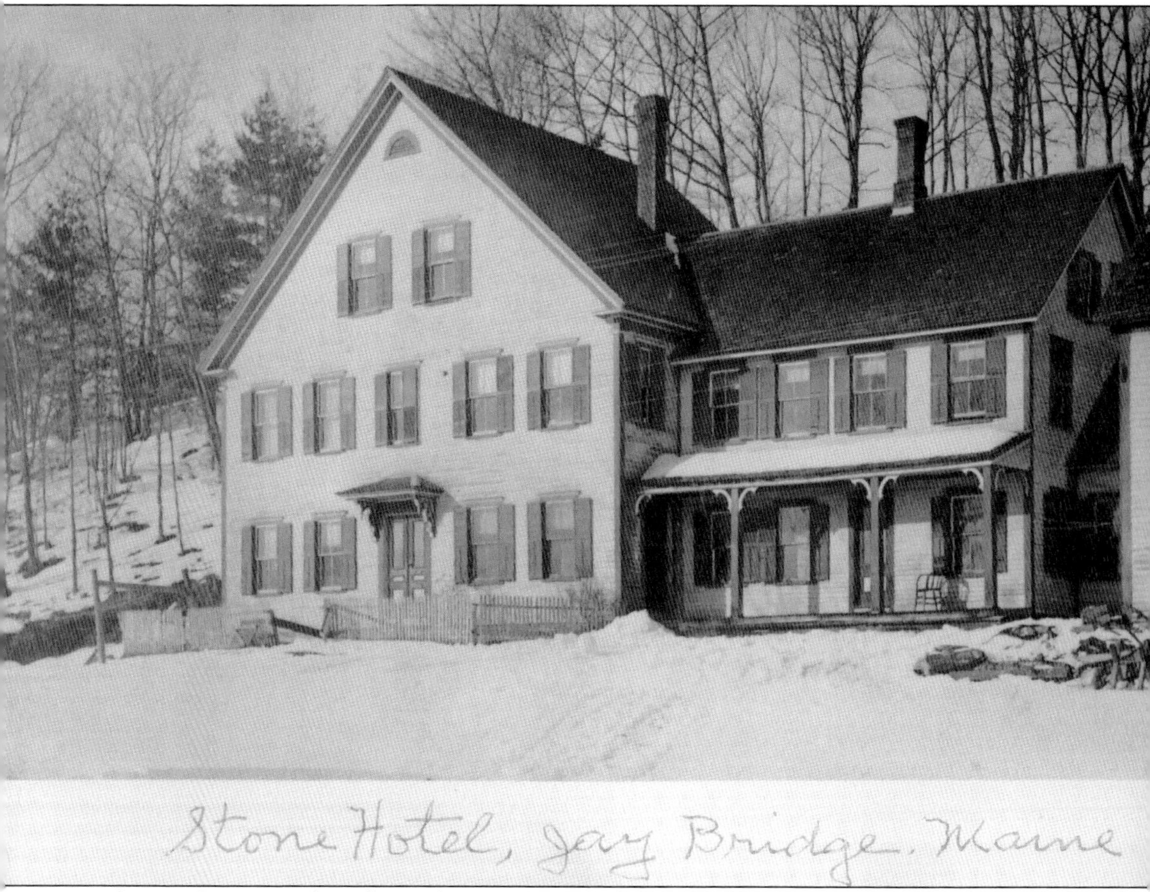

STONE HOTEL. In the village of Jay Bridge, this building was owned by M.V. Stone. The Stone family ran a motel here starting in 1892. This photograph was taken in 1900.

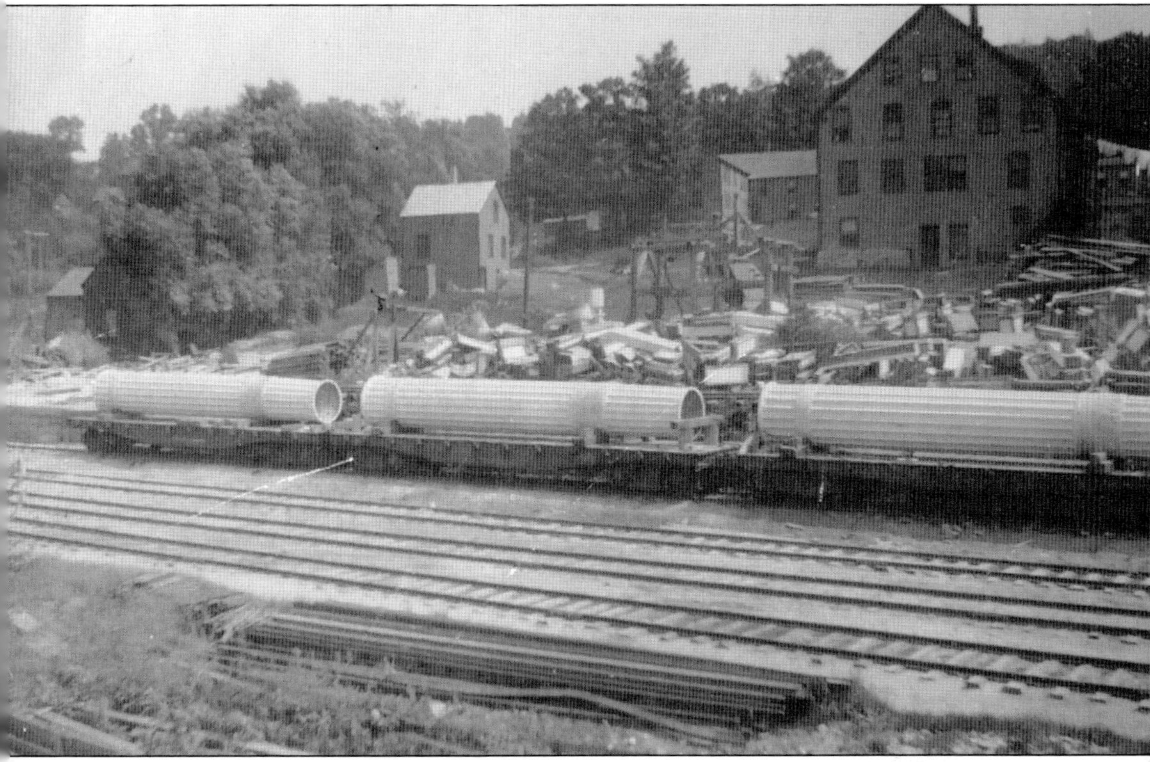

North Jay Boardinghouse. This was a boardinghouse for men who worked in the quarry. Notice the columns of granite on the railroad bed. There were a number of boardinghouses built around this area. People came from around the world to work in North Jay, and many stayed in the old Kyes' Barn, which had been converted to a large boardinghouse for the workers. Company offices were at the rear, and the company store was located in the front. The second floor had a kitchen and dining room. Sleeping quarters were upstairs. As there were no indoor bathrooms, there was a long outhouse behind the building. Dennis McGillicuddy and his family operated the store and shared cooking responsibility with Mrs. Hawkins. They were well known for home-cooked meals from their large cook stoves. Three meals a day were served for 35 to 40 workers. Mrs. Hawkins, with assistance from her helpers, changed the bedding, washing it on scrub boards.

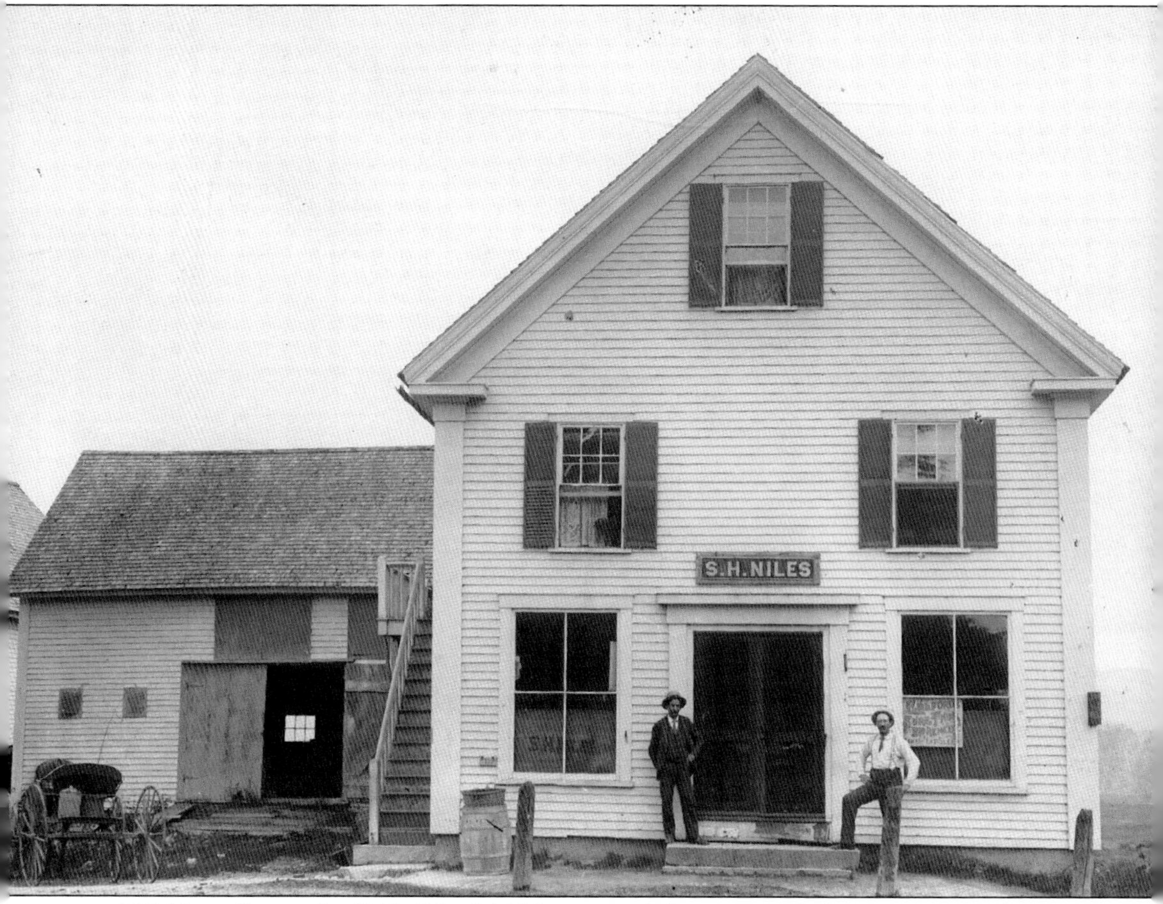

S.H Niles Store. In 1868, Silas H. Niles entered the mercantile business in North Jay as a member of the firm of Leland & Niles. Five years later, he bought his partner's interest in the store. He conducted business here until 1926, when he sold his business to Lee Morse. This was a general store. Typically, general stores had a variety of items, including food and consumables such as coffee beans, spices, flour, baking powder, eggs, sugar, milk, butter, fruits, vegetables, honey, and molasses, as well as dry goods such as bolts of cloth, thread, buttons, undergarments, hats, shoes, and essential items such as guns and ammunition, lanterns, rope, pots and pans, farm and milking equipment, and even coffins. Many also have apothecary sections where one could find medicines, tonics, soaps, toiletries, and elixirs. There is evidence that the first social lending library was founded at this store in 1850. Niles was also president of the Livermore Falls Trust & Banking Company.

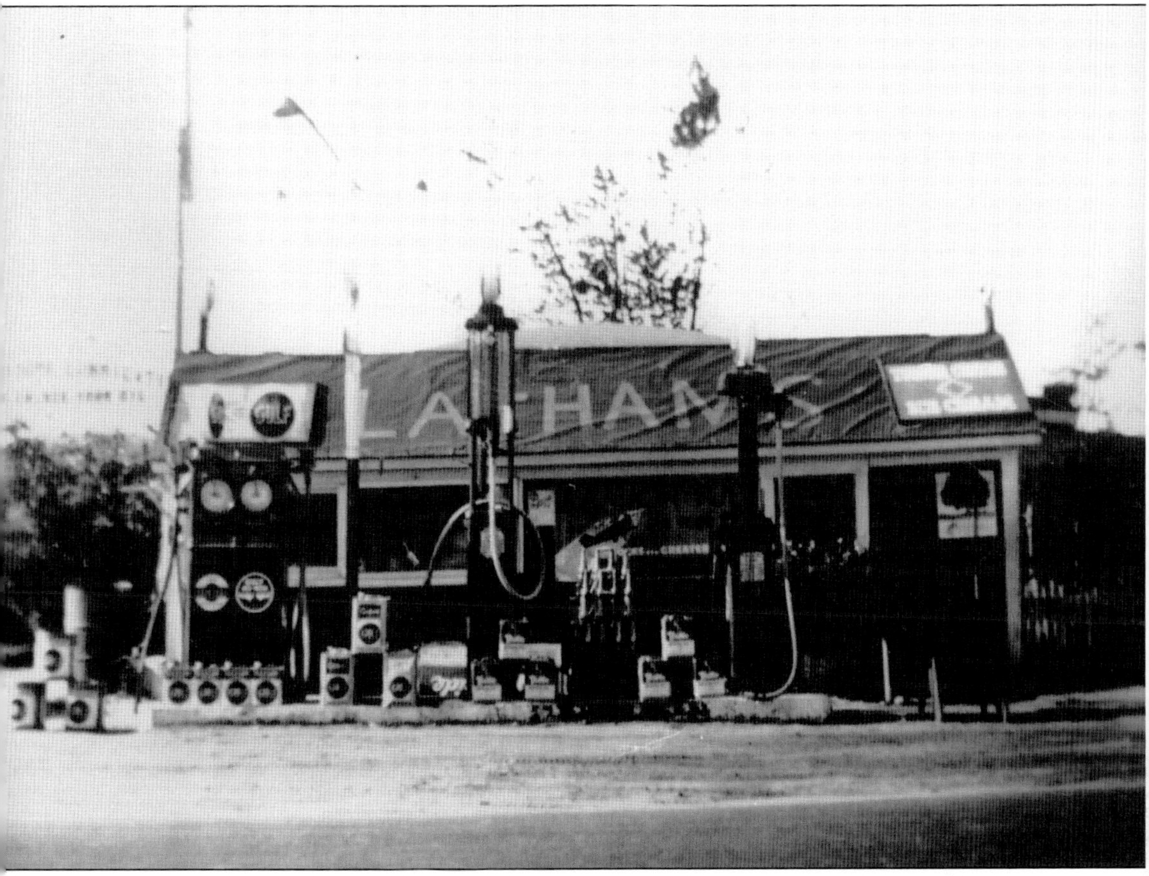

LATHAM'S FILLING STATION, OWNED AND OPERATED BY MAURICE LATHAM, 1928. Latham ran the filling station from 1928 to 1950. New pumps were added in 1930. Gerald Walsh, Latham's son-in-law, ran the filling station from 1950 to 1980. William "Chummy" Walsh ran it from 1980 until it closed.

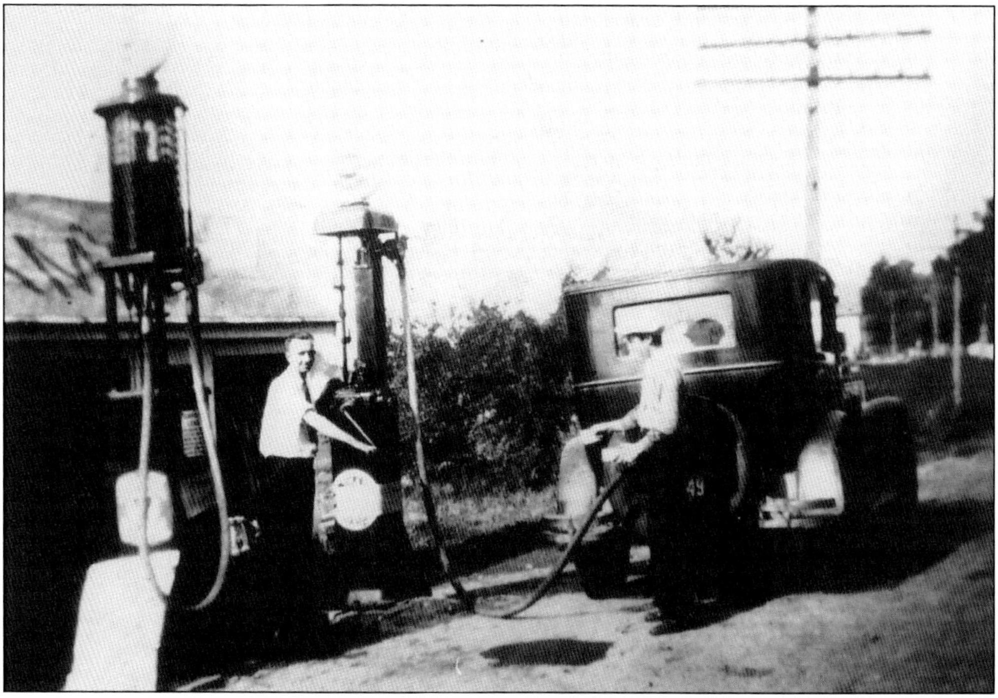

Fill It Up. Maurice Latham, left, and Gerald Walsh fill the gas tank of a 1929 Buick at Latham's in this image. This was more than a simple filling station. Other services were provided, making it more accurately a service station.

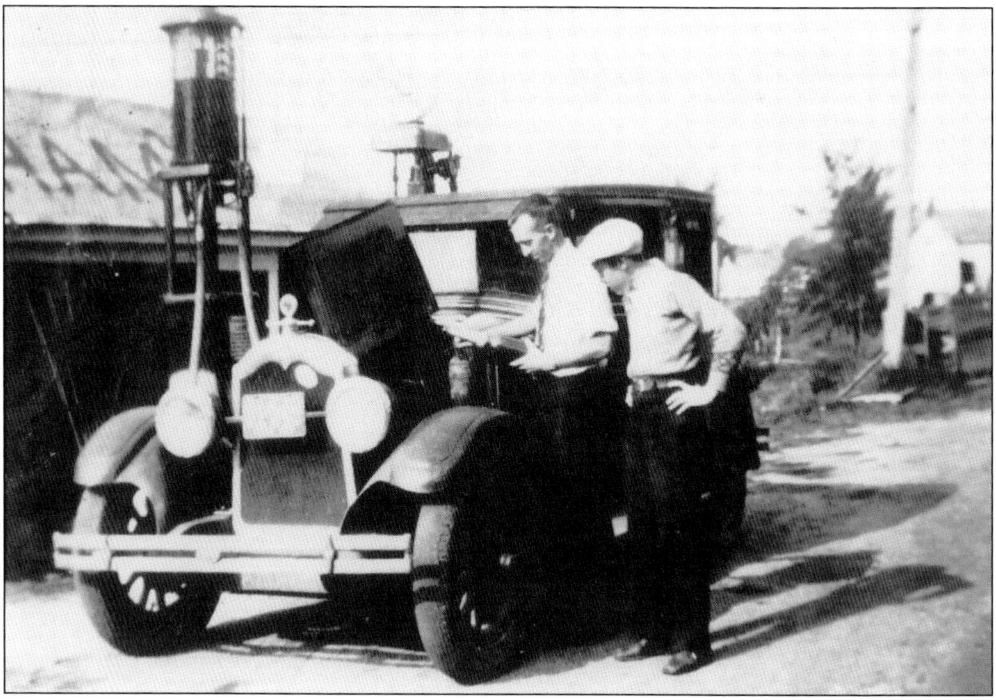

Filling and Service Station. Stations such as this became popular in the 1920s. Maurice Latham and Gerald Walsh are servicing a car in this photograph.

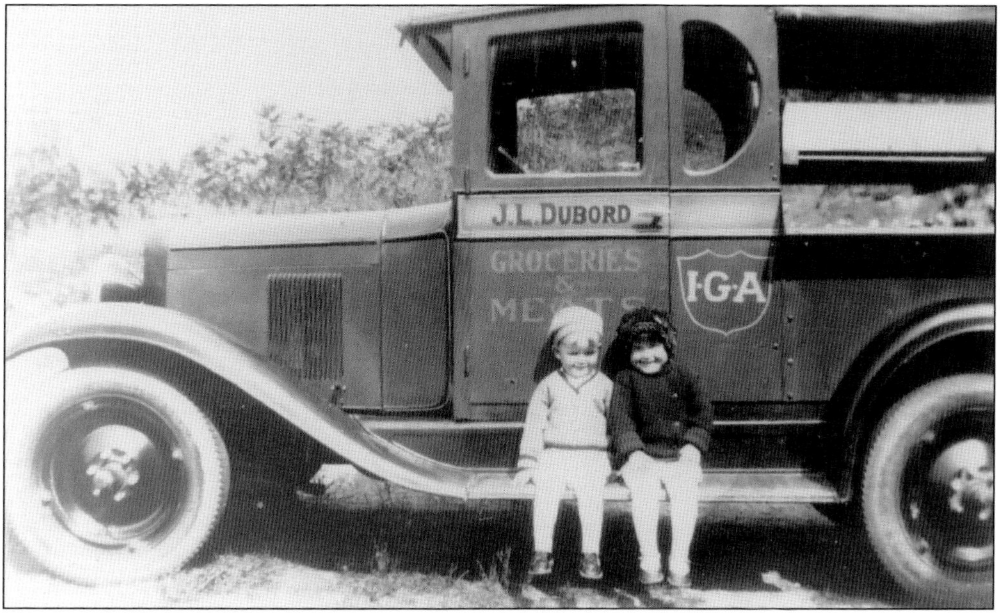

J.L. Dubord Groceries and Meats Vehicle, c. 1930, and Dubord's Market in Chisholm, c. 1940. Norman Dubord and Pauline Dubord Guerin, above, were the son and daughter of Joseph Louis and Melvina Valerie Fournier Dubord, who also had eight other children. They are sitting on a vehicle used by their parents to do business for their store, Dubord's Market, below.

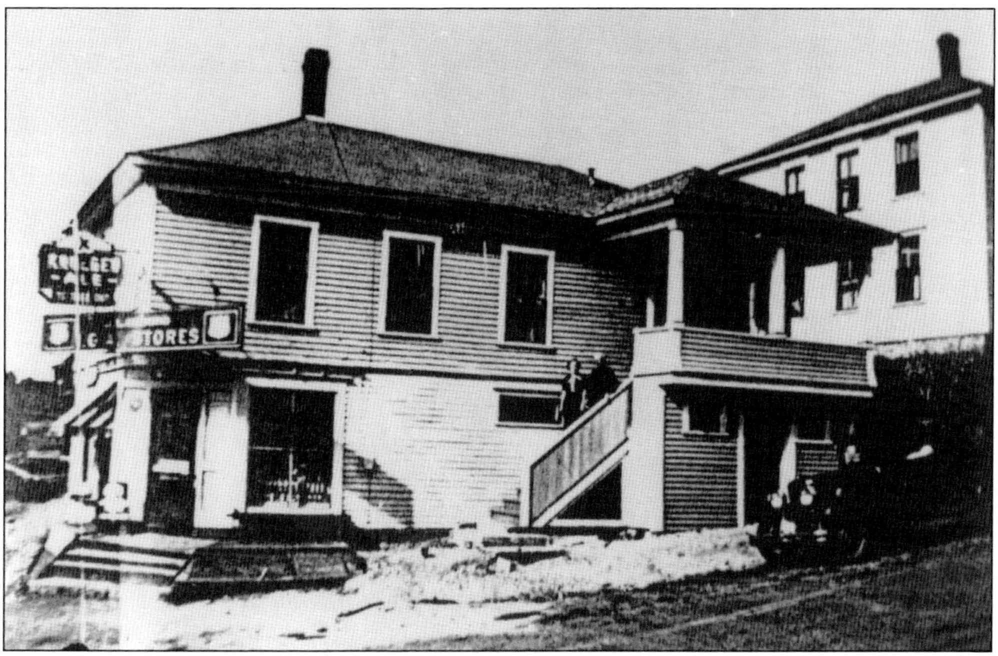

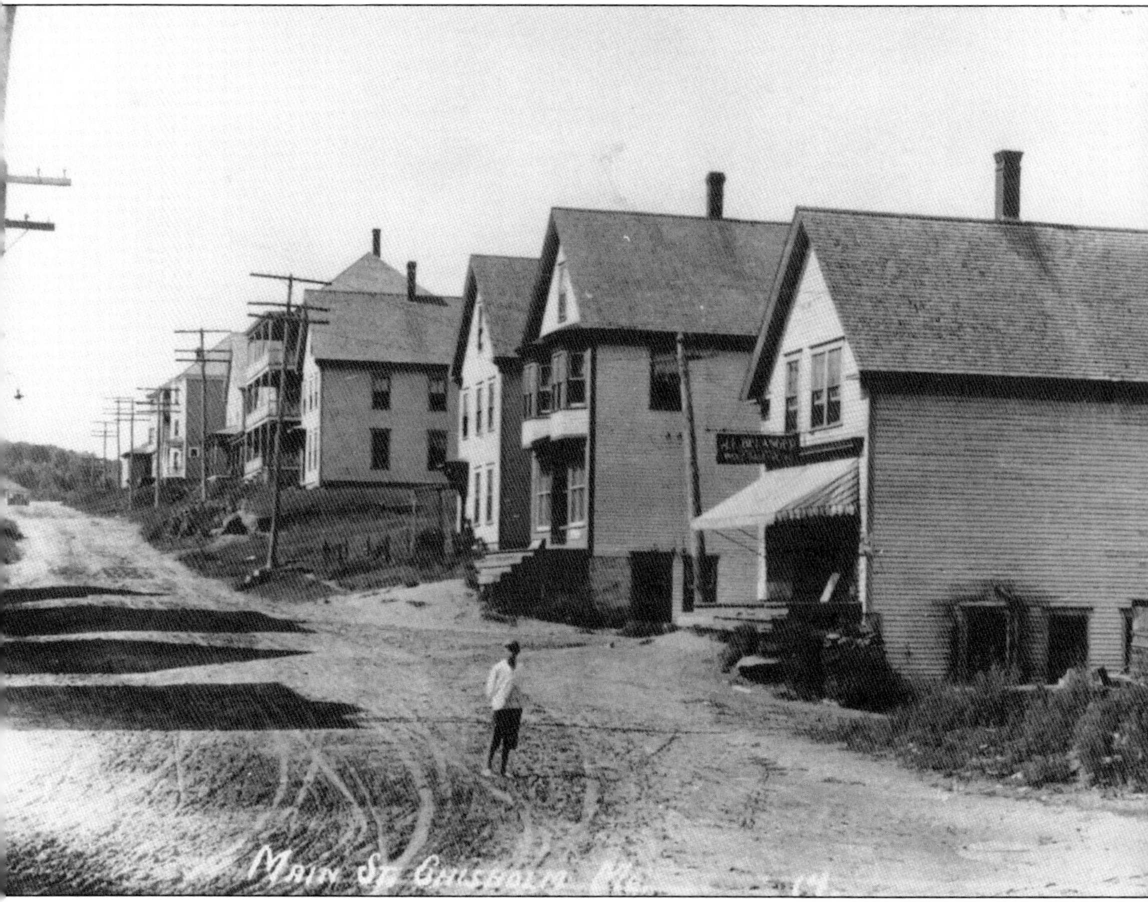

J.E. Belanger Wholesale and Retail. This photograph was taken in 1916 on Main Street in Chisholm, looking south. J.E. Belanger was a baker who also ran a confectionery from this location.

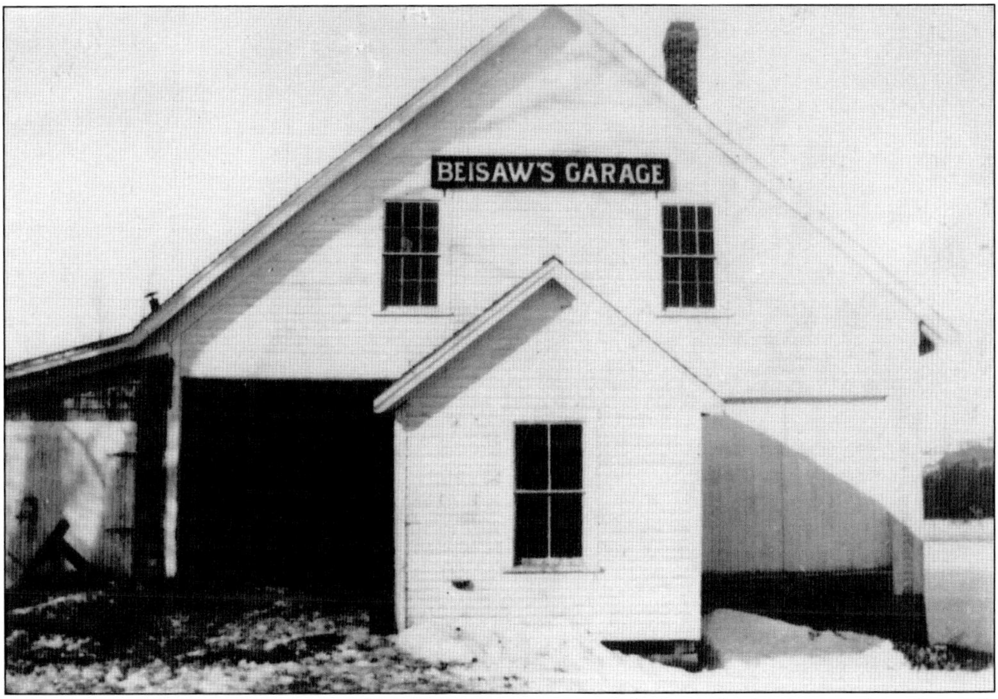

BEISAW'S GARAGE. The building above was a creamery, a blacksmith shop, and then Beisaw's Garage. Owned by Clifford Beisaw, it was located on Route 17 across from the post office and burned in 1925 or 1926. Beisaw established the new Beisaw's Garage at North Jay in 1926 and sold it to his son Harold in 1968. The garage is no longer in operation. In the photograph below is Beisaw's Garage at its second location. Clifford Beisaw is standing in front of the garage.

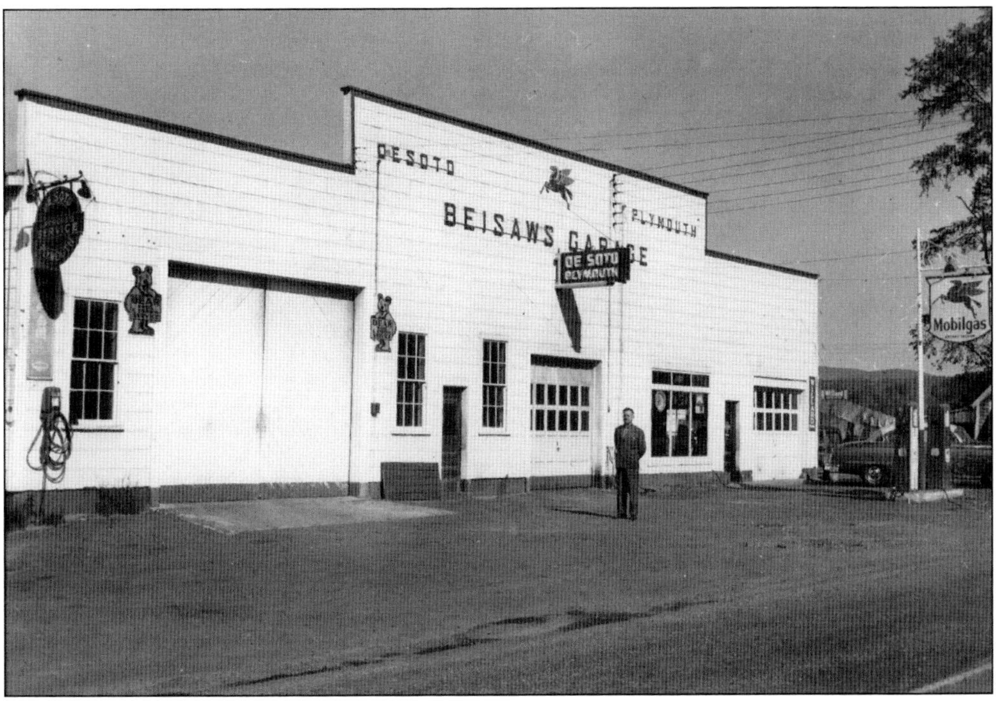

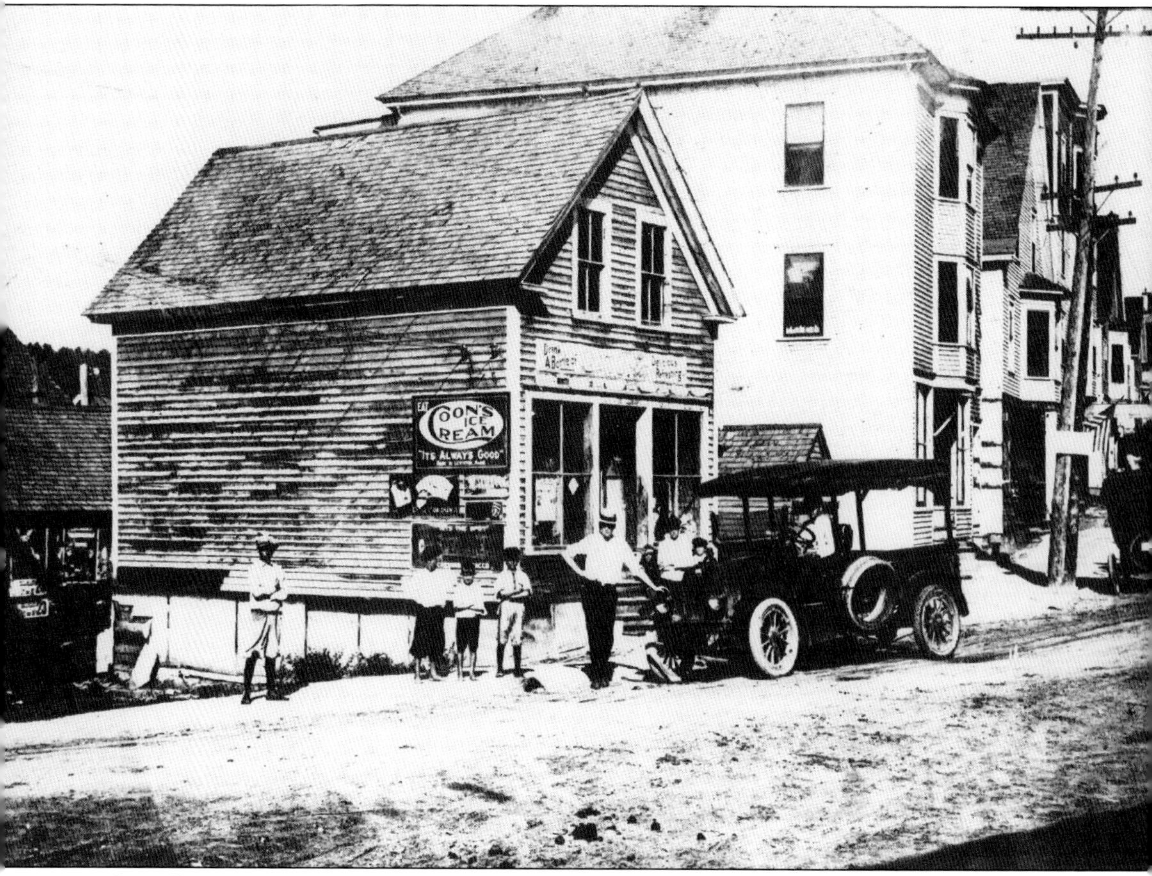

John Pineau's Restaurant. Johnnie Vaillencourt is pictured leaning on an ice truck in front of John Pineau's Restaurant in the 1920s. This is the building where the post office later stood.

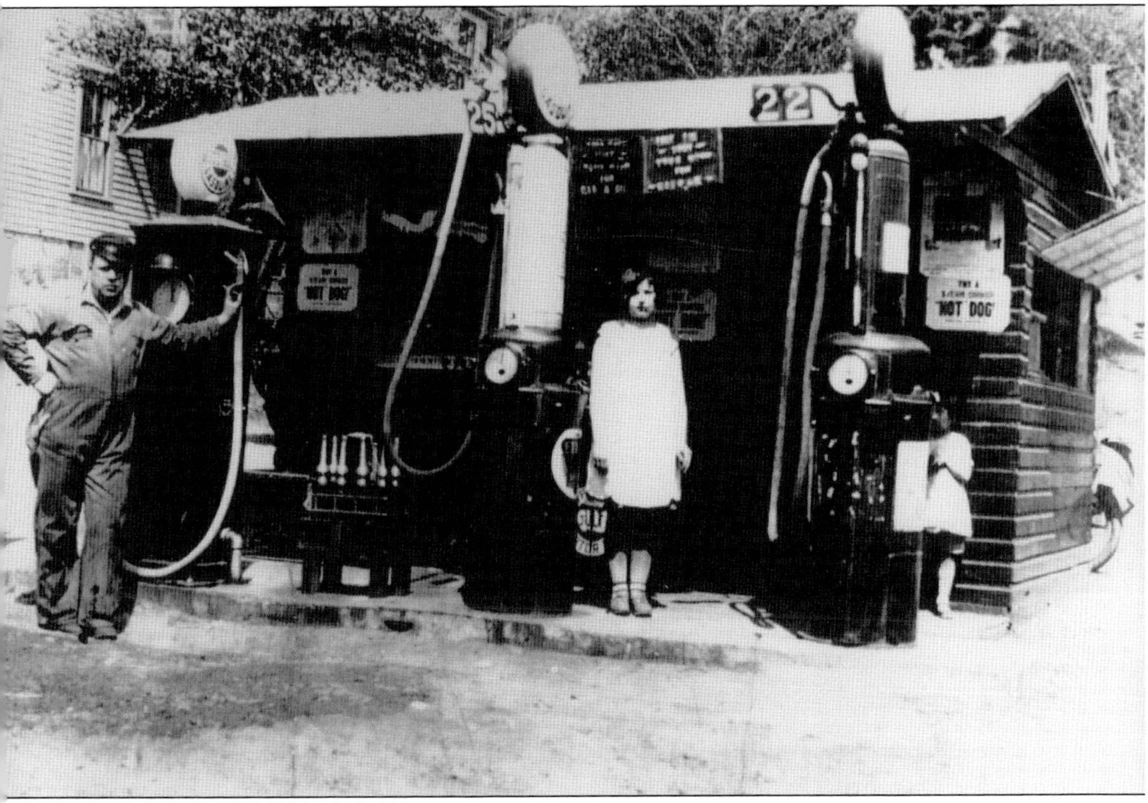

Irving Strout's Filling Station in Chisholm. In this photograph from 1930 are Irving Strout and his clerk Carmen Berube. Filling stations sprung up around the country, even in rural areas, after the sales of automobiles increased.

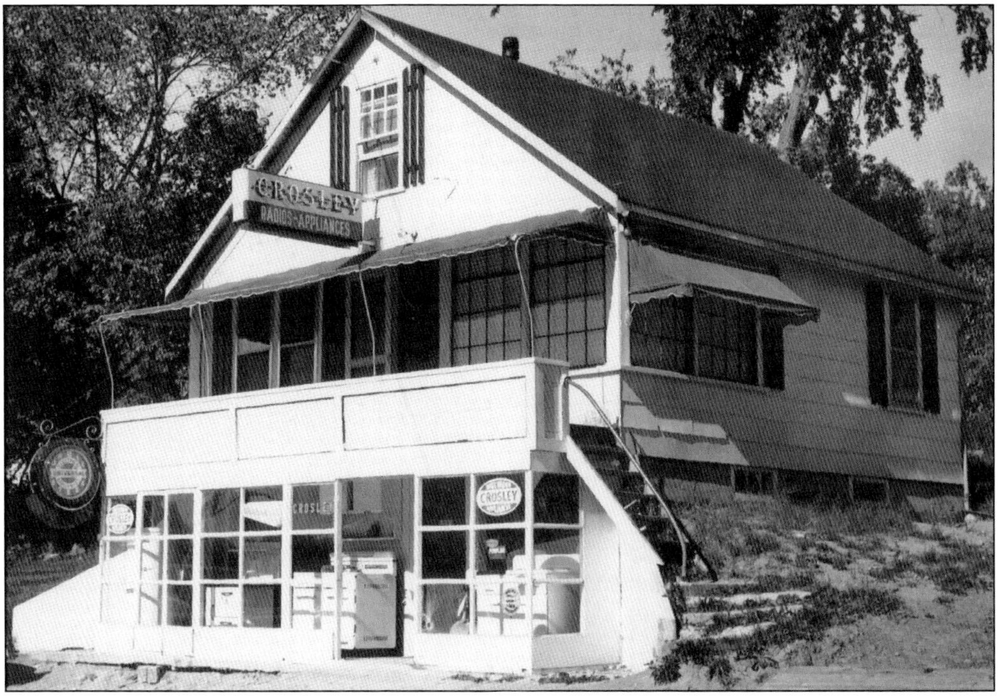

Crosley Radios Appliances. Charles Bodge Jr. was the proprietor of this store starting in 1947. He was a self-employed appliance dealer and master electrician. This photograph was taken in 1953 by Harold Karkos.

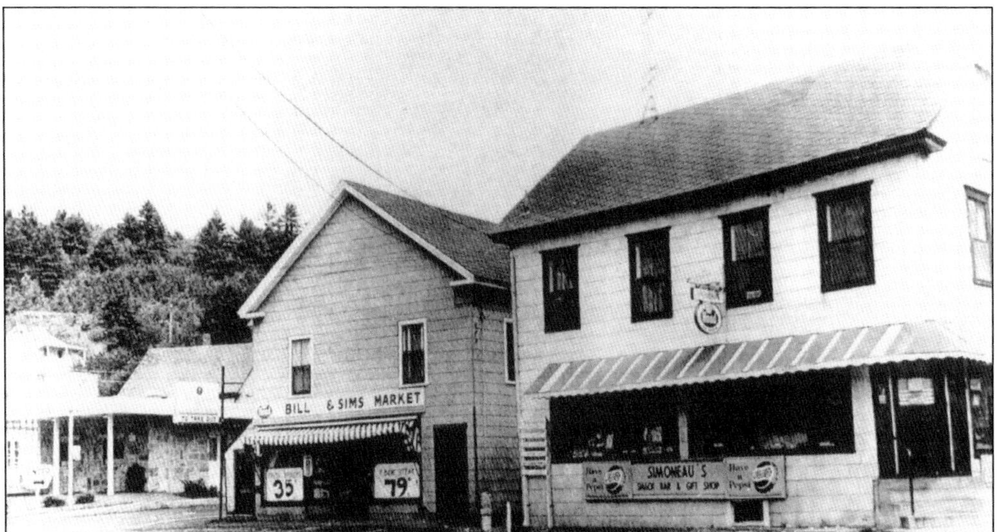

Bill and Sims Market and Simoneau's Snack Bar and Gift Shop, 1960. The Livermore Falls Trust Chisholm office is to the left in this image. The market was a popular place to shop in the 1960s, and the snack bar was well patronized.

Seven

EDUCATION AND LEARNING

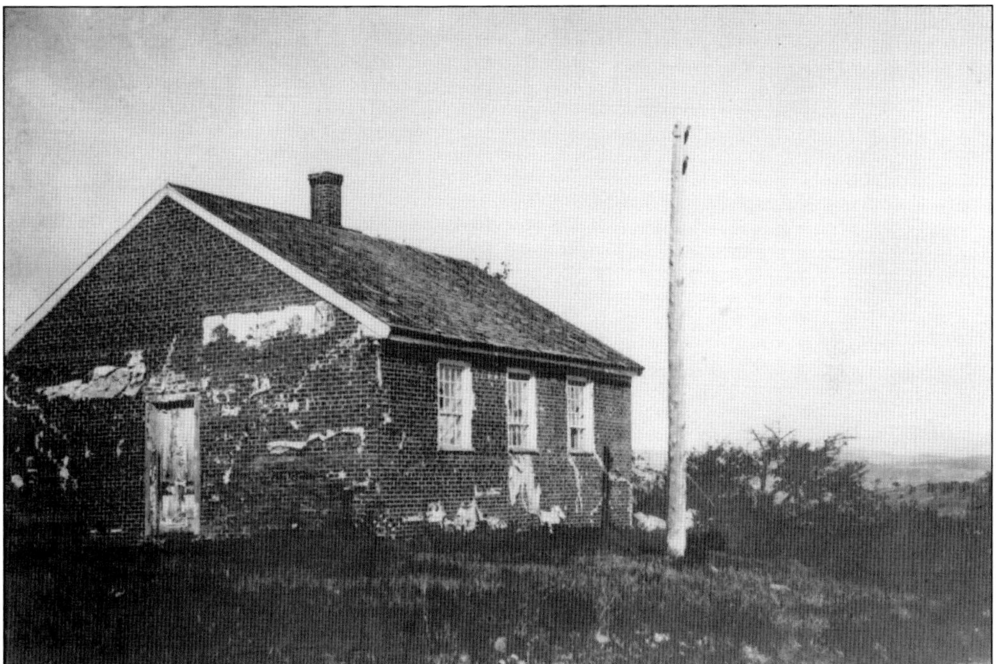

JAY HILL SCHOOLHOUSE, C. 1890. This was possibly the first schoolhouse erected in the town of Jay. It was paid for with money from a town warrant in 1798 and cost $100 to construct. The warrant allowed for four schoolhouses to be built in the town—one on Jay Hill, one in the Canton area, one on Bean's Corner, and one on Stone's Corner.

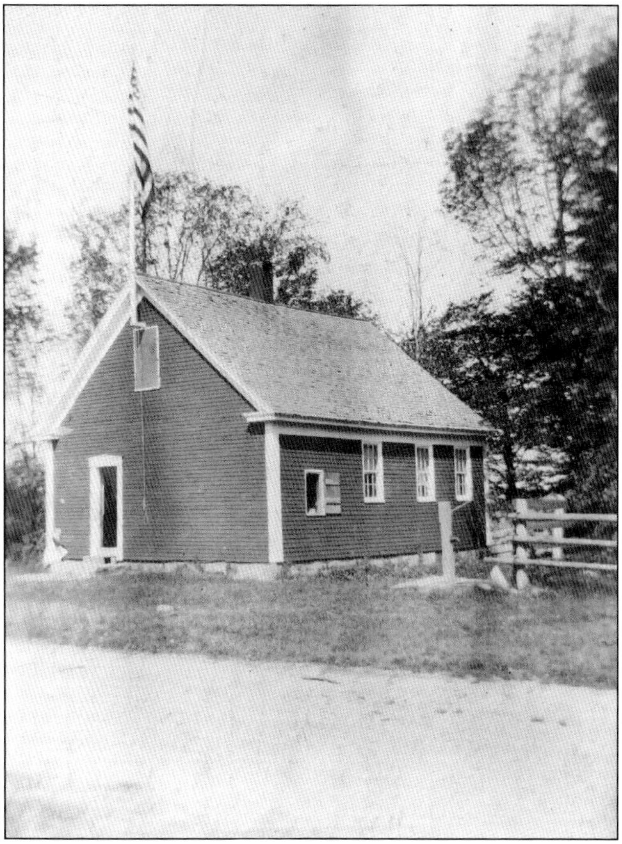

Bean's Corner Schoolhouse, Photographed September 26, 1894. Children of all ages learned in these one-room schoolhouses. This is one of the first four school buildings in Jay. Starting in 1912, the schools were all graded, with different classrooms for various ages and levels. The school superintendent, Rev. S.M. Nieveen, introduced a uniform course of study and textbooks and made the change to graded classrooms.

Stone's Corner School before the Belfry Was Added. Stone's Corner was in the southeastern part of town and was part of District No. 3. At one point, there were 19 districts in Jay, with 22 schools in all.

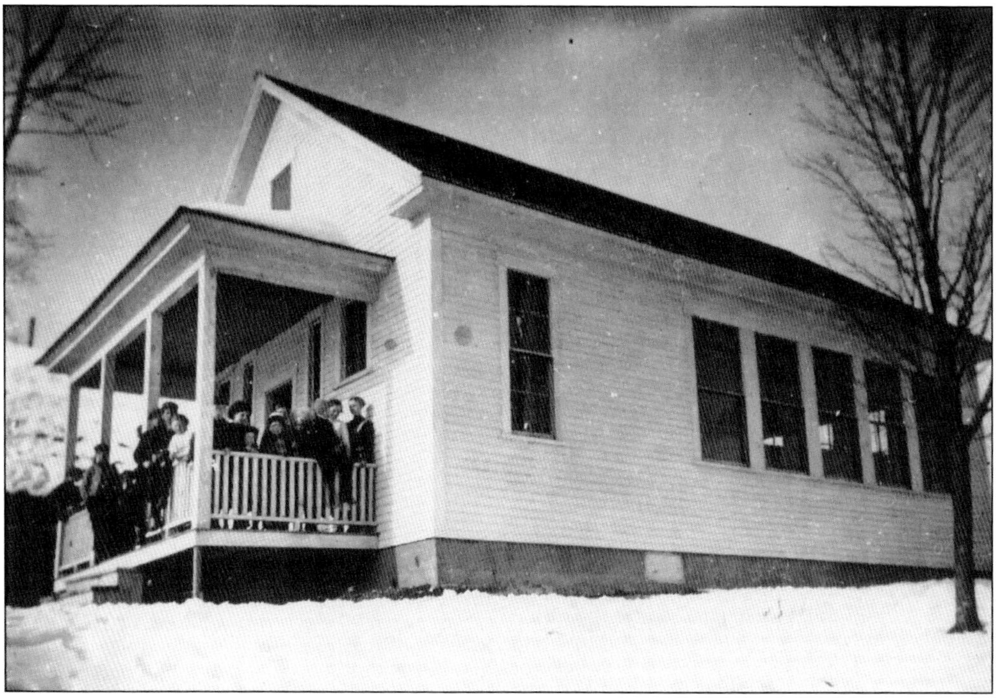

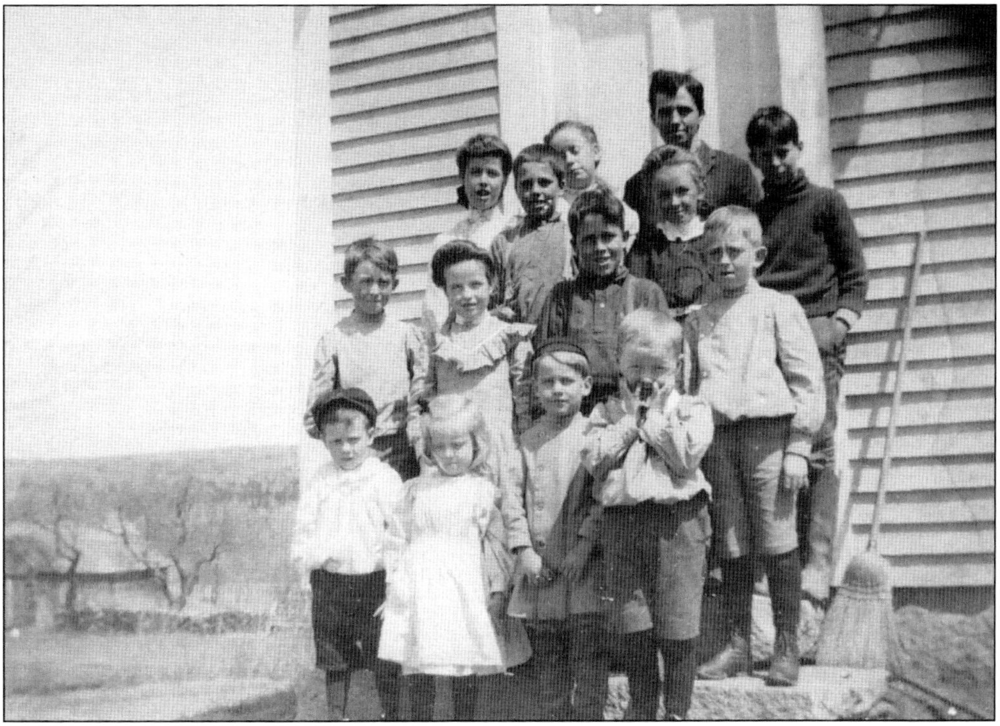

MORSE HILL SCHOOL, ABOUT 1908. In this school photograph are, from left to right, (first row) ? Leighton, Methyl Wilkins, Dunkin Trask, and Cleo Mosher; (second row) Lawrence Mosher, Ethel Leighton, Irving Leighton, and Verne Mosher; (third row) Forest Leighton and Elizabeth Mosher; (fourth row) Tena Simmons, Lelia Wilkins, Ralph Foster, and Harry Trask.

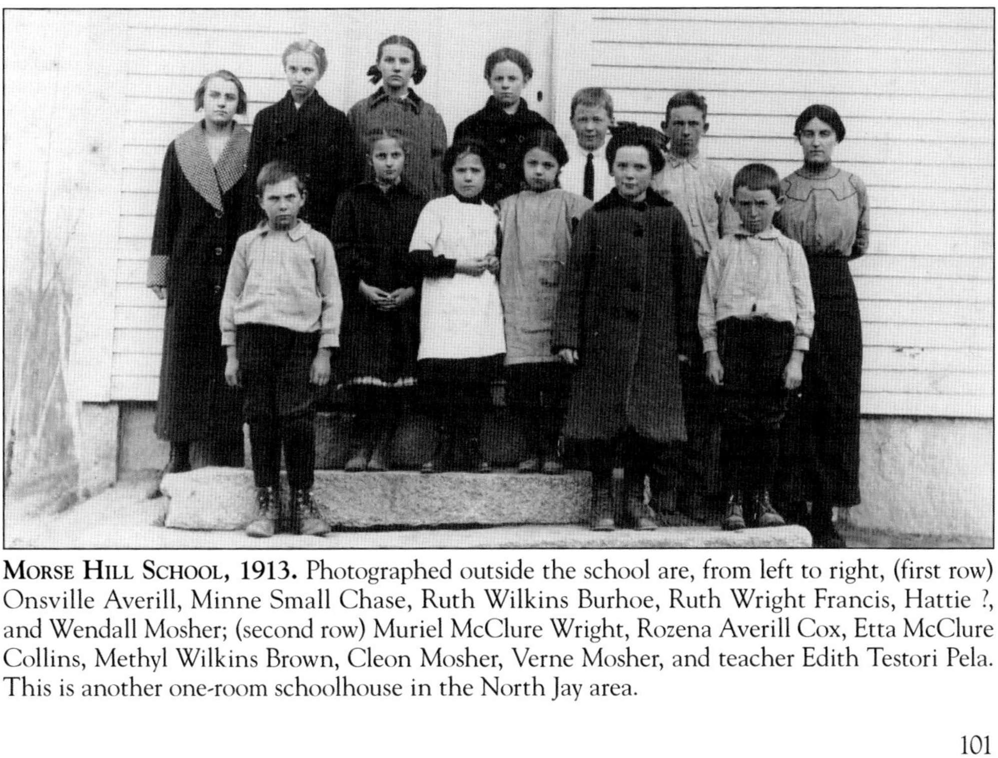

MORSE HILL SCHOOL, 1913. Photographed outside the school are, from left to right, (first row) Onsville Averill, Minne Small Chase, Ruth Wilkins Burhoe, Ruth Wright Francis, Hattie ?, and Wendall Mosher; (second row) Muriel McClure Wright, Rozena Averill Cox, Etta McClure Collins, Methyl Wilkins Brown, Cleon Mosher, Verne Mosher, and teacher Edith Testori Pela. This is another one-room schoolhouse in the North Jay area.

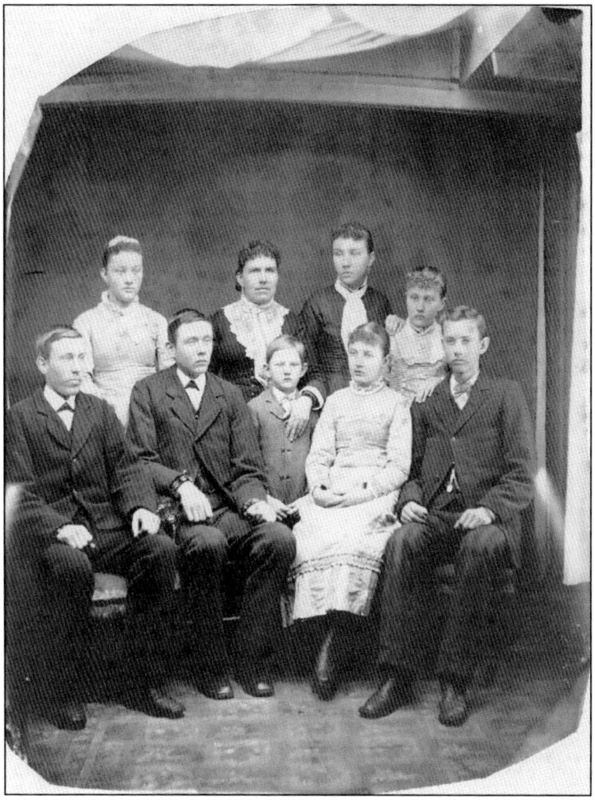

Davenport Hill School. Posing for this school photograph are, from left to right, (first row) Elroy Gray, Horace Gray, Wallace Davenport, Ella Davenport, and Charley Davenport; (second row) Emma Davenport, teacher Mary Allen, Helen Gray, and Ada Gray.

Jay Intervale School. In the foreground is Jay's first school transportation, a horse and cart, on Canton Mountain in the early 1900s. The school is visible in the background.

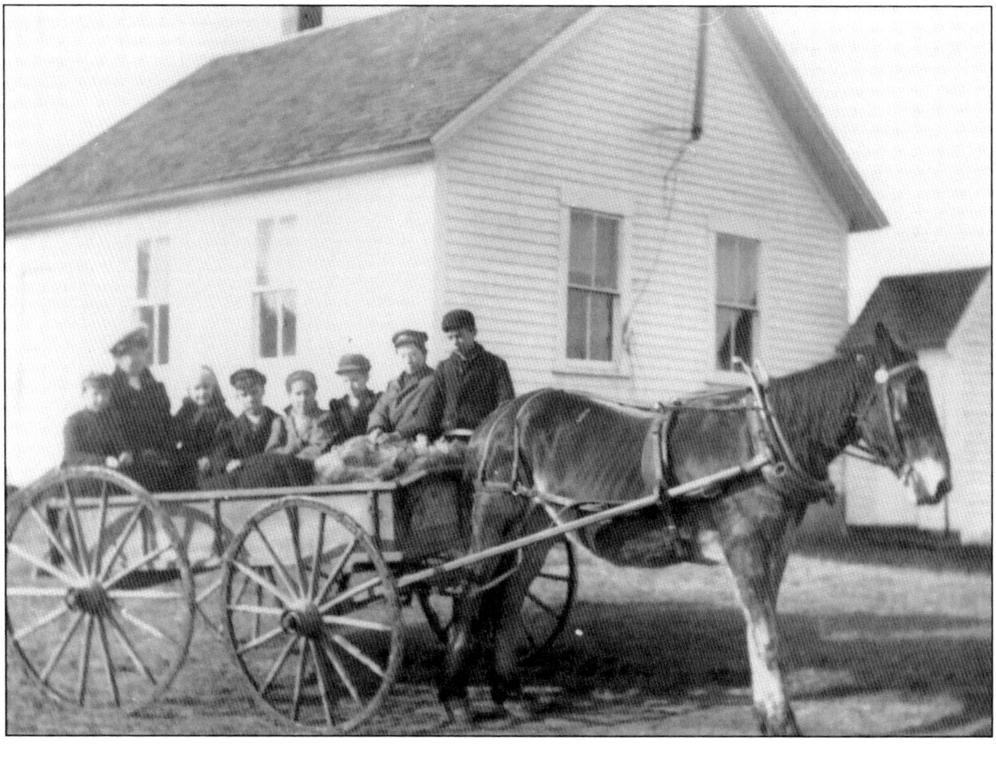

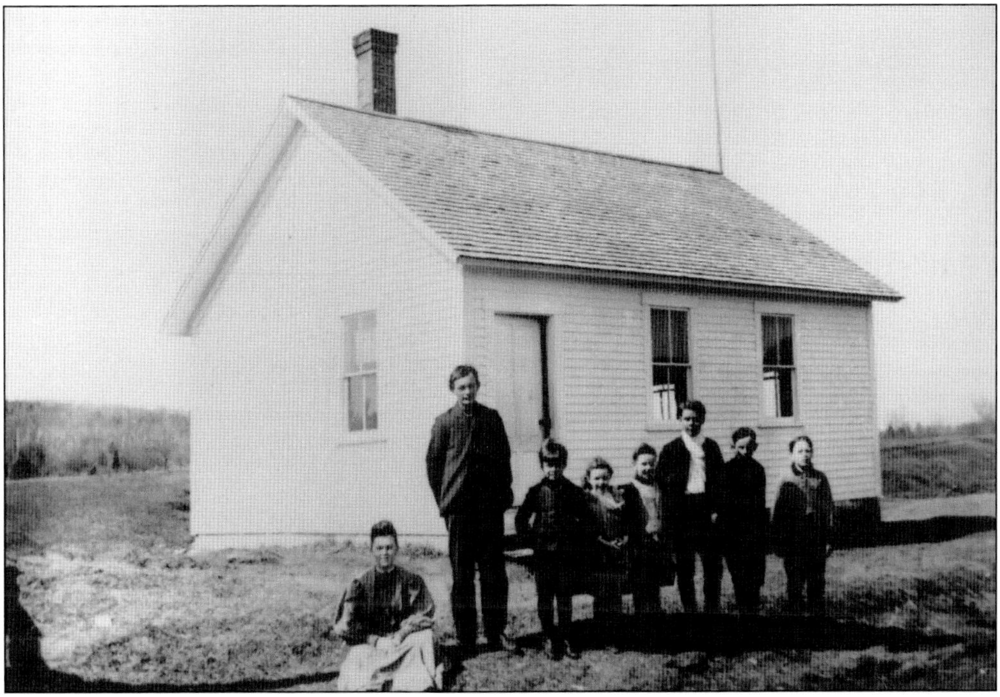

JAY INTERVALE SCHOOL, C. 1906. Many of these early schoolhouses continued to exist until after World War II, at which point most were consolidated.

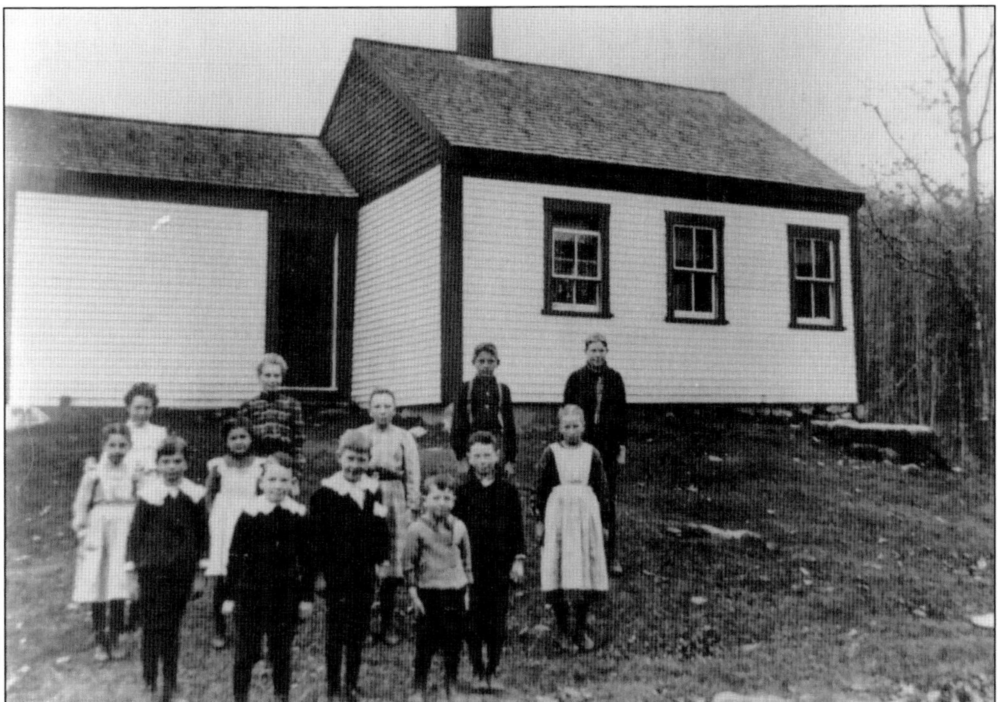

EAST JAY SCHOOL. Photographed in October 1904, this building appears to have been a two-room schoolhouse.

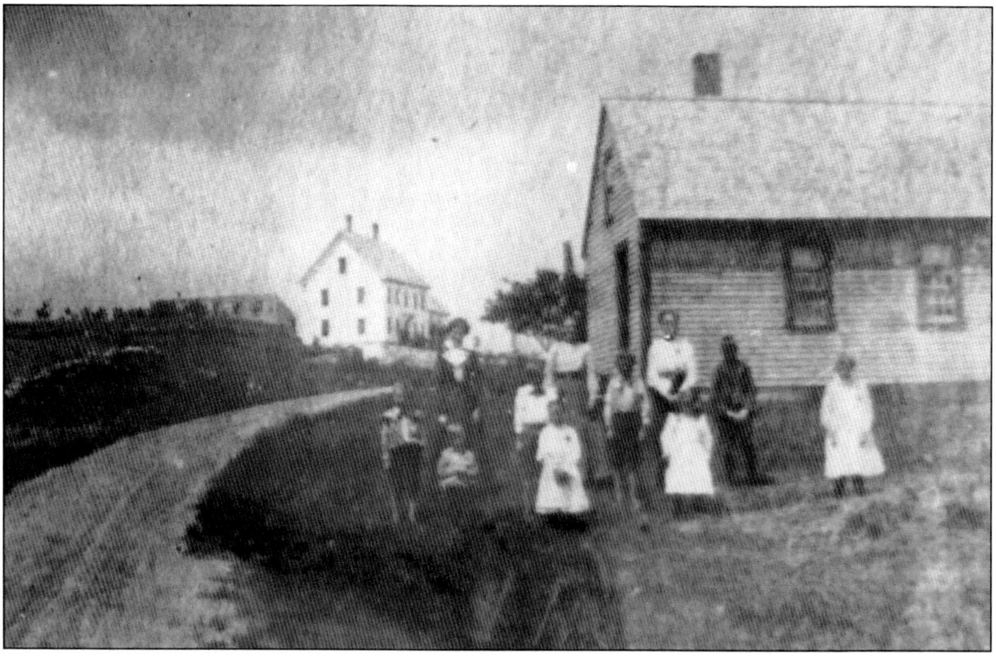

Clay Brook School. This photograph was taken July 12, 1909, at which point the school was run in the summer. Typically, schools ran during winter, spring, and summer months, closing in the fall so that the children could help with the harvest.

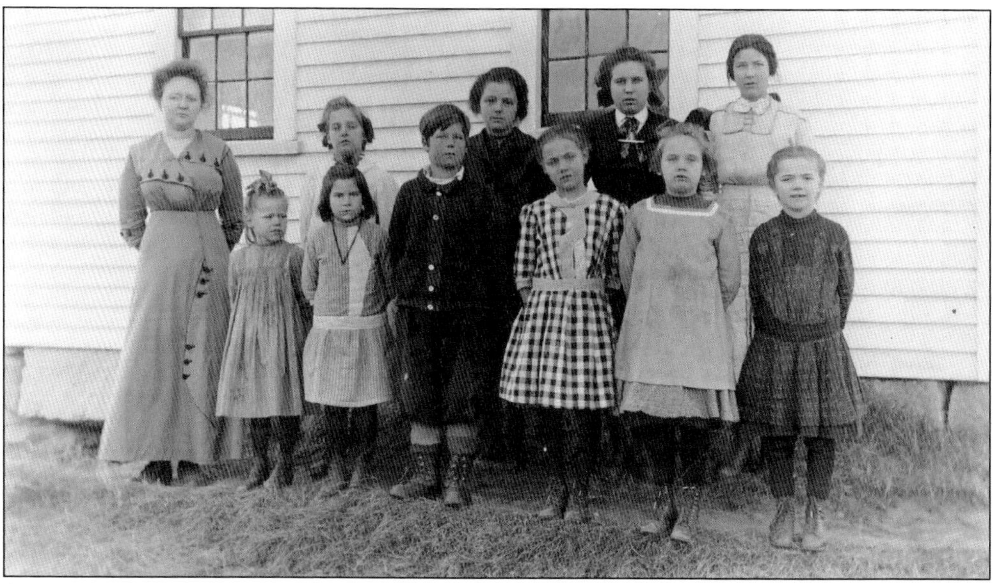

Clay Brook School Class Picture, 1914–1915. Irene Look was the teacher during this school year.

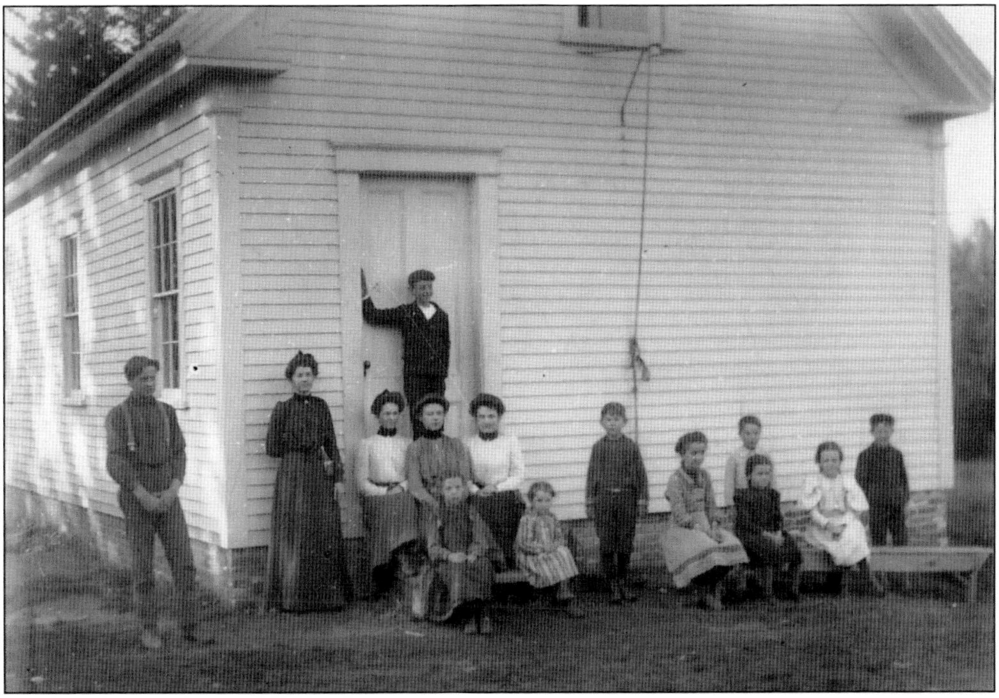

SEVERY HILL SCHOOL. Judging by the caption on the back of the photograph, this was taken during recess. As of 1897, seventeen schools were in existence in the area.

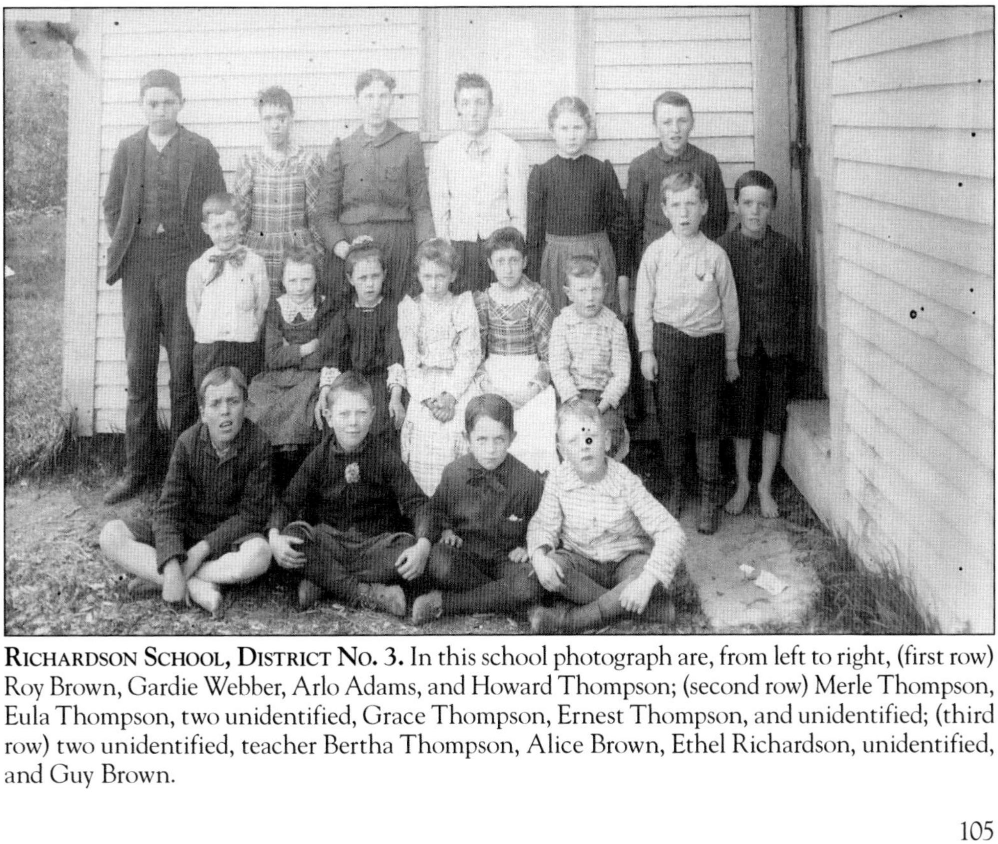

RICHARDSON SCHOOL, DISTRICT NO. 3. In this school photograph are, from left to right, (first row) Roy Brown, Gardie Webber, Arlo Adams, and Howard Thompson; (second row) Merle Thompson, Eula Thompson, two unidentified, Grace Thompson, Ernest Thompson, and unidentified; (third row) two unidentified, teacher Bertha Thompson, Alice Brown, Ethel Richardson, unidentified, and Guy Brown.

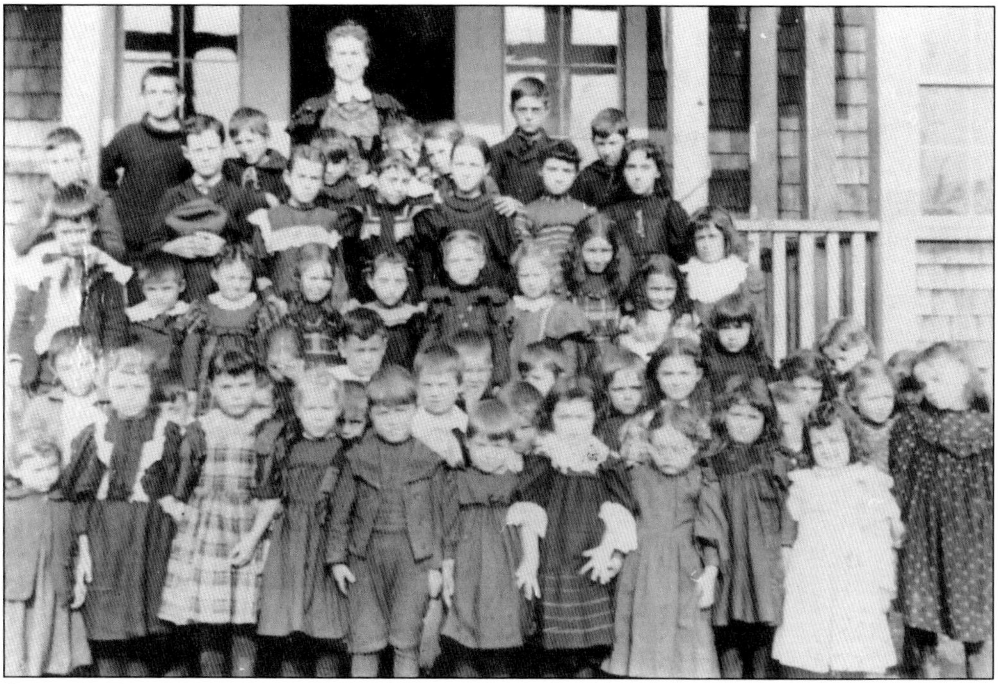

CHISHOLM SCHOOL, C. 1898. A school had to be built to educate the children of the mill workers, which explains the number of students in this image. Gertrude Chase is the teacher.

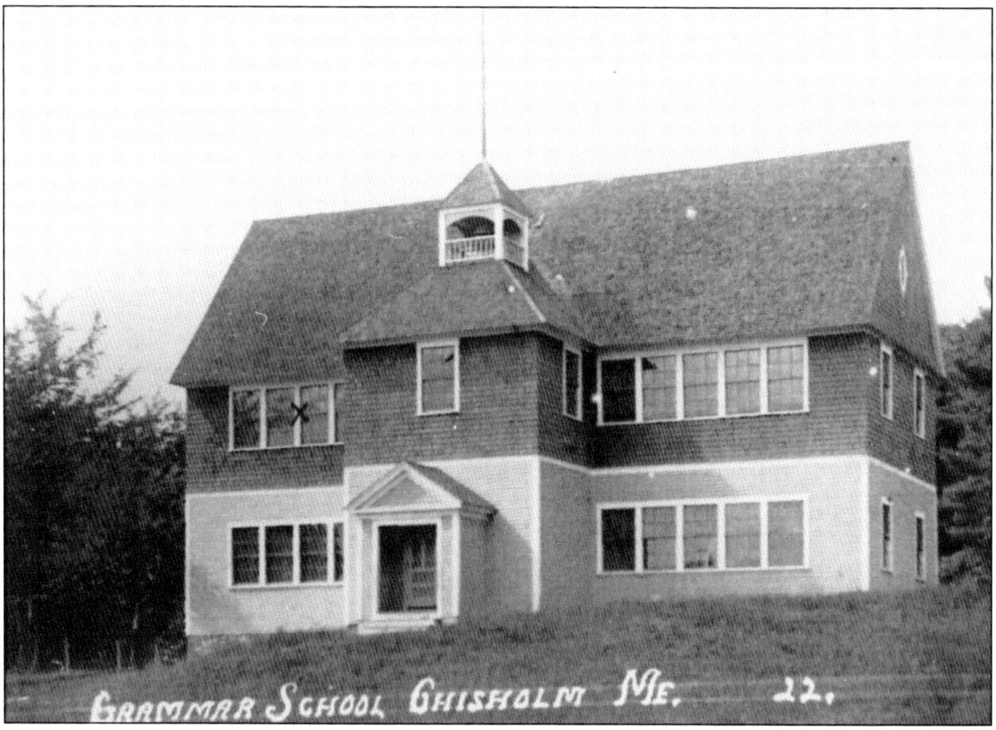

JEWELL STREET GRAMMAR SCHOOL. This school later became Jay High School. This was one of the first graded schools in town.

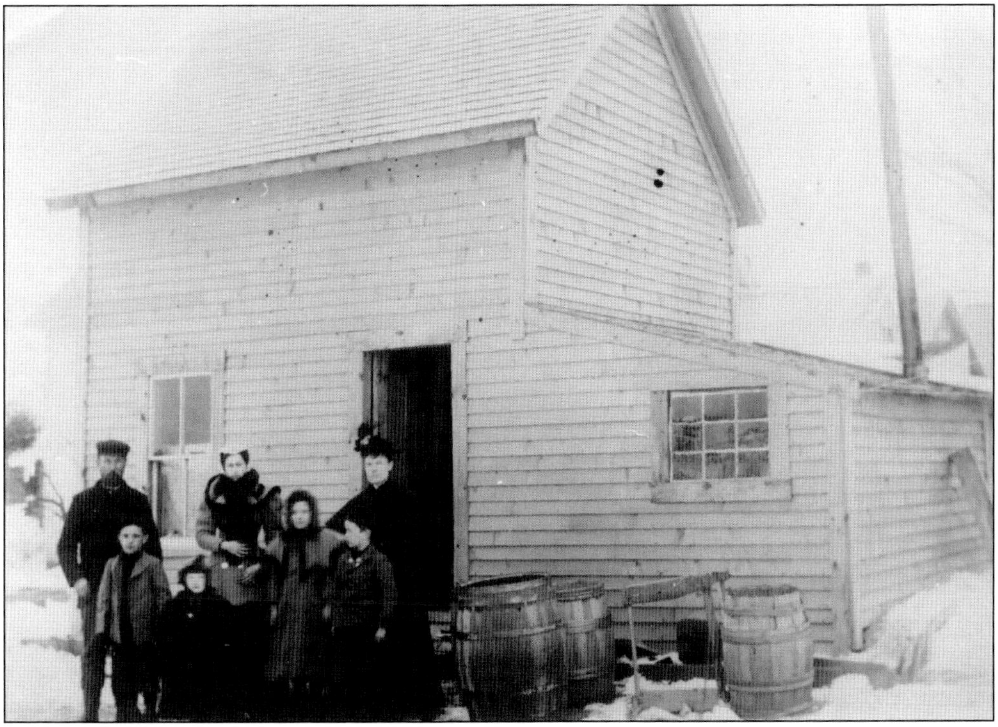

Riley School. The first school in Riley was actually on the second floor of David Alexander's Store. The picture above is of the first school building in Riley. Maude Bean Hobbs was the teacher in 1896. Grades one through eight were taught here. The Works Progress Administration (WPA) built a baseball field for the school in the 1930s. Below is a photograph showing the building after the 1910 addition.

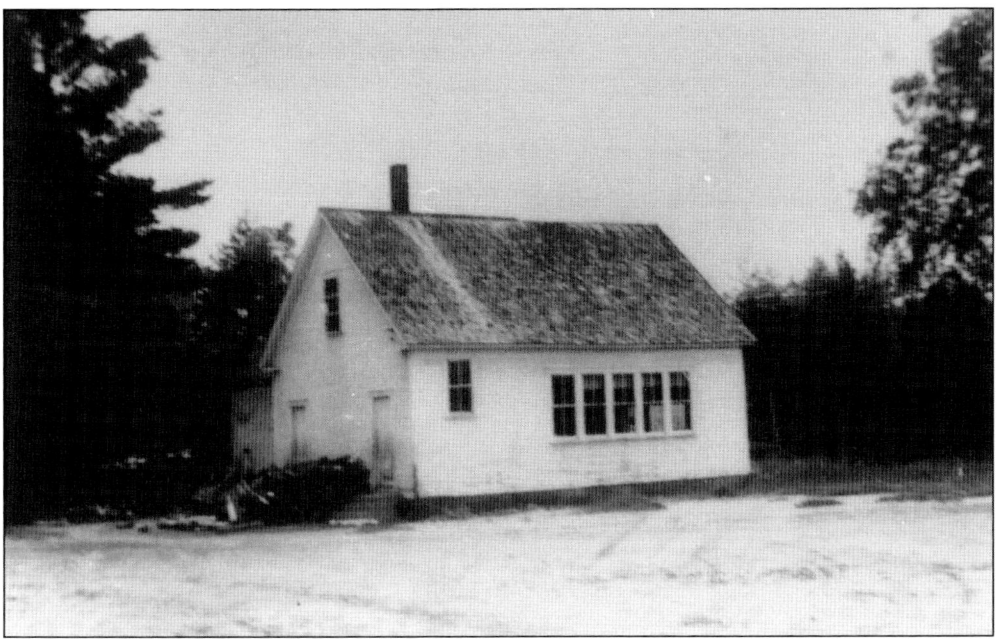

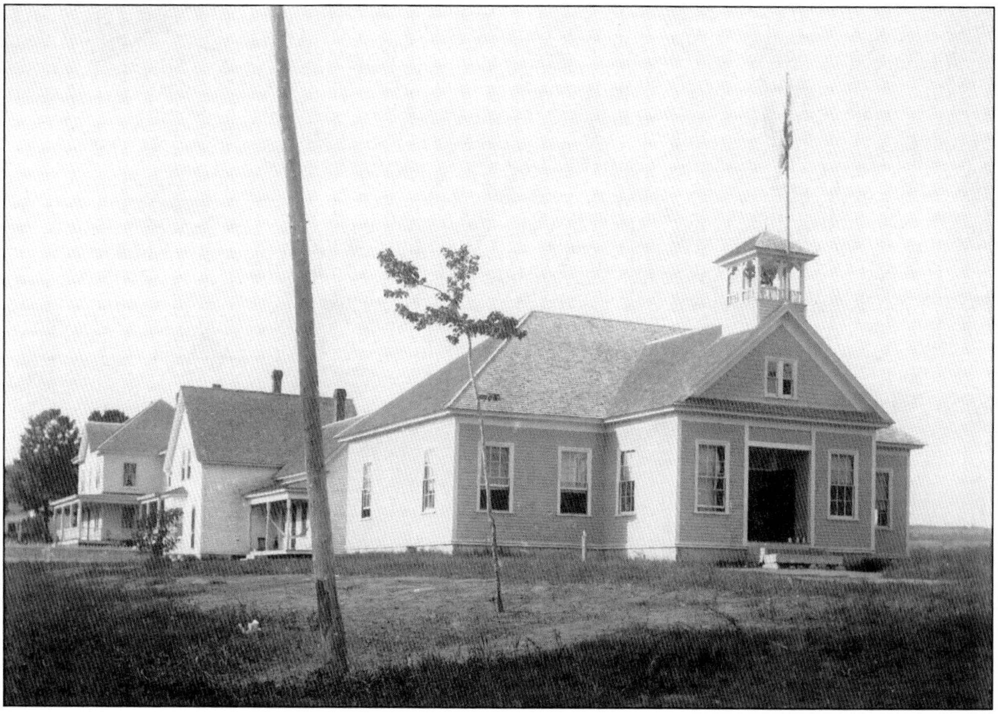

EMERSON SCHOOLHOUSE. The Emerson School in North Jay was built around 1915 and later became the parish house for the Bartlett Methodist Church. This was one of the first multiple-room, graded schoolhouses. Below is one of the classrooms in the Emerson School. Dorothy Keep (standing) was the teacher at this time, and some of the students shown are Recherio Vangelli, Beatric Clement, Lempi Lilja, Toga Carlson, Margarita Palmiotti, Alice Wilkins, Daniel Wilkins, Alice Miller, Wilfred Holt, Herbert Sprague, Impi Salmela, Ollie Wilson, Kenneth Holt, Edith Clark, Margaret McKay, Barbara Farnham, Ruth Sprague, Philip Welch, Claude Palmiotti, Angelina Palmiotti, and Emelio Vangelli.

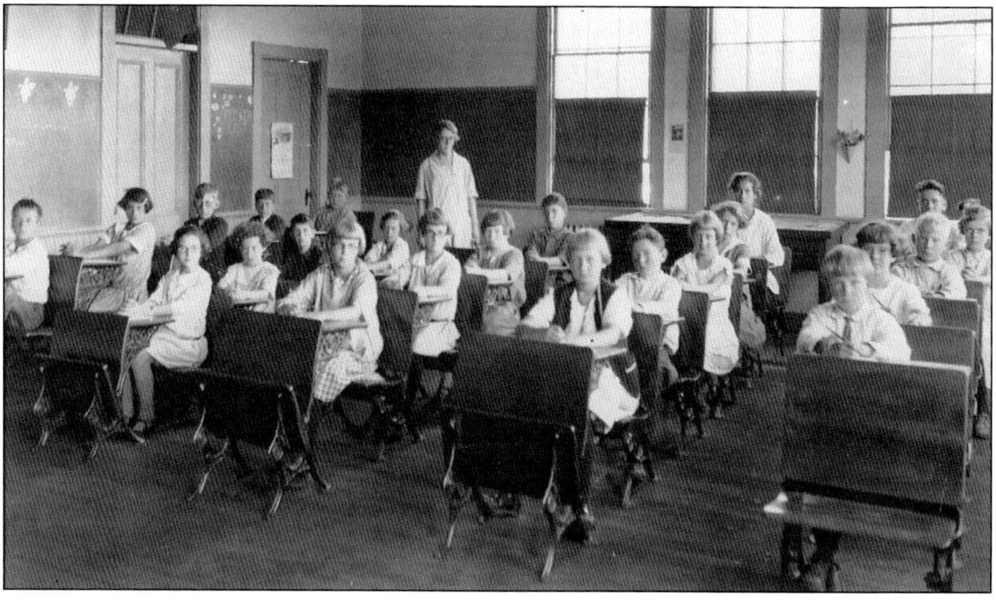

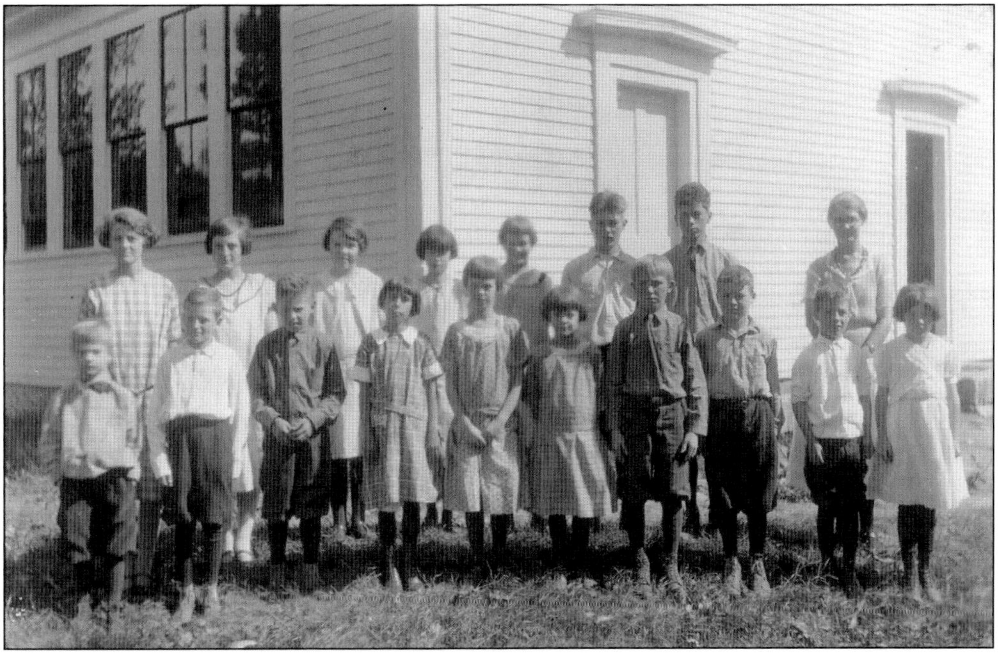

Lake School, 1924. In this school photograph are, from left to right, (first row) Elliot Clark, Allen McCourt, Ralph Noyes, Geneva Hill, Winona Kathyrn Clark, Allie Jones, Cecil McCourt, Walter McCourt, unidentified, and Catherine McCourt; (second row) Alice Purington, Tola Whitman, Margaret Patterson, Margaret Charles, Ruth Purington, Clinton Noyes, Herman Charles, and teacher Dorothy Millett.

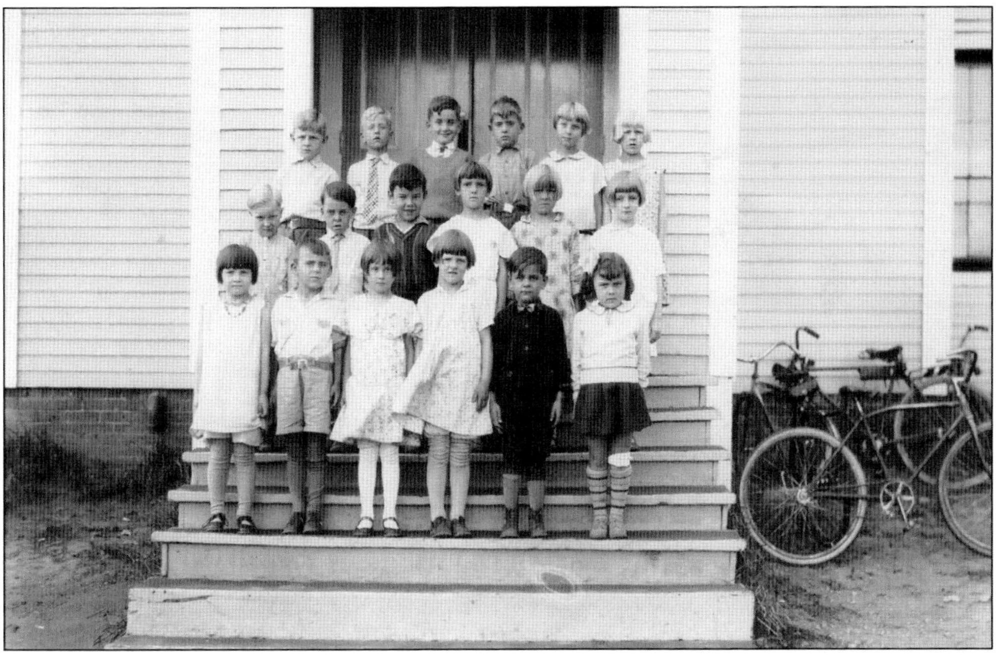

Jay Village School, 1930–1931. This school had four rooms. In the downstairs area, the primary school was held in one room and the grammar school in the other. The high school was in the upstairs rooms.

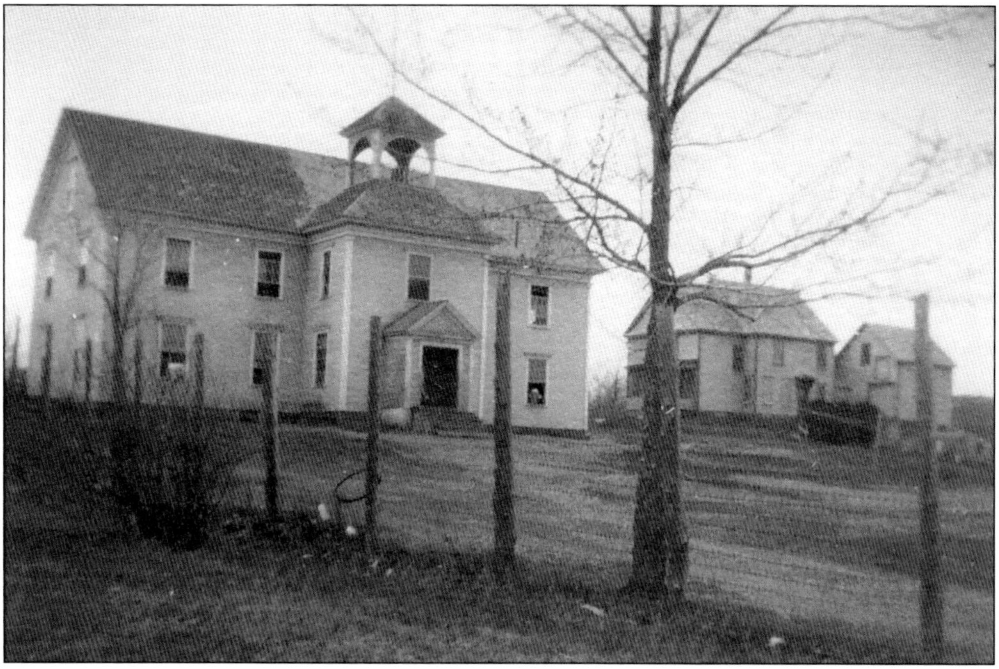

JAY HIGH SCHOOL. This school was located in the Jay Bridge area and was at one time the grammar school. A new high school was built in 1929.

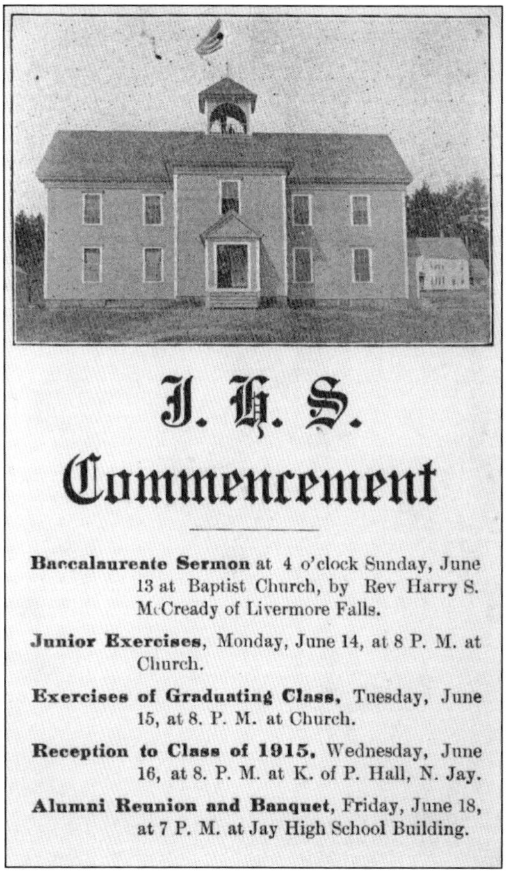

J. H. S.

Commencement

Baccalaureate Sermon at 4 o'clock Sunday, June 13 at Baptist Church, by Rev Harry S. McCready of Livermore Falls.

Junior Exercises, Monday, June 14, at 8 P. M. at Church.

Exercises of Graduating Class, Tuesday, June 15, at 8. P. M. at Church.

Reception to Class of 1915, Wednesday, June 16, at 8. P. M. at K. of P. Hall, N. Jay.

Alumni Reunion and Banquet, Friday, June 18, at 7 P. M. at Jay High School Building.

JAY HIGH SCHOOL COMMENCEMENT ANNOUNCEMENT. This card was postmarked on June 11, 1915, and tells of the impending graduation exercises.

Eight

People, Places, Events, and Leisure

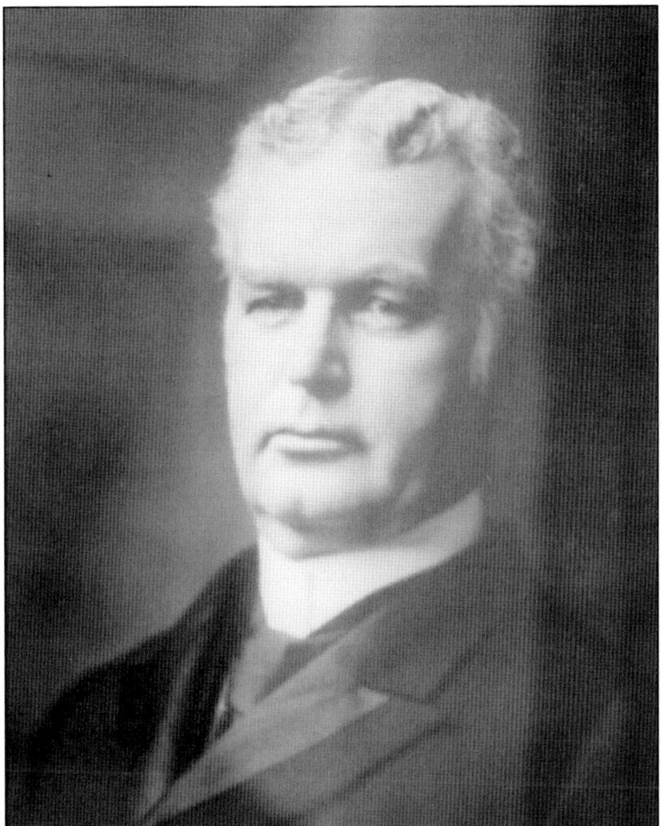

Hugh Chisholm. Hugh Chisholm came to Maine from Ontario, Canada, and was the founder of the Rumford Paper Mill. He built a small groundwood mill at the Otis Falls in the early 1880s. He also constructed the mill in Riley and acquired the Umbagog Mill. In 1898, he convinced 20 independent mills in five states to become part of the International Paper Company.

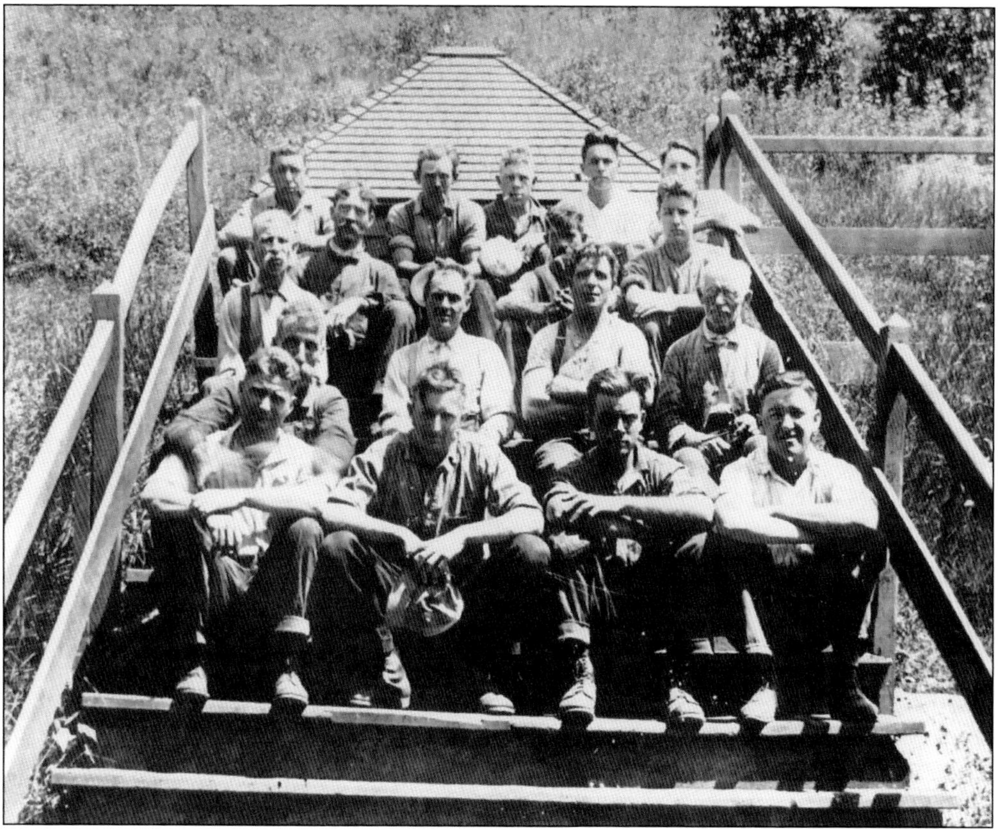

Riley Mill Workers, 1919. In this photograph taken on the steps at Riley Mill are, from left to right, (first row) Earnest Strout, John Hickey, Earl Howes, and Arthur Poland; (second row) Pat Knowles, ? Morrell, Ed Ross, and Ed Bartlett; (third row) ? Vallaire, John Bowie, ? Greenward, and Victor Knowles; (fourth row) Bob White, Frank Mason, Chauncey Thompson, Dick White, and Roy Harlow.

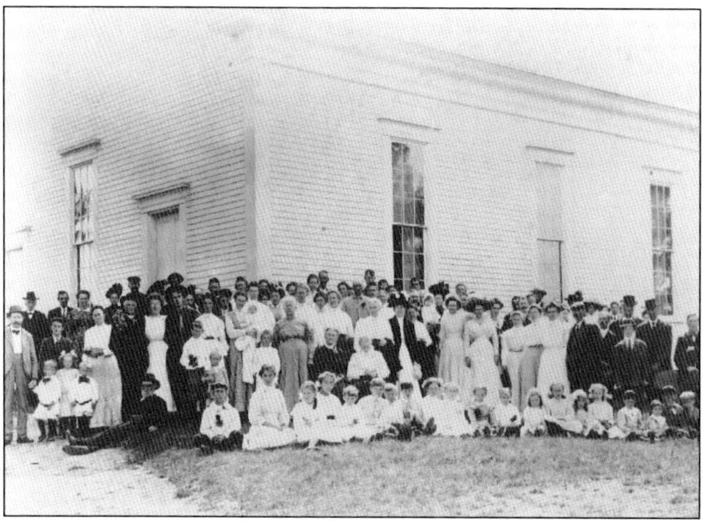

Bean Reunion. The Beans were Quakers. One Bean and his several sons, their wives, children, cattle, horses, and all their worldly goods moved from Readfield to the northeast part of Jay and founded Bean's Corner. Within a short period, this family increased exponentially, explaining why there is such a large gathering on this day at the Jay Hill Baptist Church.

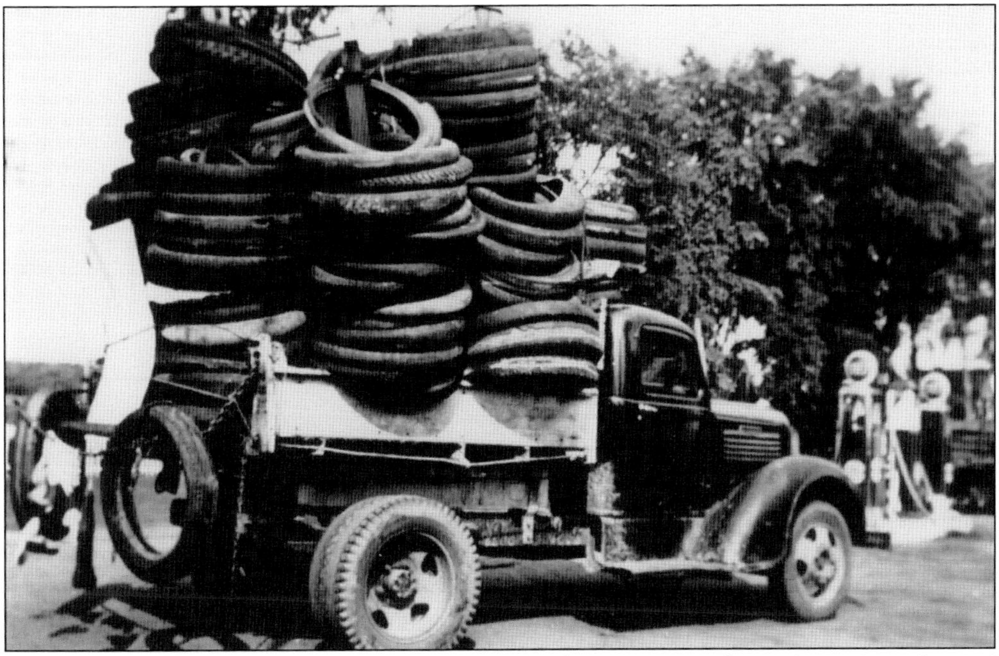

RATIONING RUBBER. These used tires, photographed sometime in the early 1940s in front of Latham's Filling Station, were to be put to use in the World War II salvage effort. The Japanese had seized plantations in the Dutch East Indies, which produced 90 percent of America's raw rubber. President Roosevelt called on citizens to help by contributing scrap rubber to be recycled. Much of this rubber was needed to make weapons, and towns would have rubber drives, such as the one pictured.

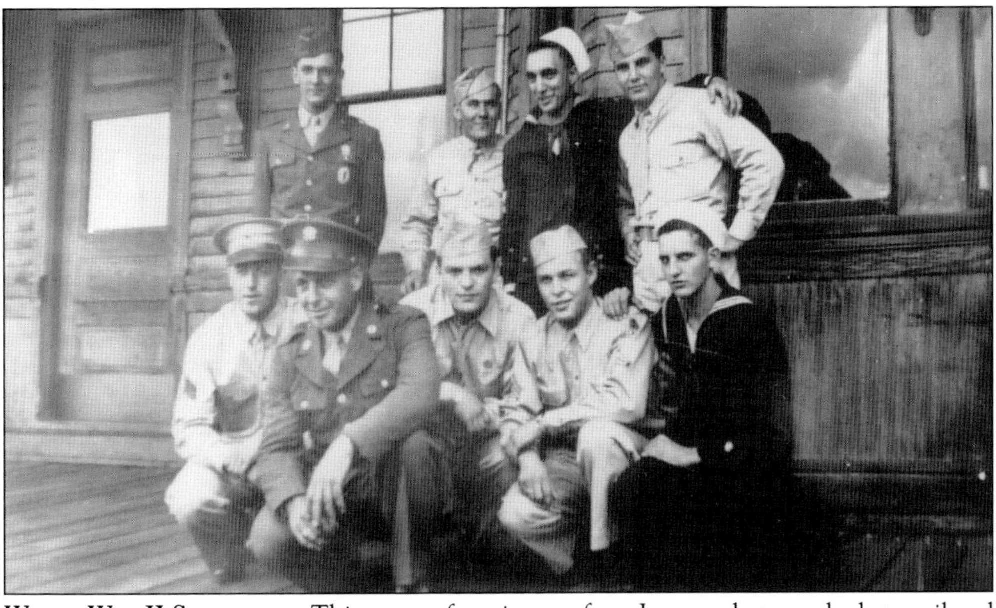

WORLD WAR II SERVICEMEN. This group of servicemen from Jay was photographed at a railroad station in Livermore Falls in 1943. The men are, from left to right, (first row) Paul Berube, Bill Berube, Lucien Chabot, Eugene Pomerleau, and Erlon Rose; (second row) Robert Guerin, Armand Pineau, Ely Duguay, and Lawrence Gagnon.

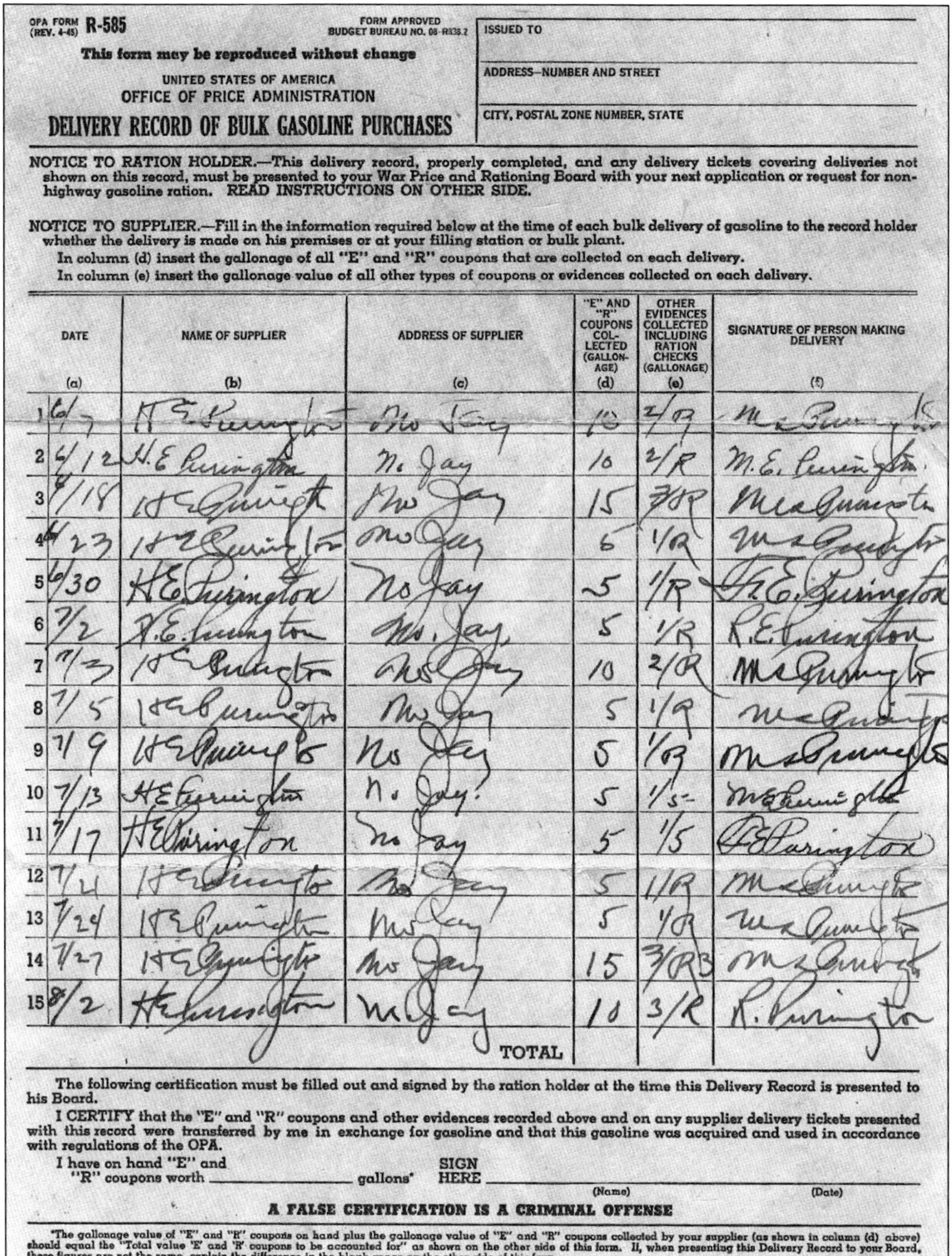
OPA FORM R-585 (REV. 4-45)

FORM APPROVED BUDGET BUREAU NO. 08-R338.2

This form may be reproduced without change

UNITED STATES OF AMERICA
OFFICE OF PRICE ADMINISTRATION

DELIVERY RECORD OF BULK GASOLINE PURCHASES

ISSUED TO

ADDRESS—NUMBER AND STREET

CITY, POSTAL ZONE NUMBER, STATE

NOTICE TO RATION HOLDER.—This delivery record, properly completed, and any delivery tickets covering deliveries not shown on this record, must be presented to your War Price and Rationing Board with your next application or request for non-highway gasoline ration. READ INSTRUCTIONS ON OTHER SIDE.

NOTICE TO SUPPLIER.—Fill in the information required below at the time of each bulk delivery of gasoline to the record holder whether the delivery is made on his premises or at your filling station or bulk plant.
In column (d) insert the gallonage of all "E" and "R" coupons that are collected on each delivery.
In column (e) insert the gallonage value of all other types of coupons or evidences collected on each delivery.

	DATE (a)	NAME OF SUPPLIER (b)	ADDRESS OF SUPPLIER (c)	"E" AND "R" COUPONS COLLECTED (GALLONAGE) (d)	OTHER EVIDENCES COLLECTED INCLUDING RATION CHECKS (GALLONAGE) (e)	SIGNATURE OF PERSON MAKING DELIVERY (f)
1	6/7	H E Purington	No Jay	10	2/R	M E Purington
2	6/12	H.E Purington	No. Jay	10	2/R	M.E. Purington
3	6/18	H E Purington	No Jay	15	3/R	M E Purington
4	6/23	H E Purington	No Jay	5	1/R	M E Purington
5	6/30	H E Purington	No Jay	5	1/R	H E Purington
6	7/2	H.E. Purington	No. Jay	5	1/R	R.E. Purington
7	7/3	H E Purington	No Jay	10	2/R	M E Purington
8	7/5	H E Purington	No Jay	5	1/R	M E Purington
9	7/9	H E Purington	No Jay	5	1/R	M E Purington
10	7/13	H E Purington	N. Jay	5	1/S	M E Purington
11	7/17	H E Purington	No Jay	5	1/S	H E Purington
12	7/21	H E Purington	No Jay	5	1/R	M E Purington
13	7/24	H E Purington	No Jay	5	1/R	M E Purington
14	7/27	H E Purington	No Jay	15	3/R	M E Purington
15	8/2	H E Purington	No Jay	10	3/R	R. Purington
			TOTAL			

The following certification must be filled out and signed by the ration holder at the time this Delivery Record is presented to his Board.

I CERTIFY that the "E" and "R" coupons and other evidences recorded above and on any supplier delivery tickets presented with this record were transferred by me in exchange for gasoline and that this gasoline was acquired and used in accordance with regulations of the OPA.

I have on hand "E" and "R" coupons worth ________ gallons* SIGN HERE ________ (Name) (Date)

A FALSE CERTIFICATION IS A CRIMINAL OFFENSE

*The gallonage value of "E" and "R" coupons on hand plus the gallonage value of "E" and "R" coupons collected by your supplier (as shown in column (d) above) should equal the "Total value 'E' and 'R' coupons to be accounted for" as shown on the other side of this form. If, when presenting this Delivery Record to your Board, these figures are not the same, explain the difference in the blank space on the other side of this form.

16—43320-1

DELIVERY RECORD OF BULK GASOLINE PURCHASES, 1945. This is from the War Price and Rationing Board in Farmington, Maine. The form was for gas delivered to the Purington store. There is a note on the back that reads, "Gasoline (and other petroleum products) takes half the cargo space on ships bearing supplies to the fighting fronts. Gasoline Powers the Attack. Rationing protects the gasoline supply. Play square with rationing." Gasoline was rationed in the United States from May 1942 to August 1945.

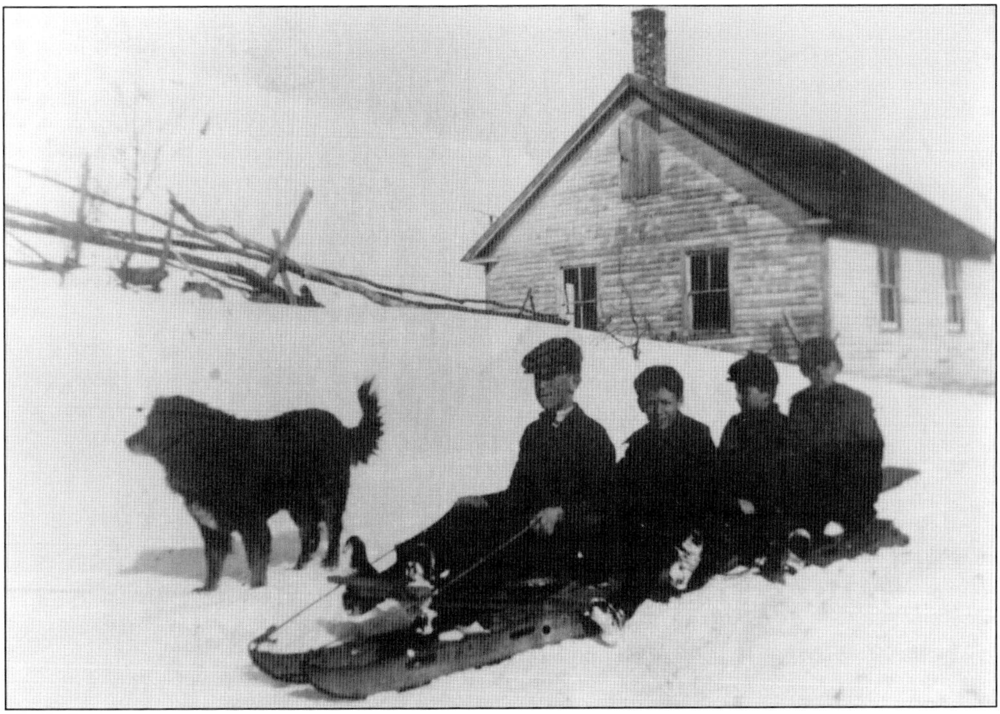

Four Boys on a Double Runner Sled in front of the East Jay School. This is also known as a bobsled. Bobsleds, or double runners, are made by placing a long, narrow platform above two single sleds. The person at the front steers by placing his feet on a crossbar attached to the front sled or by using two ropes fastened to the points of the forward runners.

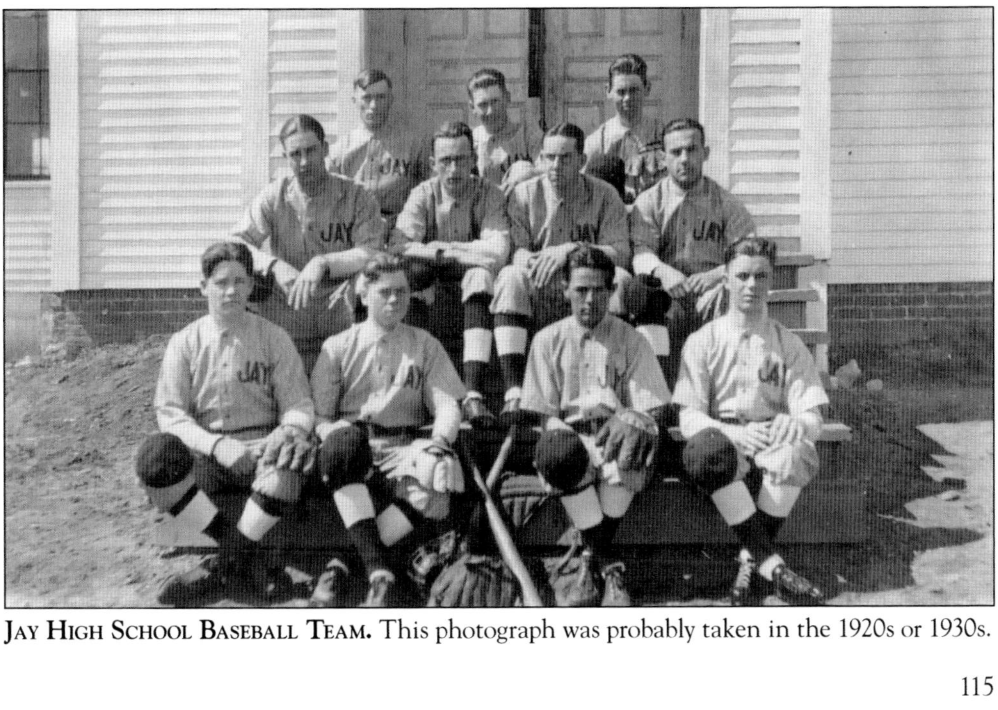

Jay High School Baseball Team. This photograph was probably taken in the 1920s or 1930s.

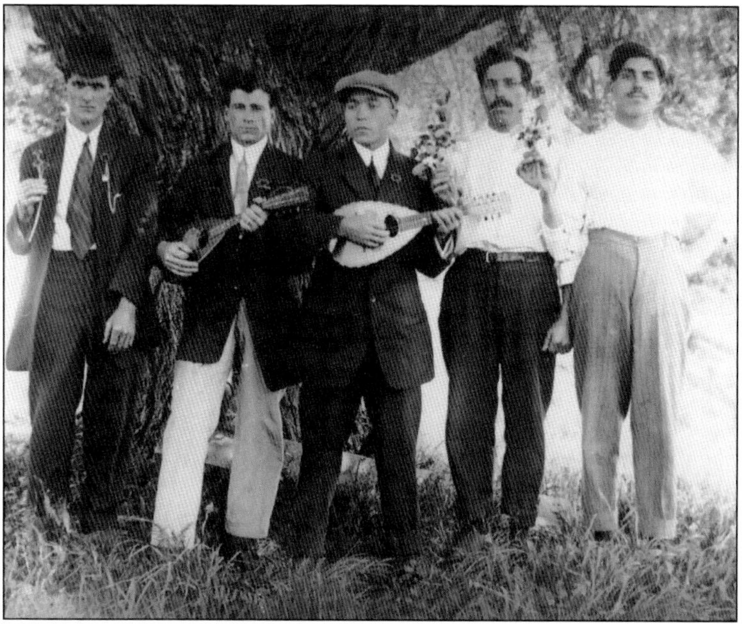

Riley Troubadours. This group of Riley workmen, photographed in 1897, performed as off-hour troubadours. One of the men was Rocco DiPompo. He and his fellow troubadours were immigrants from Italy who all worked at the Riley Mill.

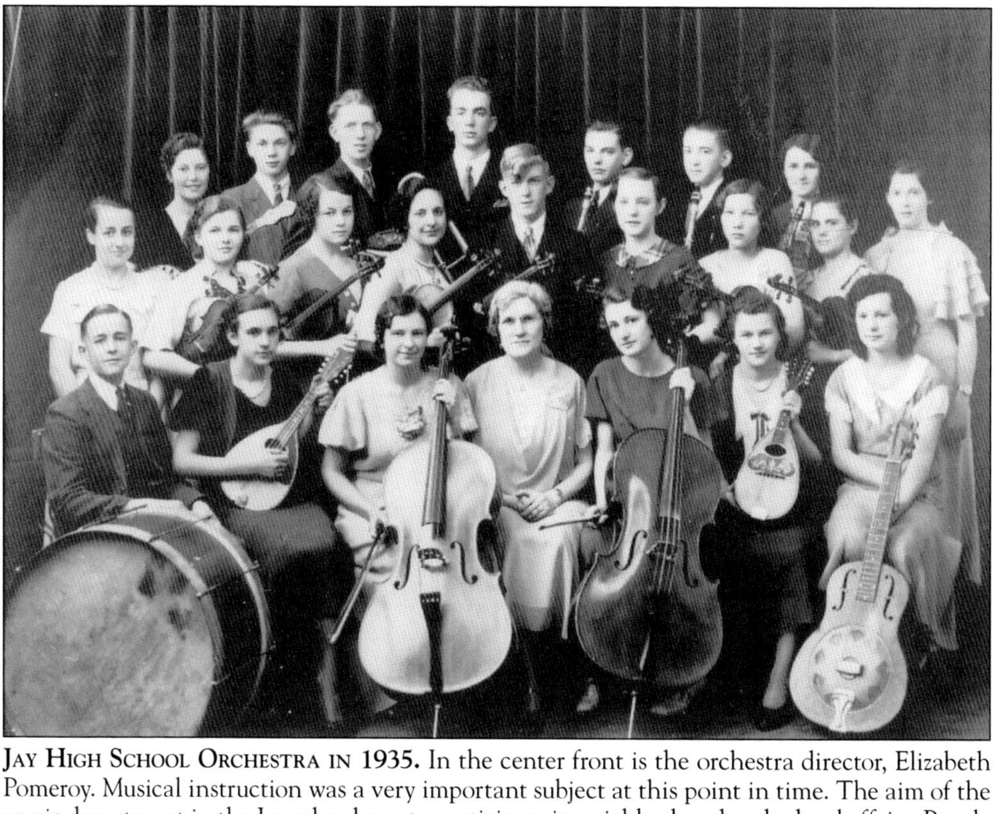

Jay High School Orchestra in 1935. In the center front is the orchestra director, Elizabeth Pomeroy. Musical instruction was a very important subject at this point in time. The aim of the music department in the Jay school was to participate in neighborhood and school affairs. People also requested the musical services of the orchestra at memorial services, clubs, and churches.

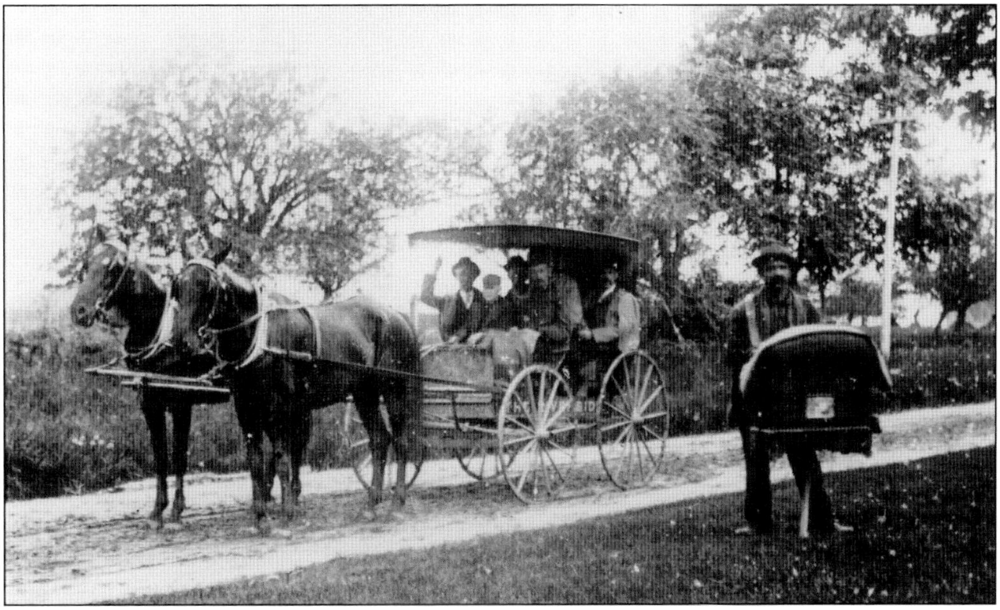

Hand Organ Music Man at the Home of Silas Jones in the Early 1900s on Jay Hill. Hand organs, also known as barrel organs, were small and portable and played by turning a handle. The name barrel organ is named for the cylinders on which the tunes are pricked out with pins and staples of various lengths. Each revolution played one tune. In this image, a carriage stops to enjoy the entertainment.

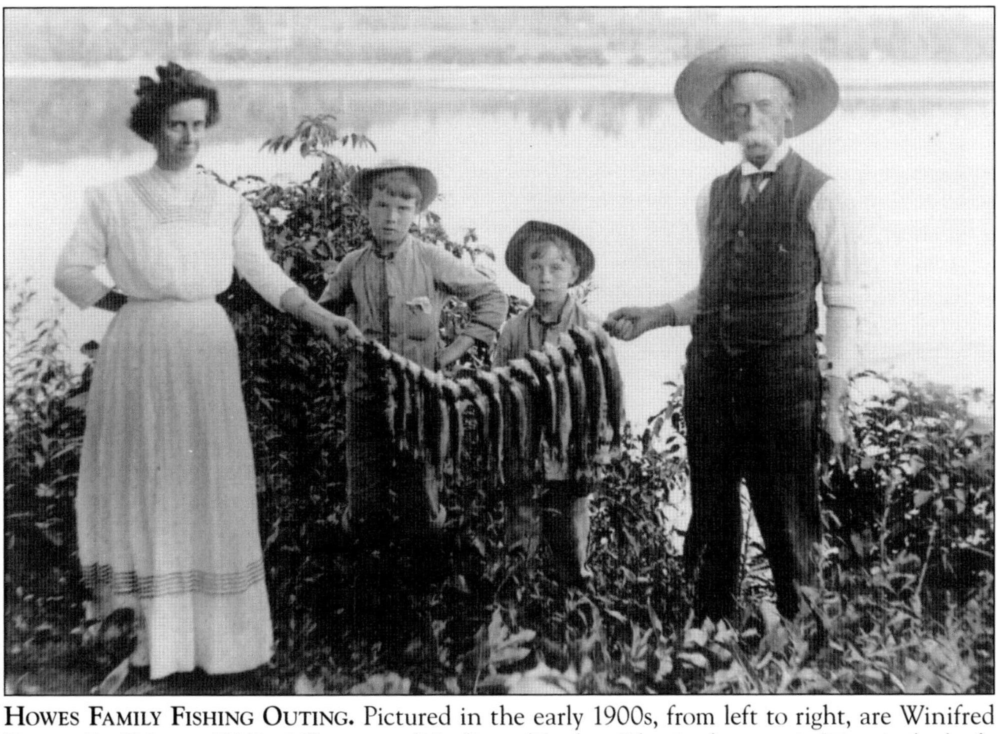

Howes Family Fishing Outing. Pictured in the early 1900s, from left to right, are Winifred Howes, Earl Howes, Wilfred Howes, and Ferdinand Jordan. The Androscoggin River is the body of water in the background.

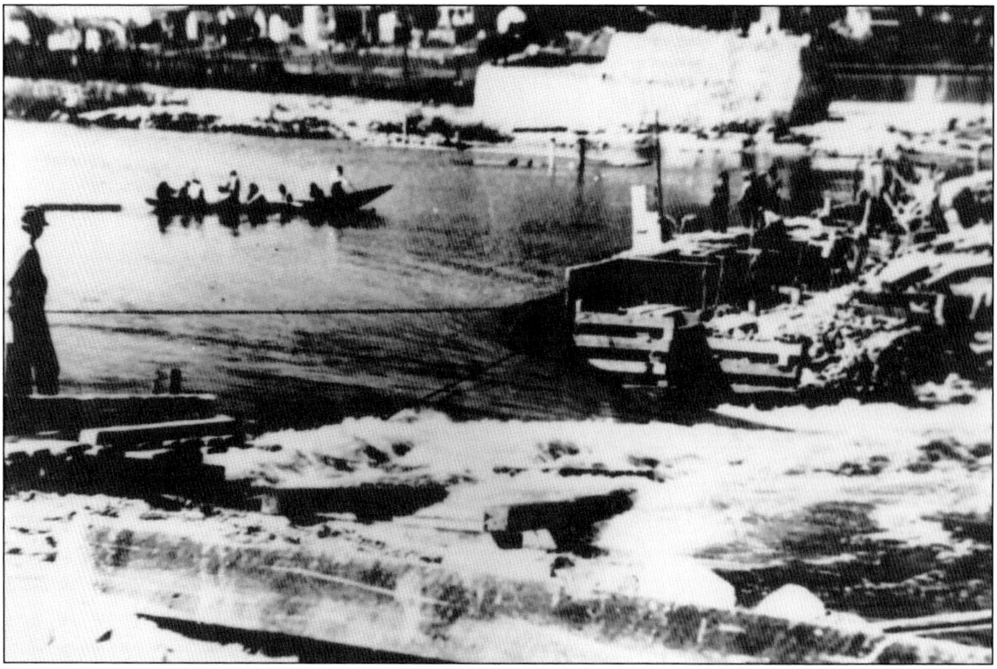

Flood of 1936. The flood caused a great deal of damage in Jay. It followed a very snowy and cold winter. The ice in the Androscoggin River was over three feet thick. Rain started on Tuesday, March 10. It turned warm and foggy and rained steadily for four days. By Friday, March 13, waters hit flood level on the river. There were huge ice jams and lowlands flooded.

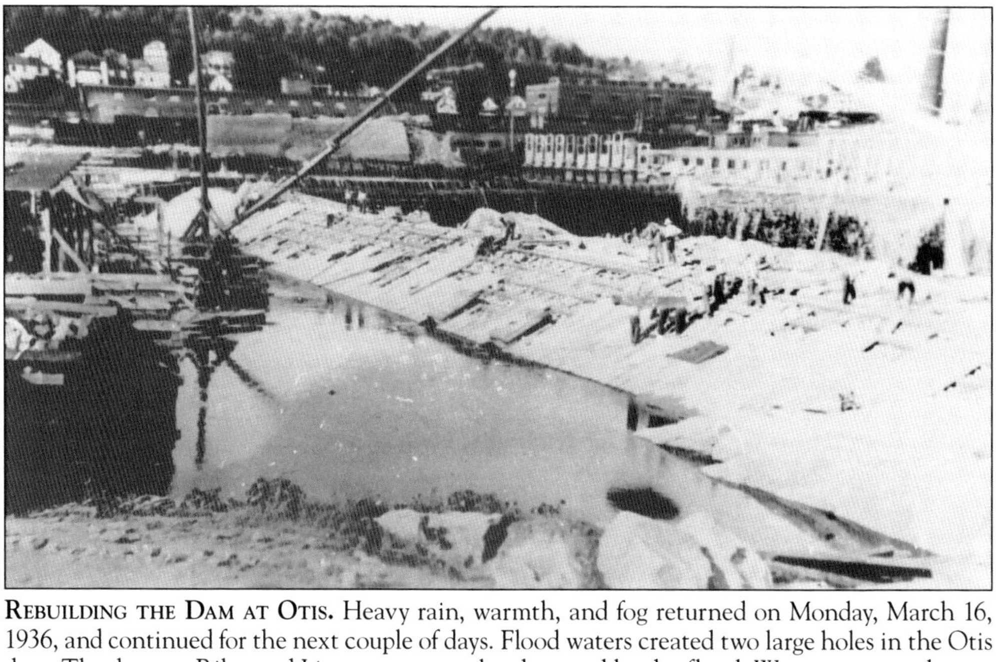

Rebuilding the Dam at Otis. Heavy rain, warmth, and fog returned on Monday, March 16, 1936, and continued for the next couple of days. Flood waters created two large holes in the Otis dam. The dams at Riley and Livermore were also damaged by the flood. Water was over the top of the grinders at the Riley Mill, and the Jay Power House was completely flooded.

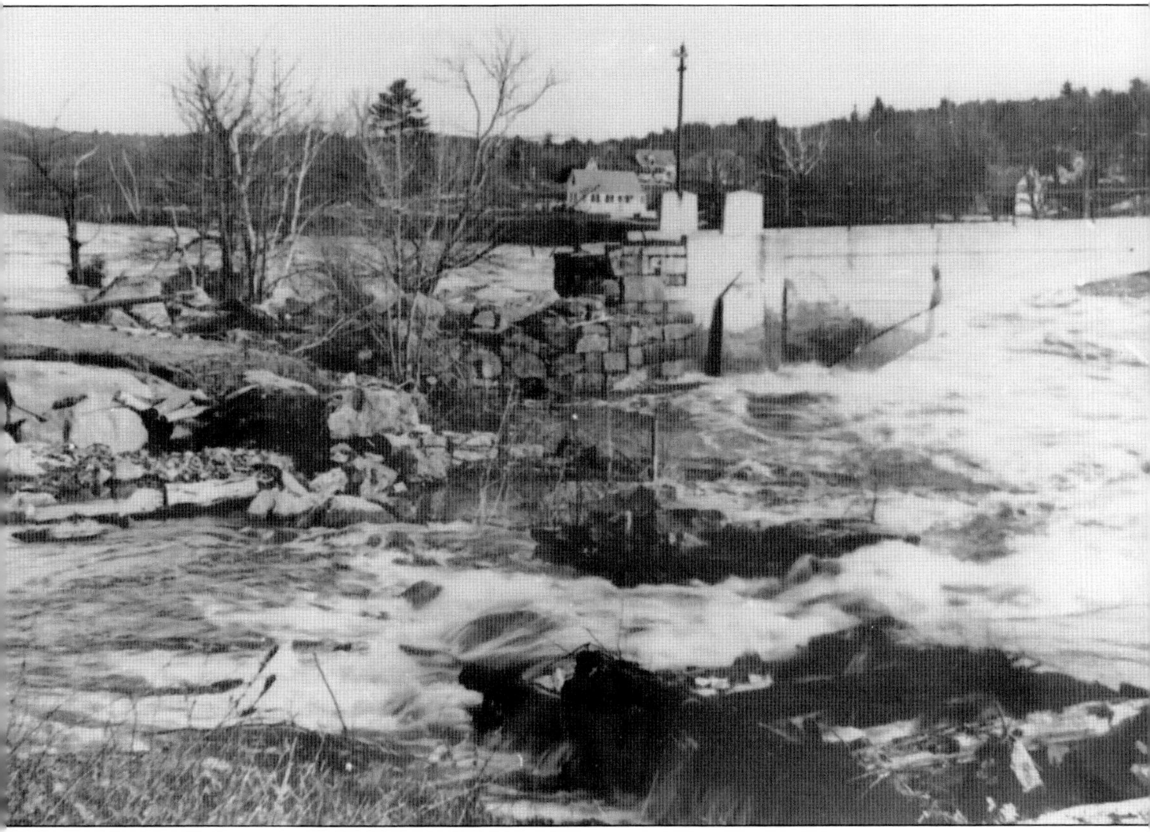

FLOOD DAMAGE. As can be seen in this image, the flood took out abutments on the cement bridge. Waters also washed away two large coffer dams at the Otis Mill. It carried seven men over the dam and falls. Six were recovered, but the seventh was never found.

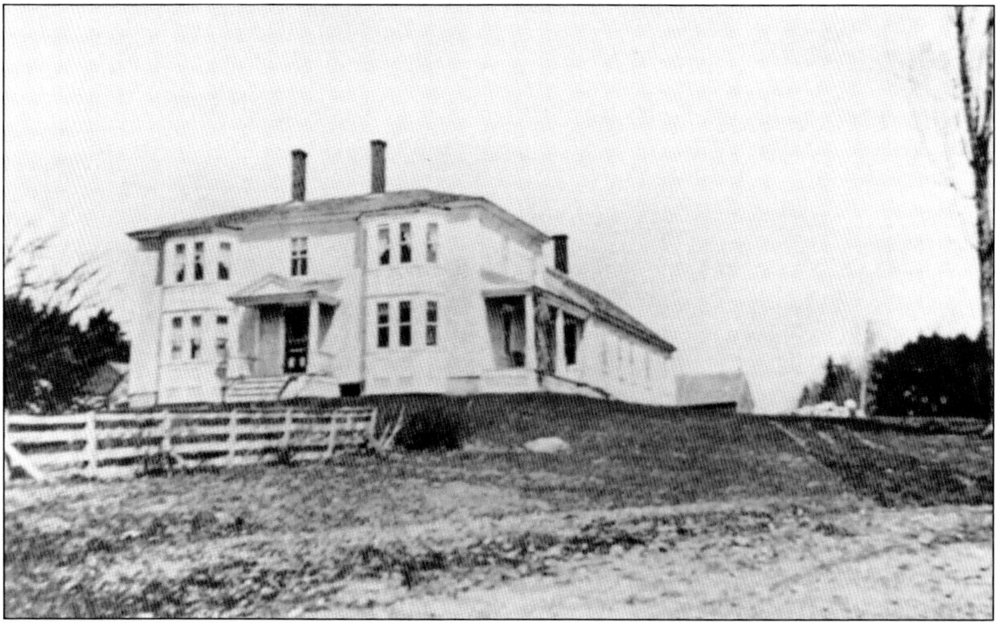

Moses Stone's Home. Maj. Moses Stone was one of the first settlers in Jay. This is the home he lived in with his wife, Elizabeth Brown, and their two children. He was very active in the affairs of Jay and represented the town in the general court of Massachusetts. Stone became a member of the Maine Legislature and was a pastor of the Methodist Church. This photograph of his home was taken around 1910.

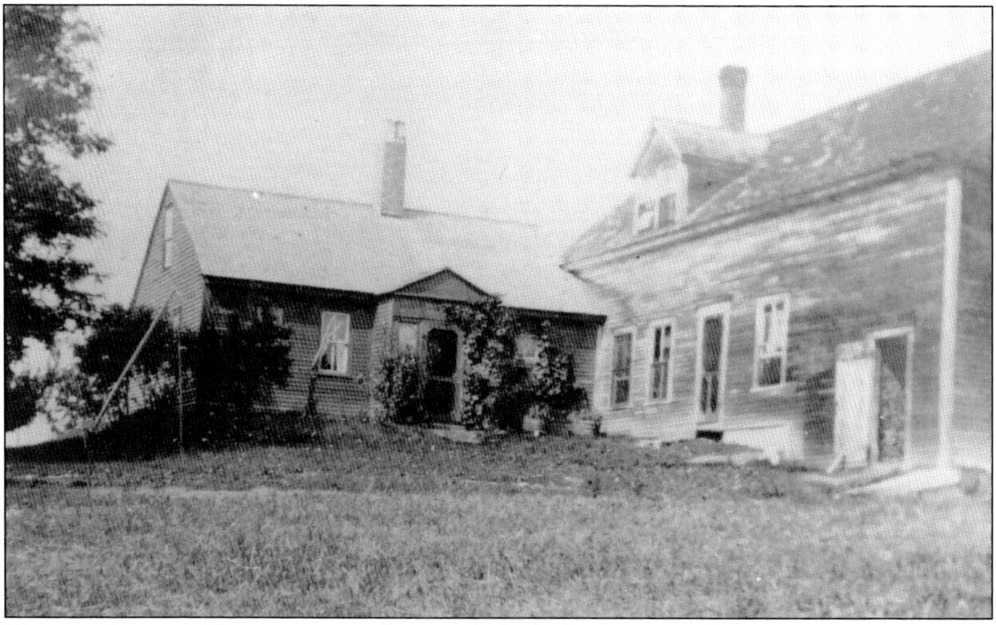

Nathan Crafts's Homestead. Nathan Crafts built this house in the late 1700s or early 1800s. Crafts was one of the first settlers on Jay Hill. It is said that he and others, such as James Starr Jr., Ezekiel Richardson, Simon Coolidge, Oliver Fuller, Samuel W. Eustic, Joseph Hyde, Scarborough Parker, Nathaniel Jackson, Samuel Jackson, Joseph Macomber, Samuel Whiting, Moses Crafts, and Moses Stone, all settled in Jay around this time.

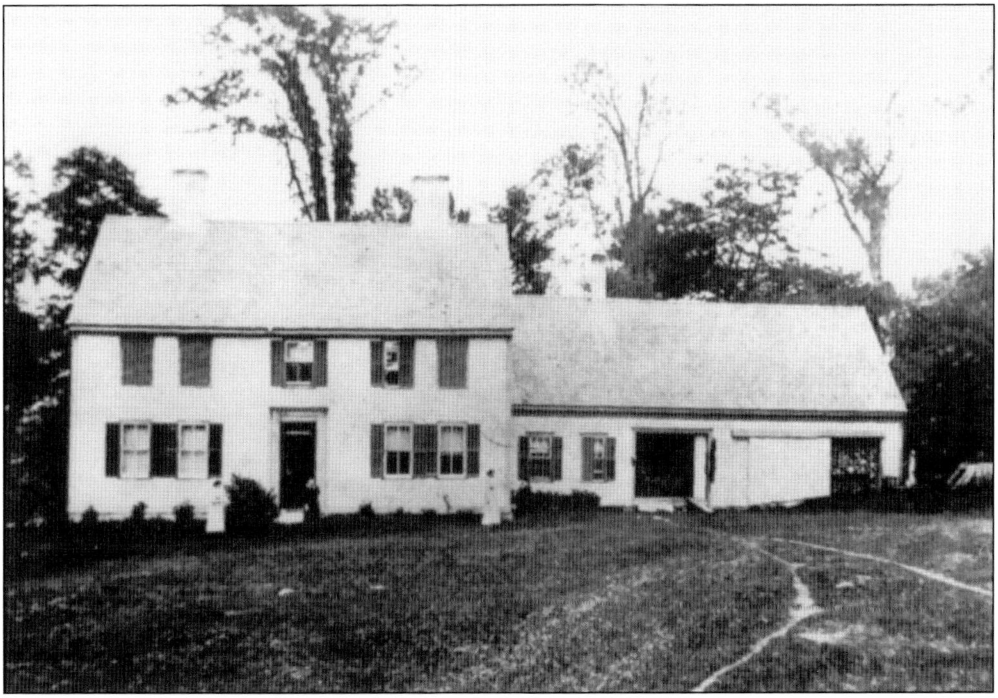

CAPT. EDWARD RICHARDSON'S HOMESTEAD. This house was built in 1794 on what is now called the Brackett Road in Jay. Captain Richardson was one of the minutemen who fought the British at Concord and later served in the Continental army in the Revolutionary War. He and his wife, Lucinda Goding, had four sons. He was a prosperous farmer who cultivated apples and other fruit.

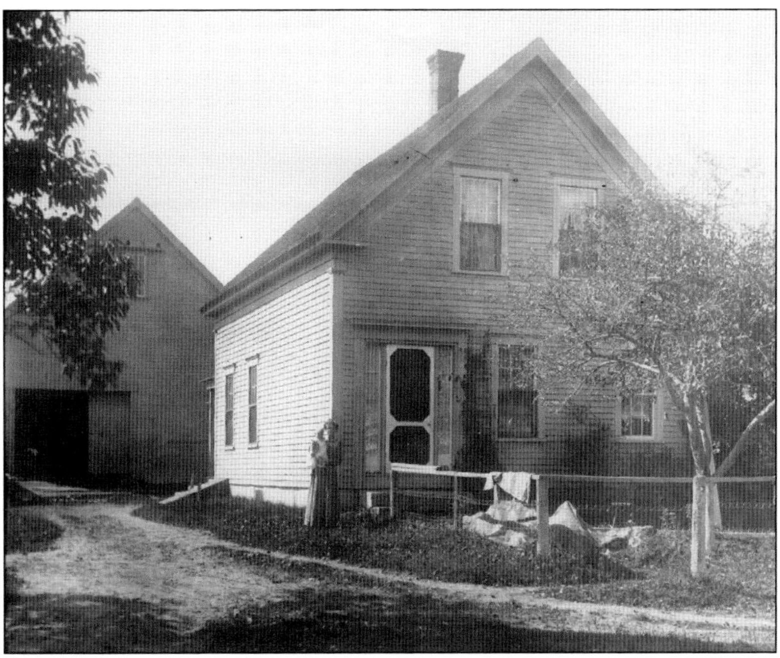

BRAD CRAFTS'S HOMESTEAD. This structure was located in North Jay. Virginia Crafts is possibly the woman in this photograph, perhaps holding Brad Crafts, her son. Brad Crafts was a town historian and photographer who dedicated his life to collecting Jay history. He was born in the early 1900s.

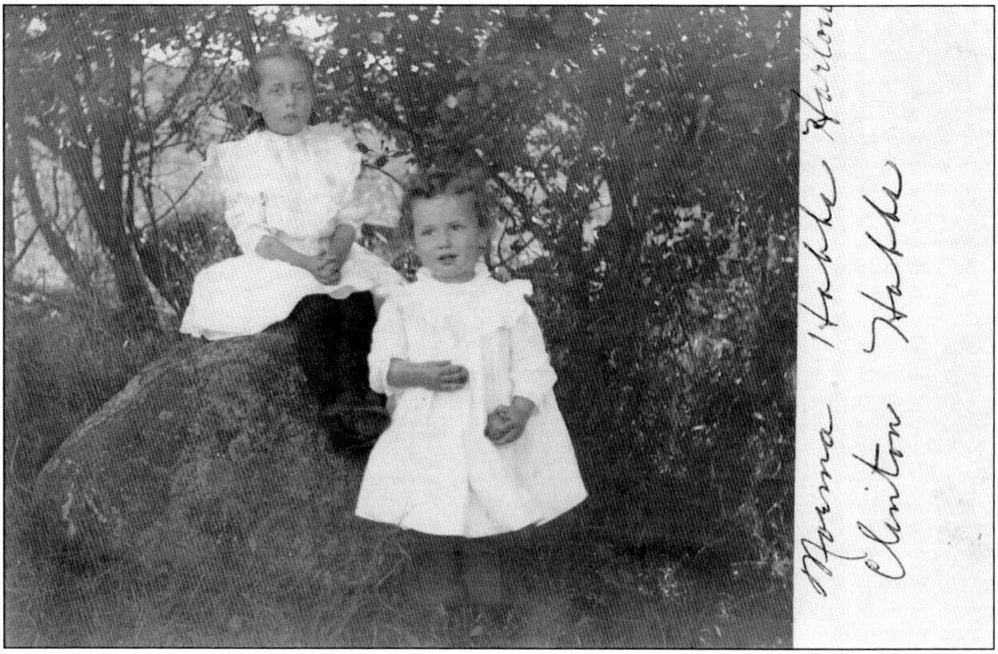

HOMEMADE CLOTHING. These dresses were made about 1902 or 1903 by Nina Maud Bean Hobbs for her children Clinton and Norma. Nina was married to LaForest Hobbs, a wheelwright and electrician. Many made their own clothing during this time.

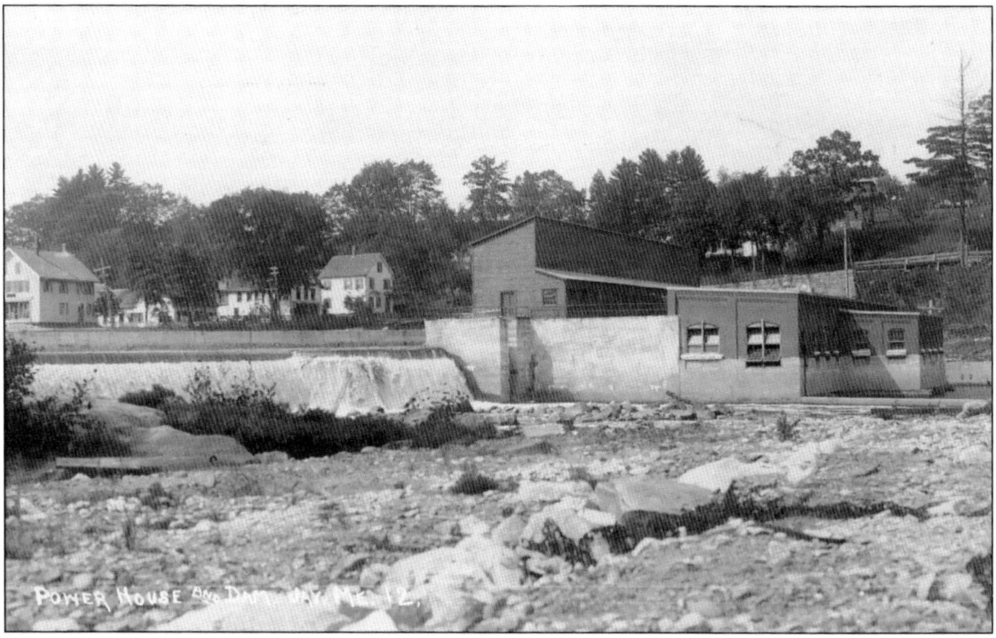

POWERHOUSE. The powerhouse at Jay Bridge has been home to three water powers: Otis Falls (Chisholm), Peterson's Rips (Riley), and Jay Bridge. This particular powerhouse was built by International Paper Company on the site of the Falmouth Mill at Jay Bridge.

Nine

Many Villages, Many Main Streets

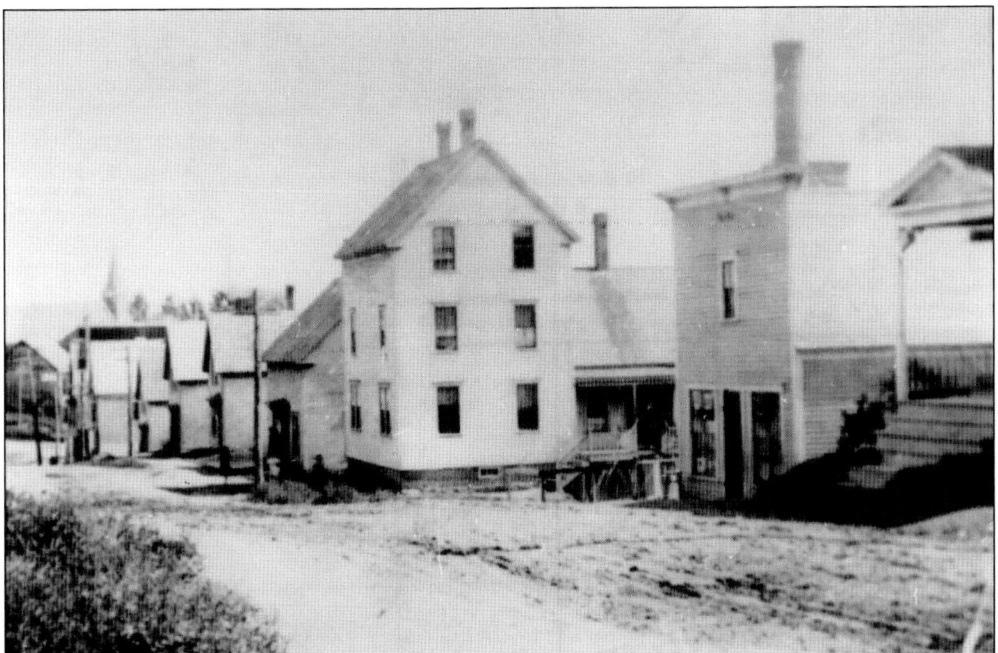

Main Street in Chisholm in 1914, Looking North. In 1883, Chisholm only had three houses; by 1912, there were around 1,000 inhabitants. Around the mill, new apartment buildings and stores were built. Chisholm also had a new Catholic church and two-room schoolhouse in the town.

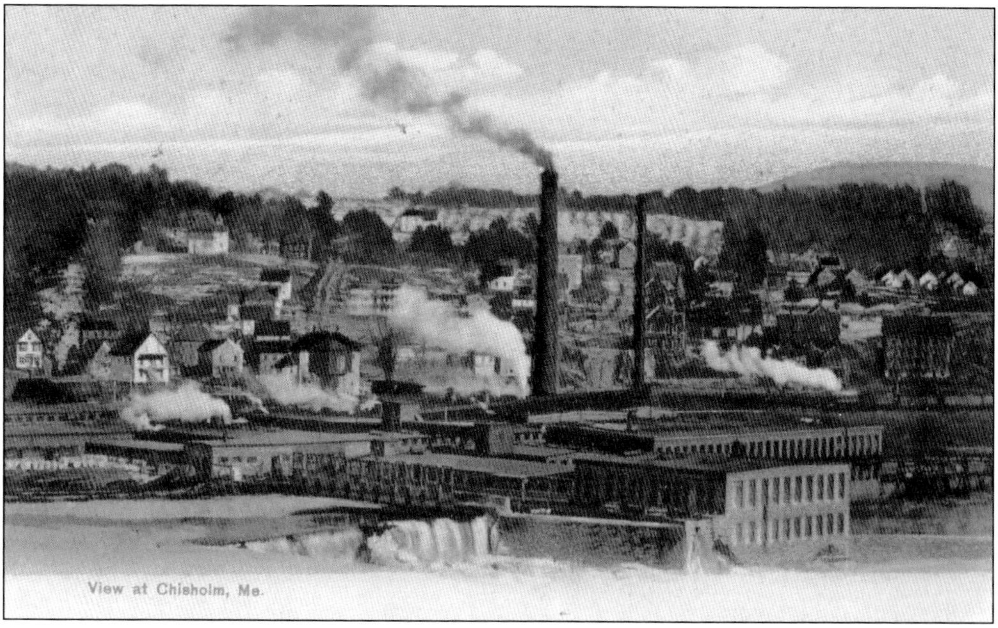

CHISHOLM VILLAGE IN THE EARLY 1900S. This image was taken when the population was just starting to grow. The Otis Mill is in the foreground and a few houses are visible on the hillside.

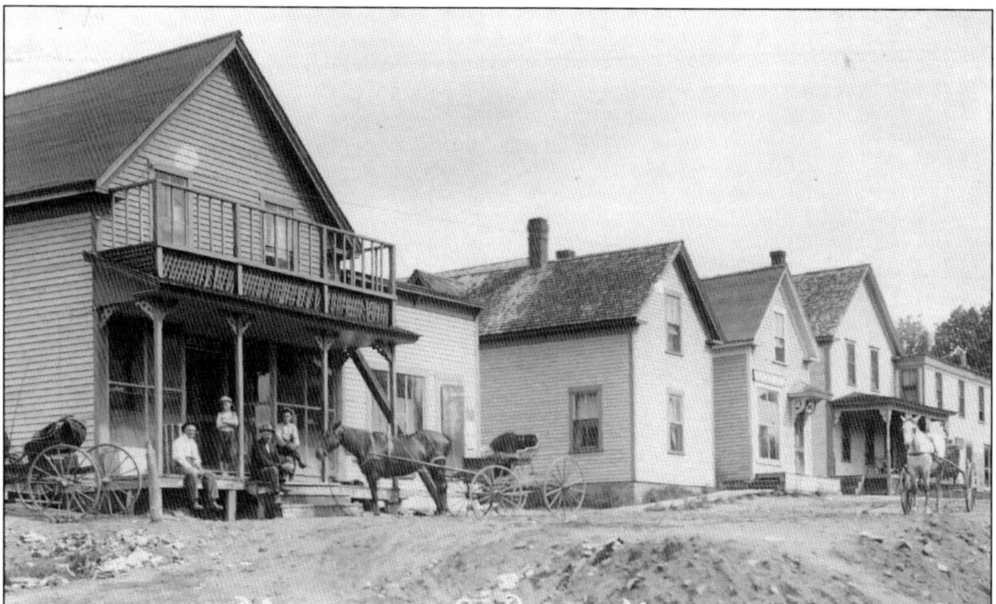

MAIN STREET, RILEY. In this photograph is Main Street in Riley before the fire of 1911. The third, fourth, and fifth building were destroyed by fire. The first building from the left was a store owned by David Alexander. It was also the site of the first Riley post office. The first school was held here on the second floor, as were church services. The second building, with the flat roof, was a boardinghouse for mill workers.

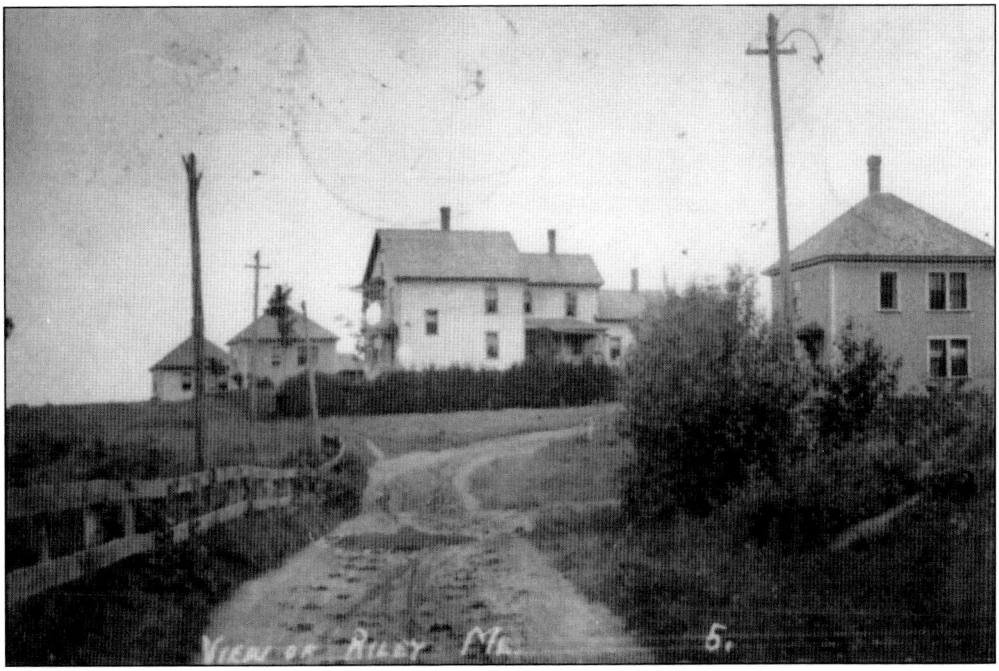

RILEY VILLAGE. Riley had its own post office, a barbershop, a poolroom, an ice cream parlor, and a number of general stores over the years. The population of this small village was made up of people of many nationalities, including Czechs, Lithuanians, Italians, Poles, Finns, and French Canadians. The village was named after the mill manager, Edwin Riley.

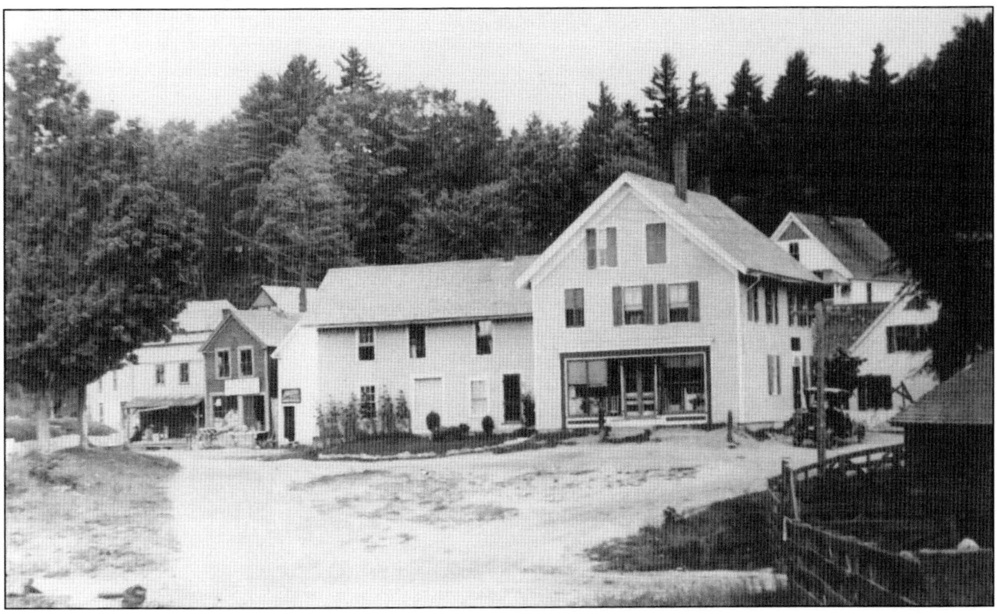

JAY VILLAGE, AROUND 1904. This building housed Adams' Store and the Jay Post Office. Jay Village had its own railroad station, called Depot Flat. The village had a number of shops, two grocery stores, a hardware store, a courthouse, and a blacksmith. During the winter, streets in town were plowed. In outlying areas, two long rollers were drawn by three pairs of horses to roll the roads, packing down the snow.

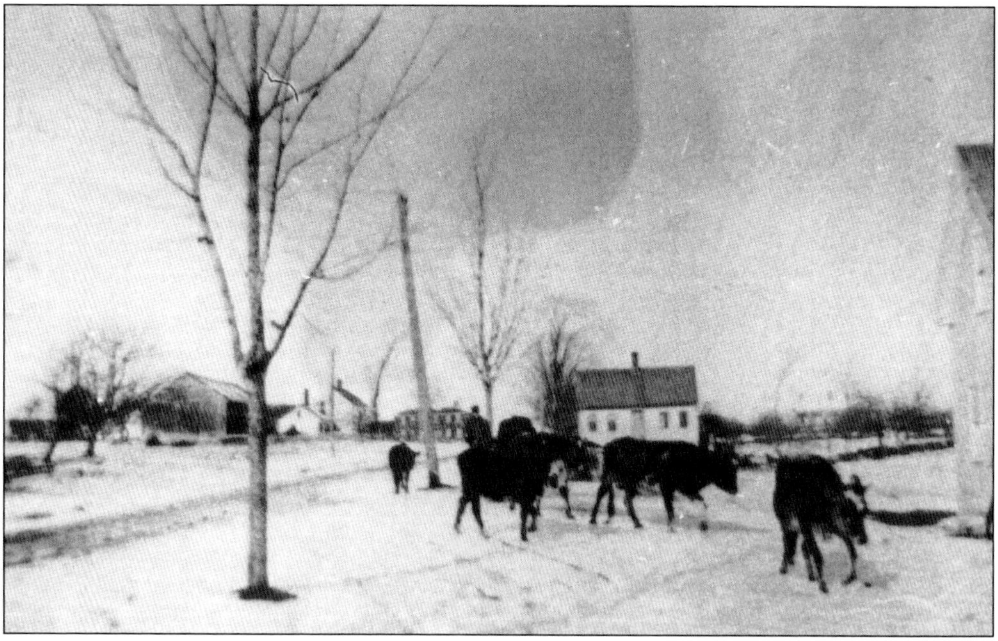

Jay Hill Village Near the Turn of the 20th Century. Jay Hill was the first settled area in Jay, and for some time, it was considered the center of town. The first meetinghouse and tavern were built here. There was also a village blacksmith shop, cabinet shop, a cooper, a shoemaker, village stores, a lawyer's office, and a courtroom. The first doctor and minister for the town also settled here. With the advent of industry, the center of town transferred to the area where the most jobs were—North Jay, Chisholm, and Riley.

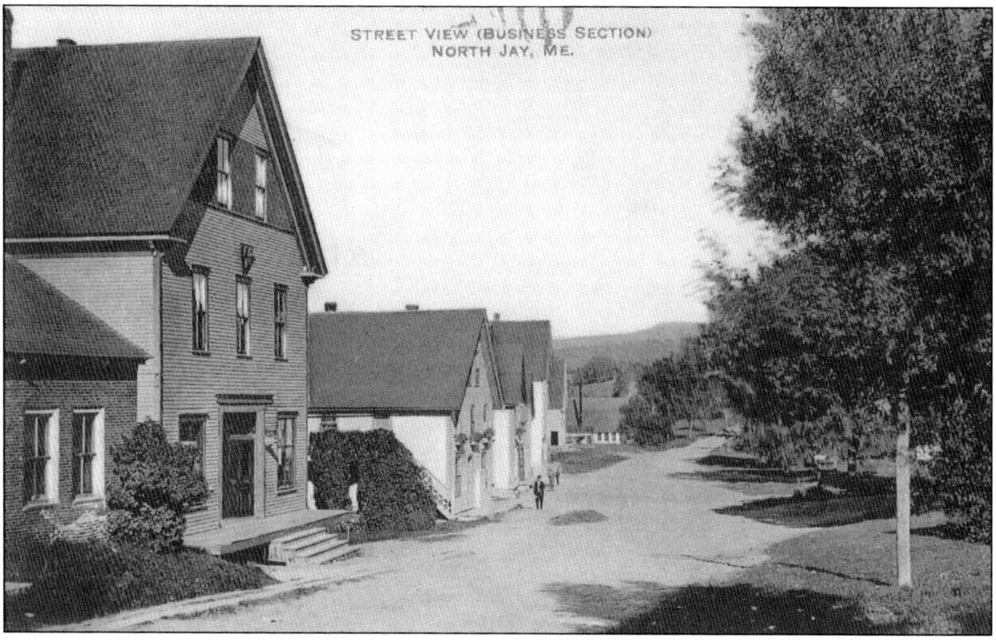

North Jay Business District. The business district of North Jay in the early 1900s is captured on this postcard. The card is postmarked in 1912, dating the photograph to before that year. North Jay was once a bustling little village.

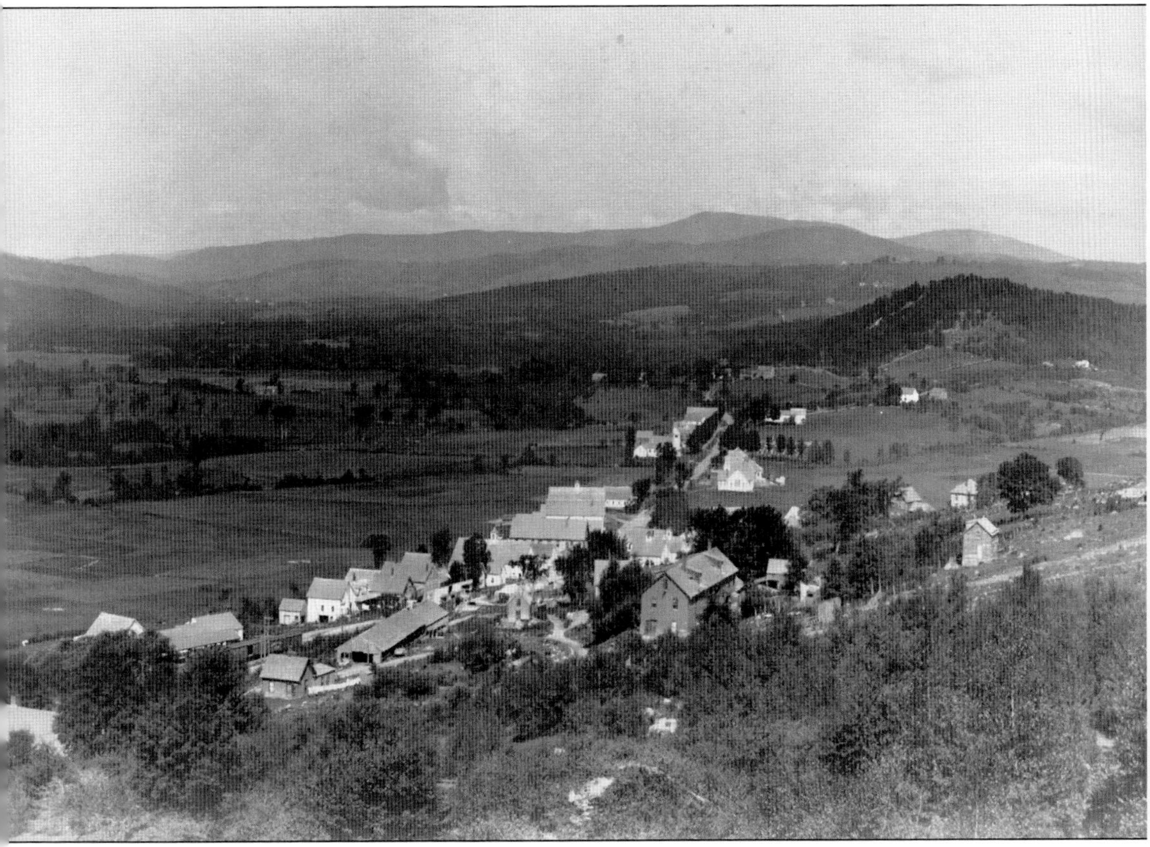

View of North Jay Village, Early 1900s. The Maine and New Hampshire Company cutting sheds and office, churches, and the downtown business district pictured here. North Jay was a thriving village with its own stores, churches, fraternal organizations, and schools. A beautiful library was built in 1916. North Jay had only a few scattered households in 1820. By 1900, there were about 1,000 people living in the village.